Gender and
the Environment

For my students

GENDER AND THE ENVIRONMENT

Nicole Detraz

polity

First published in 2017 by Polity Press
Reprinted: 2020

Polity Press
65 Bridge Street
Cambridge CB2 1UR, UK

Polity Press
350 Main Street
Malden, MA 02148, USA

ISBN-13: 978-0-7456-6382-1
ISBN-13: 978-0-7456-6383-8 (pb)

A catalogue record for this book is available from the British Library.

Library of Congress Cataloging-in-Publication Data

Names: Detraz, Nicole, author.
Title: Gender and the environment / Nicole Detraz.
Description: Cambridge, UK ; Malden, MA : Polity Press, [2016] | Includes bibliographical references and index.
Identifiers: LCCN 2016017578| ISBN 9780745663821 (hardback : alk. paper) | ISBN 9780745663838 (pbk. : alk. paper) | ISBN 9781509511969 (Epub) | ISBN 9781509511952 (Mobi)
Subjects: LCSH: Women and the environment. | Environmental policy–Social aspects. | Environmental management–Social aspects. | Environmental protection–Social aspects. | Global environmental change–Social aspects.
Classification: LCC GE195.9 .D47 2016 | DDC 304.2081–dc23
LC record available at https://lccn.loc.gov/2016017578

Typeset in 10.5 on 12 pt Sabon
by Toppan Best-set Premedia Limited
Printed and bound in the United States by LSC Communications

For further information on Polity, visit our website: politybooks.com

Contents

Acknowledgments

This book is dedicated to my students. I love teaching global environmental politics (GEP), and I have been fortunate enough to do so at two institutions. While there are positives to each of the classes I teach, I am the happiest in my GEP classes. This is because my students inevitably challenge me to think differently on issues that I have been grappling with since graduate school. They ask questions and push discussions of topics like the politics of sustainability, justice, security, and resource use in directions that I didn't necessarily anticipate, but that enrich my lectures immeasurably. This is important not only for my teaching, but also for my research, as I reevaluate taken-for-granted assumptions. I am a better teacher and scholar for my interactions with each class.

There are a number of people I would like to thank for their support, help, and friendship as I worked on this manuscript. I would like to begin by thanking Mark Johnson and Hannah Guess for their research help. I am very fortunate to have had such hard-working graduate assistants. I would also like to thank Sera Babakus for coming out of GA retirement and agreeing to read a complete manuscript draft for me. Sera, you are completely wonderful.

Thanks to the GEP and FTGS international relations communities for the great work that you do. It is wonderful to be part of two different groups of scholars who show such passion and dedication to making our field, and our world, a bit better. I am most grateful to Sonalini Sapra and Annica Kronsell for reading over some early thoughts on the book project quite some time ago.

My colleagues at the University of Memphis also deserve a great many thanks for providing encouragement and assistance in all that I do. As far as I am concerned, there are no better people to work with than each of you. It is a great feeling to enjoy the company of the people I work with and consider them friends.

Thanks also to my family and friends for being there for me. Your love means the world to me. Thanks to Kirby, Brenda, Paige, John, Alexander, and Aubrey for the sandcastles, and snow angels, and cookouts. You have shaped my appreciation of multiple places and spaces. Thanks also to Dursun and my Turkish family for showing me the natural beauty of your amazing country so that I might reflect on human–environment connections in an entirely new place. Hepinizi cok seviyorum (I love you all).

Last, but never least, I would like to thank Nekane Tanaka Galdos and Louise Knight at Polity for being absolutely fabulous to work with. Your patience and support are most appreciated. I have really loved finding such a great home for two of my books at Polity.

Abbreviations

CEDAW	Convention on the Elimination of All Forms of Discrimination against Women
COP	Conference of the Parties
CRED	Centre for Research on the Epidemiology of Disasters
DRC	Democratic Republic of the Congo
EPA	Environmental Protection Agency
ESS	environmental security studies
EU	European Union
FAO	Food and Agriculture Organization
GAD	gender and development
GDP	gross domestic product
GED	gender, environment, and development
GEP	global environmental politics
ICISS	International Commission on Intervention and State Sovereignty
IFPRI	International Food Policy Research Institute
IGO	intergovernmental organization
IPCC	Intergovernmental Panel on Climate Change
IUCN	International Union for Conservation of Nature
IR	international relations
MEA	Millennium Ecosystem Assessment
NGO	nongovernmental organization
PCB	polychlorinated biphenyl

R2P	responsibility to protect
UCC	United Church of Christ
UN	United Nations
UN DESA	United Nations Department of Economic and Social Affairs
UNDP	United Nations Development Programme
UNDSD	United Nations Division for Sustainable Development
UNEP	United Nations Environment Programme
UNESCO	United Nations Educational, Scientific and Cultural Organization
UNFCC	United Nations Framework Convention on Climate Change
UNGA	United Nations General Assembly
WAD	women and development
WED	women, environment, and development
WEDO	Women's Environment and Development Organization
WGC	Women and Gender Constituency
WHO	World Health Organization
WID	Women in Development
WILPF	Women's International League for Peace and Freedom
WWF	World Wildlife Fund

1
Introduction: How Are Gender and the Environment Connected?

Environmental challenges are widely recognized as important issues for the international community to address. Climate change, loss of biodiversity in forests and oceans, natural disasters, dependence on polluting energy sources: all of these are environmental issues that have captured the attention of people and policymakers around the world. Environmental issues are typically understood to be complex and transboundary, but they are not always recognized as being gendered. This book provides an introduction to the links between gender and the environment by analyzing some of the key issues and topics within global environmental politics (GEP) through gender lenses. In particular, it identifies sustainability and justice as two central goals within GEP in general. Actors seek sustainable solutions to environmental challenges, and many also strive to ensure that these solutions are fair and just. Including gender in discussions and evaluations of these aims is both necessary and helpful.

There are both instrumental and ethical reasons for reflecting on the connections between gender and environmental politics. The instrumental reason relates to the overall goal of sustainability: halting environmental change requires consulting multiple perspectives and understanding a diverse range of experiences. Humans have a strong incentive to identify and pursue effective paths toward sustainability. The chapters of this book make the case that we are unlikely to get there unless we incorporate gender into our understanding of sustainability. The ethical reason for including gender is that current distributions of environmental ills and environmental benefits are uneven across the international system. People who are most likely to suffer from environmental change are also those who experience discrimination and marginalization at multiple levels and based on multiple categories (gender, race, class, ethnicity, etc.). Gender lenses allow us to examine specific gendered manifestations of injustice that have been underexplored in GEP.

By examining debates about population, consumption, security, and governance, the book considers how looking at the environment through gender lenses pushes us to ask different questions and broaden our sphere of analysis. It specifically claims that the concepts of sustainability and justice can shape how we see gender in these debates. These topics are appropriate to include because of the fact that they (1) are central concepts within GEP debates, and (2) have important gender components that are often ignored in both scholarship and policymaking. The central argument running through the text is that considering the environment through gender lenses challenges the primacy of some traditional environmental concepts and shifts the focus of sustainability and justice goals to be more inclusive.

Exploring the objectives of sustainability and justice through gender lenses is particularly important because society's understanding and enforcement of gender norms influence how we interact with the environment in numerous ways. Men and women are typically differently placed in terms of both their vulnerabilities to environmental change and their agency in addressing environmental issues. Without exposing the relevance and presence of gender in these kinds of discussions, important debates may continue without the inclusion of a key element. This book highlights gendered understandings of key environmental issues and topics and reveals the complexities of these discussions. It argues that a feminist perspective will help advance the GEP field by highlighting the gendered assumptions that go into scholarship and policymaking, and thus should help us come to a more complete understanding of and response to global environmental problems. These contributions directly relate to goals of sustainability and justice. Environmental processes and experiences are gendered – meaning that gender currently (and historically) intersects with power relations, which influence, among others, political processes of environmental decision-making; economic processes, which can help or hinder environmental sustainability; and social processes, which determine which tasks members of society will be expected to perform. The objective of the current volume is to reveal this gendering in order to facilitate dialogue across academic disciplines but also to better inform policymaking.

This undertaking is particularly important now because environmental issues are the subject of high-stakes policymaking in states across the globe. Issues like climate change, energy independence, green jobs, etc. have had a central place on the agenda of policymakers in recent years. These environmental debates have included several of the topics that are explored in the chapters of this book, including population, consumption, and environmental security. It is essential that students and the general public understand the role of gender in these topics so that they can better comprehend the ongoing discussions about environmental change and environmental policymaking.

Also, this undertaking is important because environmental issues have profound implications for human well-being. Rather than the repercussions of environmental change simply being a theoretical issue, these concerns are also often survival issues for those living in many parts of the world. Much feminist work has focused on the particular gendered implications of environmental change for marginalized populations in society, focusing especially on the unique hardships that women face because of environmental degradation. This includes women having to travel farther from home to collect water or fuelwood, women's unique experiences as environmental refugees, or women suffering food insecurity in greater numbers than men. These examples are important to understand because they offer insight into the gendered complexities of environmental issues.

This book is situated in the field of GEP. As an intellectual tradition with many connections to international relations (IR), GEP assess the politics of identifying, coping with, and addressing environmental protection and change. For many years, feminist scholars have claimed that IR has been slow to incorporate gender into its analysis (Tickner 2001). Since many GEP scholars have been trained within IR, it is not very surprising that gender does not factor into the work of most GEP scholars in a consistent and sustained fashion. This is not to say that there is necessarily a hostility to looking at environmental issues through gender lenses, but rather that there is a silence about gender. For example, most foundational texts within GEP contain very little attention to gender. Again, this is not to suggest that the authors and editors of these texts have specifically excluded gender on purpose. Rather, it is indicative of larger silences about gender within the field as a whole.

Understanding environmental politics

What is the environment? This is a question that I pose to my students, and which receives a wide array of responses. Many claim that "the environment" encompasses humans and the places and spaces in which they live. Others argue that the environment is a forest or field that is largely untouched by human hands. Since the Enlightenment in particular, there has been a tendency in many societies to think of nature as an entity that is external to humanity, and in many cases, something for humans to dominate (Hartmann et al. 2005; Plumwood 2002). Those who are critical of this tendency claim that terms like "nature," "environment," and "wilderness" must be understood as being historically contingent. The chapters of this book adopt a wide perspective on what "counts" as the environment. They draw on critical scholarship that sees discourses used in environmental debates as fluid entities that shape our understandings of global environmental political issues and the solutions we propose to address them.

Discourses are powerful forces within both academic and policy debates. The use of one discourse over another has very real implications for how we understand and seek to address international concerns (Ackerly and True 2010).[1] For example, there are multiple discourses around the concept of "genetically modified food." One discourse may include narratives of genetic modification as a solution to food shortages, while a second discourse may include narratives of genetic modification as a dangerous source of food insecurity. Policies made about the genetic modification of food will be supportive of the practice if the first discourse is used, and are likely to prohibit the practice if the second is used. Discourses shape our understanding of the terms of a debate, and are therefore important to how policies about environmental issues will be made (Detraz 2014).

There is a very long history of humans being concerned about perceived negative changes in their "environment." The late 1800s and early 1900s saw individuals and groups call attention to the radical changes that accompanied processes of industrialization. During this timeframe, well-known authors in the global North[2] like Henry David Thoreau, Ralph Waldo Emerson, and others reflected on the impacts of industrialization on pastoral landscapes, wilderness, and simple ways of life. John Muir challenged the society of the time to consider the meaning and necessity of preservation of wild spaces. Gifford Pinchot raised questions of conservation in the face of industrialization's hasty use of resources (Wapner 2012). In fact, the timeframe associated with the rapid spread of industrialization is frequently cited as a turning point in humanity's relationship with "nature," as well as our understanding of that relationship. In the face of these debates, some governments began to manage natural resources "scientifically" through policies such as sustained yield management for timber and other resources.

Despite the attention of some, the environment was not considered a central political issue for much of the history of the modern state system.[3] It was not until the 1960s and 1970s that public demand for safer and cleaner spaces, coupled with the rise of environmentally focused nongovernmental organizations (NGOs), resulted in states paying increased attention to the environment as a political issue. Environmental NGOs have had a strong presence in the environmental issue area. The first environmental NGOs emerged in the late nineteenth century, including the International Union of Forestry Research Organizations in 1891 and the International Friends of Nature in 1895 (Betsill 2014). In later years, Greenpeace, Earth Island Institute, Rainforest Action Network, World Wildlife Fund and Conservation International, along with others, emerged as examples of transnational environmental activist groups working to protect environmental quality across the globe (Wapner 2012).

By the late 1970s and 1980s many governments had created environmental departments or ministries to specifically tackle environmental policymaking (Chasek et al. 2006). Early examples include the US Environmental Protection Agency (EPA), which was created in 1970, and the Canadian Department of the Environment and the French Environment Ministry, both established the following year. Singapore's Ministry of the Environment followed in 1972. The 1970s also saw the United Nations (UN) Conference on the Human Environment held in June 1972 in Stockholm, Sweden. This conference was heralded as reflecting a growing recognition of the seriousness of environmental issues, as well as their transboundary nature. One important outcome of the conference was the establishment of the United Nations Environment Programme (UNEP), located in Nairobi, which adopted a mission to "provide leadership and encourage partnership in caring for the environment by inspiring, informing, and enabling nations and peoples to improve their quality of life without compromising that of future generations" (UNEP 2015).

Two additional global environmental conferences are regarded as significantly shaping the trajectory of environmental politics: the 1992 United Nations Conference on Environment and Development held in Rio de Janeiro, Brazil (popularly known as the Earth Summit), and the 2002 World Summit on Sustainable Development in Johannesburg, South Africa. These global conferences witnessed heated debates about which environmental issues should be on the global agenda, who is responsible for protecting the environment, and how best to halt or reverse environmental change. In the years from 1972 to the present, the governance of global environmental issues has involved both state and non-state actors working on a diverse range of problems related to environmental processes (Betsill 2014; Stevis 2014).

GEP scholarship   The environment came to be recognized as a central topic of scholarship within political science during a similar timeframe. Scholars of the late 1960s and early 1970s began to reflect on issues like the role of states and global institutions as well as the global economy with regard to the environment. GEP emerged as a specific topic of study under the umbrella of IR. As a subfield of political science, IR focuses on political relations that reach across political boundaries. GEP scholars within IR examine the nature of these associations as they relate to the global environment. The focus of GEP scholarship has included work on environmental actors and regimes, studies of the ecological impact of the global political economy, and work on the ethics of environmental politics, among many other topics (Dauvergne and Clapp 2016). Many GEP scholars are political scientists who draw from existing work in their field, as well as reach across disciplinary boundaries in order to build theories about why environmental change occurs and how best to approach it. While not all GEP scholars are explicitly associated with political science, this book largely focuses its attention on debates within this particular academic community.

Over the years, the types of issues on the radar of scholars and policymakers have changed. Early concerns included the extraction and use of resources and species and the implications of population growth for them (Stevis 2014). "Worries about energy supply, animal rights, species extinction, global climate change, depletion of the ozone layer in the upper atmosphere, toxic wastes, the protection of whole ecosystems, environmental justice, food safety, and genetically modified organisms" have been added to these early concerns (Dryzek 2005: 3). As this extensive list suggests, there is a wide variety of environmental issues that have gotten global attention. Each of these issues has been the subject of intense debate at multiple levels in society, including the global, national, and local levels. GEP as a distinct field of study came of age in the early 1990s. This was partly motivated by the enthusiasm and attention given to environmental concerns after the 1992 Rio Conference (Betsill 2014). Rio helped to place environmental issues on the agenda of policymakers and academics alike. In the past twenty-plus years, GEP has become broader and deeper in terms of the geographical and disciplinary origins of its researchers, as well as its research agendas, substantive concerns, and theoretical approaches (Betsill et al. 2014).

Gender–Environment connections

This book is premised on the idea that environmental, social, economic, and political processes are all related, and are all gendered. In the context of this project, gender refers to socially constructed understandings of what people identified as men and women ought to be. Elsewhere I have argued that there are two important components of this definition: the idea of social construction, and a difference between sex and gender (Detraz 2012). Understanding gender to be a product of social construction means that assumptions of "masculine" and "feminine" behavior are not to be taken for granted. There is not a normal or natural way to be, but rather we are all exposed to expectations about what a man or woman is supposed to be, or how a man or woman is supposed to act. These expectations are fluid – they shift over time and across societies – and there are multiple forms of masculinity and femininity that exist within a given society at a given time. The difference between sex and gender is that sex typically refers to biological differences, while gender refers to the behaviors that are understood to be appropriate or acceptable for people who are identified as male and those identified as female. Both sex and gender are complex concepts that are frequently essentialized in both everyday conversations and much academic work.

Gender is of fundamental importance for understanding global politics because gender is intimately connected to power relations within society through patriarchal systems. Patriarchy is "the structural and ideological system that perpetuates the privileging of masculinity" (Enloe 2004: 4). Patriarchal systems exist because they become viewed as the only option by many men and women alike. Cynthia Enloe (2007: 80–1) explains that patriarchy relies on social constructions of gender to exist.

Any patriarchy survives and thrives only if its leaders and members can perpetuate a widely accepted standard of "proper" femininity. A dominant notion of "proper" femininity is especially potent when it becomes the basis by which women (and girls) judge, or "police," each other... Second, if the promoters of a patriarchal system are skillful, they will manage to make "femininity" appear natural – not the product of human decisions. This feat makes their own uses of power harder to see.

Patriarchy likewise requires the policing of masculinity in similar ways. Gender becomes seen as something fixed when its socially constructed nature is veiled. When this occurs, those individuals who are viewed as violating gender norms become seen as unnatural, and even potentially dangerous in some cases.

Gender intersects with race, class, sexuality, caste, and ethnicity in the ways that society understands difference, acceptance, and value. The term "intersectionality" was coined by critical race and legal scholar Kimberlé Crenshaw (1989, 1994) in the 1980s to highlight the various ways that forms of marginalization interact. Since this time, intersectional analysis has become widely adopted and adapted across multiple disciplines. Various feminist scholars have argued that intersectionality is an essential component for analyzing how multiple kinds of power differentials work together within society (Lykke 2009). In addition to paying attention to gender as a multifaceted concept, the present volume also considers ways that gendered marginalization and agency intersect with race, ethnicity, class, sexuality, national origin, and other forms of "difference." Intersectional research focuses on the simultaneous and interactive effects of these categories of difference. It explores multiple, co-constituted differences.

Gender is a central concept within feminist perspectives. Anne Sisson Runyan and V. Spike Peterson (2013) have popularized the idea of examining issues in world politics through gender lenses. Gender lenses are plural due to the fact that there are multiple and fluid versions of masculinity and femininity. Gender lenses allow us to examine issues in ways that go beyond what is typically visible and present in IR scholarship. To use gender lenses is to focus on gender as a specific kind of power relation, and to trace out the multiple ways that gender is central to understanding practices and processes within world politics. Gender lenses allow us to focus on the gendered nature of international institutions, and, at the same time, allow us to focus on the everyday experiences of men and women.

Much important insight into the connections between gender and the environment has come from feminist scholars, who approach the issue from a variety of perspectives. That is to say, there is not only one form of feminism, and this book draws on multiple forms. Feminist scholars highlight the specific associations between the relative position of people in society and the ways that they experience and/or contribute to environmental change. This necessitates reflecting on lived experiences through an understanding of the power relations and social norms that shape those experiences. Feminist authors often claim that the systems of domination that contribute to the marginalization of women are frequently the same systems of domination that contribute to treating the non-human world as inferior. According to Val Plumwood (2006: 54), "[a]n ecological form of feminism must be willing to mount a more thorough challenge to the dominant models of culture and humanity which define them against or in opposition to the non-human world, treating the truly human as excluding characteristics associated with the feminine, the animal and nature." This calls attention to the importance of unraveling multiple forms of power relations in order to understand how they influence drivers and experiences of environmental change and policymaking to address these in particular contexts.

Feminist environmental scholars specifically seek to understand the unique experience of women *and* men in the face of environmental damage. Rather than assume that environmental change impacts everyone similarly, or even that it impacts the marginalized in the same ways, feminist environmental scholars conclude that our relationships to nature are gendered – and that this often serves to make women more vulnerable than men to environmental change. Much environmental scholarship and policymaking treats environmental damage as a gender-neutral phenomenon, which masks the complexity of human–nature connections as well as opportunities for effective and just environmental policies.

There is a danger, however, in a simplistic analysis that automatically views women as victims in the face of environmental change. This volume calls for a more nuanced understanding of the ways that women and men both contribute to and address environmental damage. This caution is echoed by many feminists who argue against simplistic notions of nurturing or life-giving women and destructive men (Harcourt and Nelson 2015; Sandilands 1999). The automatic connection of women with environmental protection paints a simplistic, and inaccurate, picture of environmental issues. The story of environmental change and environmental protection is a very complex one that is deeply and intimately connected to socially constructed ideas of "nature" – much the same way that the story of gender is tied to socially constructed ideas of masculinity and femininity. Focusing on gender–environment connections also does not mean thinking only about marginalization and vulnerability. It is important to think of agency when discussing these connections. We must engage in careful analysis of where agency exists, and what the obstacles to agency might be.

For this reason, this book explores gendered understandings of environmental issues rather than simply the roles and responses of women in discussions of environmental issues. Examining GEP through gender lenses involves asking how the social constructions of masculinity and femininity impact the way we relate to nature, and the perceived "appropriate" roles for men and women in addressing environmental damage. This goes beyond simply bringing women into an analysis, which can isolate women from the broader sociocultural context in which behavioral norms are embedded. Therefore, this book will not only explore the particular position of women and men within the context of the environment, but also investigate the objects of study and the specific language used in present environmental discussions for examples of gendered implications.

Gender identities are constructed in part through environmental struggles and practices. Farhana Sultana (2009: 428) claims that "gendered subjectivities are socially and discursively constructed but also materially constituted;

subjectivities are produced through practices and discourses, and involve production of subject-positions (which are usually unstable and shifting). Subjects are always embedded in multiple relations of power, and are interpellated differently across space and time." This means that while socially constructed gender norms influence our relationship to our environment, the association also goes the other way: our very ideas about masculinity and femininity can be bound up with our understandings of the environment and our place within it. For example, certain tasks often come to be categorized as "men's work" or "women's work." An individual's inability to perform those tasks then comes to suggest something about them as someone who is identified as a man or a woman. In a discussion of one woman's experience of gendered assumptions about household tasks in Nepal, Andrea Nightingale (2011: 156–7) explains that

> [A]s she was now frail, she was unable to perform many of the agricultural tasks normally seen as "women's" work, requiring male household members or hired hands to do them, and changing her long-term commitment to the ecological health of those spaces. Her inability to perform tasks required of village women in this place meant that she was now less "valuable" as a woman and in many respects her power and status diminished relative to other female relatives.

This example underscores the multiple ways that gender and environment are connected. For some people, their daily interactions with the environment are deeply connected with perceptions of gender roles. Inability to perform particular roles has implications for how the individual and their community may perceive them not only as a person, but as a man or a woman.

Connecting gender and the environment: ecofeminism

The chapters in this book explore aspects of the many connections between gender and the environment. There are numerous terms that feminist scholars use to indicate a feminism that connects to environmental issues, including ecofeminism, environmentalist feminism, feminist environmentalism, eco-critical feminism, and critical feminist eco-socialism (Lykke 2009; MacGregor 2006; Plumwood 2006).

Ecofeminism represents a widely discussed lens through which to view the combination of gender issues and the environment. The term traces back to 1974 when French feminist Françoise d'Eaubonne published the word *ecoféminisme* to refer to the movement by women necessary to save the planet. The 1970s and 1980s saw the tendency for scholars and activists to use the term "ecofeminist" to refer to their struggle to link feminism and ecology. The term "ecofeminism" covers numerous approaches to connecting feminist concerns and environmental concerns (Mies and Shiva 1993; Sandilands 1999; Sturgeon 1997; Warren 1997). Noël Sturgeon (1997: 23) states: "[E]cofeminism is a movement that makes connections between environmentalisms and feminisms; more precisely, it articulates the theory that the ideologies that authorize injustices based on gender, race, and class are related to the ideologies that sanction the exploitation and degradation of the environment." Heather Eaton and Lois Ann Lorentzen (2003) explain that while ecofeminism covers a range of gender–environment connections, three are central: the empirical, the cultural, and the epistemological. The *empirical claim* refers to the fact that women are typically disproportionately impacted by the negative consequences of environmental damage (Stein 2004). This is often because of their marginalization within society, or their gendered roles in household labor. The *cultural claim* is that cultures have established an idea of the world as dualistically and hierarchically divided. "Dualisms such as reason/emotion, mind/body, culture/nature, heaven/earth, and man/woman give priority to the first over the second...Religion, philosophy, science, and cultural symbols reinforce this worldview, making male power over both women and nature appear 'natural' and thus justified" (Eaton and Lorentzen 2003: 2). The *epistemological claim* refers to the idea that women's experiences with environmental matters, due to socially constructed roles and responsibilities, make them potentially useful sources of knowledge and expertise for solutions to environmental change.

These three claims have informed ecofeminist scholarship and critiques of issues like militarization, globalization, and status quo environmental policymaking (King 1995; Seager 1993). US ecofeminism in particular had strong connections to an activist mass movement through its relation to feminist antimilitarism (Sturgeon 1997). It is frequently understood to be both an activist and an academic movement. While it is true that some versions of "ecomaternalism" or "motherhood environmentalism" that assert a special role for women as environmental caregivers have been critiqued as essentialist (MacGregor 2006; Sandilands 1999), it is also true that the ecofeminist label is just one of a number used to describe scholarship on the connections between gender and the environment.

Connecting gender and the environment: feminist political ecology   Feminist political ecology is an intellectual tradition that is largely found within geography. It builds on political ecology, which is an area of scholarly inquiry that addresses issues such as the politics of environmental degradation and conservation, the connections between neoliberal processes and environmental change, access and control of resources, and environmental struggles around power, justice, and governance, among many others (Elmhirst 2011). *Feminist Political Ecology: Global Issues and Local Experiences*, edited by Dianne Rocheleau, Barbara Thomas-Slayter, and Esther Wangari (1996), is frequently cited as one of the foundational texts for this area of scholarship. The book outlined three key themes to emerge from feminist theorizing on gender and environment and political ecology work. The first is the existence of gendered knowledge. This refers to the ways in which gender structures access to scientific and ecological knowledge. The second is a consistent pattern of gendered environmental rights and responsibilities, including differential access to land and resources through both legal and de facto claims. The third is gendered politics and grassroots activism. This final area includes pointing out the frequent participation and leadership of women in environmental movements (Nightingale 2006).

Andrea Nightingale (2006: 169) argues that current feminist political ecology scholarship rejects the essentialization that has been associated with some forms of ecofeminism. In particular, she claims that conflating gender with women is in danger of "falling back into essentialist understandings of women and their 'natural' connection to the land. This kind of essentialism masks a variety of political-economic, cultural, and symbolic processes by which gender is produced by environmental issues as well as being implicated in the construction of the 'issue' itself." Rather, feminist political ecologists stress that environmental issues are gendered in complicated and important ways. The relation between gender and environment can be understood as twofold: "the gendered environments we signify, inhabit, and transform, and the gendered power relations implicated in the complex dynamics of resource access and control, play an important role in processes of subject formation" (Hawkins and Ojeda 2011: 237). This means that societal processes that produce difference are intimately tied to a specific place. This also means that they are intimately tied to the environments being produced.

A complex understanding of gender–environmental connections is essential if we are to comprehend the multiple ways that these issues connect with policymaking. Rebecca Elmhirst (2011) argues that essentialist notions of gender–environment connections have been used to support "sustainable development" policies that have, at times, been problematic. She claims that many sustainable development agendas treated women as a homogeneous category charged with caring for degraded environments. Some activist networks have tended to advocate more nuanced strategies; however, the tendency to reduce complexity is still witnessed in some avenues of environmental policymaking. Feminist political ecology scholarship offers important insight into the multiple, multifaceted aspects of gender–environment connections.

Plan of the book

As already discussed, there is a vibrant, interdisciplinary literature on gender and environmental issues. Existing work has made strides in illustrating the deep, complex, situated connections that exist between social ideas about masculinity and femininity, and processes and policies of environmental change. The chapters in this book continue this project of revealing gender in environmental politics. They examine central debates within GEP through gender lenses in order to contribute to more holistic scholarship and policymaking on issues that are essential for both human and ecosystem health and well-being. It is important to illustrate the ways that gender is already a part of GEP scholarship and policymaking and where it needs to be fully revealed. To this end, I argue that building on existing debates is essential. Feminist work in GEP should be thought of as critically assessing the manifestations of gender in ways that strive to contribute to more comprehensive assessments of key debates, as well as work to reduce gendered discrimination as it connects to environmental issues.

The book begins with chapters on sustainability and justice as two goals of environmental policymaking. These make up the frame of the later chapters through illustrating the ways in which gender is essential to our strategies for maintaining healthy environments, as well as to understanding how and why unhealthy environments are not evenly distributed across the international system. Chapter 2 provides an assessment of the specific connections between sustainability and gender. At a very basic level, "sustainability" refers to ensuring that ecosystems continue to function. It is a concept that has been central to environmental debates among academic, policymaking, and activist communities over the past few decades. Likewise, "sustainable development" has been a popular term within environmental politics. It is an approach to economic development that tries to reconcile current economic growth and environmental protection with the needs of future generations. Chapter 2 examines the concepts of sustainability and sustainable development as key objectives of environmental politics. It argues that through an examination of factors like knowledge production and human–nature relationships, gender contributes to our understanding of which practices are sustainable and which are not. The chapter also explores how the idea of sustainable development has been criticized by feminist scholars as "greenwashing" existing development paradigms, which are often ineffective at reaching marginalized populations who are in the greatest need of help.

Chapter 3 looks at the ways that gender informs concepts of and strategies for justice as it relates to environmental processes and policies. The environmental justice movement includes the goals of ensuring the fair distribution of healthy and damaged environments across the globe, and the protection of marginalized populations against environmental damage. These distributional concerns involve the equity of benefits and ills within a state or community, as well as across the boundaries of the global North and South. In addition to a concern with environmental justice, there have also been calls for the idea of ecological justice, or the justice or morality of the relationship between humans and the rest of the natural world. Both environmental justice and ecological justice have important gendered components, such as strategies for overcoming marginalization in environmental policymaking, and the "othering" that influences where environmental damage is most likely to occur. This chapter illustrates that understanding the gendered sources of injustice, gendered experiences of injustice, and achieving gendered procedural justice aids in gaining a more comprehensive understanding not only of men's and women's position in environmental politics, but also of larger patterns of marginalization and discrimination that connect to environmental change.

The next three chapters examine debates about three central concepts for GEP scholars and policymakers: population, consumption, and security. These topics have been the subject of intense discussion among actors who play a role in environmental politics, and continue to find a place on policymaking agendas. Each chapter features a short case study on an environmental concern in order to highlight how central environmental concepts are reflected in scholarly and policymaking debates about real-world environmental issues. These short examples are intended to illustrate how various environmental concerns are connected to the goals of sustainability and justice, as well as how reflecting on gender aids in achieving these goals.

Debates about population are some of the most heated within environmental scholarship and policymaking. Chapter 4 explores this controversial issue as fundamentally gendered. Fears about "overpopulation" resulting in environmental damage have existed for centuries. These debates are controversial for a number of reasons, including their implications about the drivers of environmental change, and the power dynamics of these implications. Reflections on population are also animated because they open the door for discussion about controversial potential solutions to these issues. Feminist scholars have focused particular attention on debates about population and the potential dangers of making women's bodies the site for environmental policymaking. At the same time, gender factors into issues like societal priorities, the perceived domination of humans over the non-human world, and the role of scientific expertise in environmental solutions. The chapter explores each of these issues as they relate to long-standing deliberations about population and environmental damage. It includes an examination of the case of natural disasters to illustrate how gendered understanding of population connects to a fuller picture of sustainable environmental practices and environmental consequences, as well as the (in)justice and (in)equity of experiences of environmental change.

Chapter 5 examines what some environmental politics voices have pointed to as an important alternative to population debates: the issue of consumption. Several actors have sought to put consumption on the global radar as a contributor to environmental damage. This includes discussions of the sustainability of global consumption patterns, the role of existing economic structures in facilitating these levels of consumption, and the potential for those structures to correct potentially damaging patterns. Gender lenses highlight the fact that consumption is not gender-neutral. They provide a framework from which to ask about the social and economic processes that directly shape what we consume and why. The case of plastic consumption sheds light on how these processes influence consumption patterns that threaten human health as well as the health of ecosystems.

Finally, environmental security is a concept that acknowledges connections between environmental change and security broadly construed. Chapter 6 explores the various ways that scholars, policymakers, and the media have linked the issues of security and the environment over the past few decades, and the gendered implications of these links. To date, there has been little incorporation of gender into debates about security and the environment. This chapter illustrates how existing security and environment discourses are gendered, and provides a blueprint for how gender can be fruitfully included in the ways that we understand issues of resource conflict, human vulnerability stemming from environmental change, and security threats to the environment itself. This chapter examines the case of food security to demonstrate how environmental issues have been securitized, and how this process is gendered. The case also shows the unique forms of insecurity that men and women experience linked to these issues.

By way of a conclusion, Chapter 7 uses global discussions of climate change to examine how current environmental governance mechanisms are gendered. The chapter includes brief discussions of climate change and sustainability, justice, population, consumption, and security to demonstrate that all of these issues are related, and each has important connections to gender norms and processes across societies. Incorporating gender into environmental debates requires rethinking some of the key assumptions and concepts of environmental scholarship and policymaking. Integrating gender involves examining how environmental debates are gendered, as well as exploring the unique experiences of men and women in situations of both environmental change and environmental protection.

Over the past several decades, a range of environmental problems and concepts have been incorporated into global policymaking agendas and IR scholarship. The international community has made strides in addressing some pressing threats to sustainability, but there is more to be done. Gender is an essential part of the story of environmental protection and environmental damage. It is tied to processes that contribute to both sustainability and degradation, and processes that ensure that certain individuals and communities are at greater risk from environmental change. It is essential that we reveal these relationships in order to achieve environmental policies that are better able to address and remove sources of environmental damage in ways that are both effective and just.

2

Sustainability and Sustainable Development as Gendered Concepts

Over the past two centuries humans have dramatically shaped ecosystems. In the early 2000s, former UN Secretary General Kofi Annan called for a wide-ranging assessment of consequences of ecosystem change for human well-being. The result, the Millennium Ecosystem Assessment (MEA), was conducted as a detailed evaluation of ecosystem health. The MEA concluded that "[o]ver the past 50 years, humans have changed ecosystems more rapidly and extensively than in any comparable period of time in human history, largely to meet rapidly growing demands for food, fresh water, timber, fiber and fuel. This has resulted in a substantial and largely irreversible loss in the diversity of life on Earth" (MEA 2005). While these changes resulted in short-term gains in human well-being and development, they are achieved at long-term cost to ecosystem health and sustainability. How best to balance these needs of ecosystems with the wants and needs of humans, often discussed in terms of sustainability and sustainable development, has been the subject of much debate in the international community.

The concept of sustainability

Sustainability is a concept that has garnered a huge degree of attention within academic, policy, and activist communities over the past few decades. As will be the case for most of the concepts discussed in the chapters ahead, sustainability evokes fierce definitional debates (Lipschutz 2009). The general concept of sustainability can be traced back as far as the mid-nineteenth century, but the actual term did not enter the more general environmental vocabulary until the 1980s. Hans Carl von Carlowitz, a German mining administrator in the early 1700s, is credited with being one of the first to publish on the sustainable use of forestry. According to Carlowitz, sustainability (or *Nachhaltigkeit* in German) was needed to guide the practice of timber collection so that overharvesting and timber shortages wouldn't threaten the mining industry. The term "sustainable" as we now know it first appeared during the 1970s, in a book edited by Dennis Pirages, and later in the 1980 *World Conservation Strategy* by the International Union for Conservation of Nature (IUCN). From here, the term gained popularity among scholars and other actors during the 1980s and 1990s (Lipschutz 2009).

The term "sustainability" derives from the Latin *sustinere*, meaning "to hold up." A limited idea of environmental sustainability essentially refers to ensuring that ecosystems can function in a way that allows them to continue, or to hold up over time. In this way, sustainability connects to the idea of resilience. Resilience is usually defined as the capacity or ability of an ecosystem to absorb disruption without shifting to an alternative state, causing loss of function and services.[1] It encompasses the processes of both resistance (i.e., the amount of disturbance needed to change an ecosystem's structure) and recovery (i.e., the speed of the reversion to the original structure) (Côté and Darling 2010). Sustainability is achieved if an ecosystem manages to avoid altering to a different state and losing function. This rather limited "do no harm" approach to environmental sustainability mandates that humans avoid altering ecosystems beyond their ability to recover. It acknowledges that ecosystems always experience change, but that there are some levels of change that inhibit them from recovering. Change must be "limited in scope, and it has to occur within an appropriate frame of time" (Thiele 2013: 4). Ensuring sustainability within this approach would mean ensuring that we do not cross beyond those levels of change. The end goal for many definitions of sustainability is none other than survival (Princen 2012; Thiele 2013).

However, ideas of sustainability can also include reflections on how human beings, and the processes and institutions that make up our interactions, impact the functioning of ecosystems. Thomas Princen (2012: 469), for example, argues that sustainability "is about reconnection, about finding ourselves in nature and nature in us. It is about infusing ecological content (intentionality) into all that is our human world, especially our economy." He goes on to say that sustainability spans a long time period, focuses on the intersection between social and biophysical systems, and is sensitive to scale (Princen 2005, 2012). This definition highlights the various connections that exist between humans and the "natural" world, and how the actions of each impact the other. Sustainability involves multiple aspects working together. It is frequently conceptualized as resting on the pillars of ecology, society, and economy (Thiele 2013).[2] The ecology part of this triad refers to the healthy functioning of ecosystems. The society part speaks to the flourishing of human communities. The economy aspect refers to thriving economic systems. How these three facets fit together is the subject of debate. The concept of sustainable development, discussed later, is one take on the connections between them.

The notion of a triad reflects the recognition that human health and well-being are connected to ecosystems. Ecosystem services are the benefits we obtain from functioning ecosystems. These include providing resources such as food, water, timber, and fiber; providing regulating services that affect climate, floods, disease, wastes, and water quality; providing support services such as soil formation, photosynthesis, and nutrient cycling; and providing cultural services that provide recreational, aesthetic, and spiritual benefits (Ekins 2000). While humans are shielded from some environmental changes due to technology and other factors, we are fundamentally dependent on ecosystem services to keep our communities alive (MEA 2005).

One definitional distinction within sustainability debates involves notions of *weak sustainability* versus *strong sustainability*.[3] Advocates of weak sustainability claim that humans can come up with alternatives to many resources, and therefore avoid catastrophe if these are depleted (Hopwood et al. 2005). Advocates of strong sustainability, on the other hand, argue that there are some benefits provided by functioning ecosystems (i.e., ecosystem services) that cannot be replaced with technological switches or approaches (Agyeman et al. 2003). These include things like the processes associated with the ozone layer, photosynthesis, or the water cycle.

Achieving sustainability   This distinction between weak and strong sustainability hints at one major component of sustainability debates: how to achieve sustainability? If society is negatively impacting the health of ecosystems, what must we do to facilitate or practice sustainability? Early answers to this question often revolved around developing and implementing a "conservation ethic." Figures like Gifford Pinchot advocated for the conservation of natural resources for human benefit. Pinchot, sometimes referred to as the "father of conservation" in the US, was the Chief of the US Forest Service in the late 1800s. He felt that natural resources like wildlife and land were best protected through scientific management in order to maximize their long-term benefits for humans.

In contrast, Scottish naturalist John Muir sought to protect the environment from human degradation. His idea of "preservationism" held that nature has intrinsic value outside of human benefit. While he recognized that humans rely on the environment for the provision of some basic needs, he also thought that we derive great spiritual fulfillment from interacting with wilderness, open spaces, and scenic beauty. It was Muir's belief in this spiritual fulfillment that led him to push for protected spaces in his home of California and beyond, as well as found the Sierra Club, an influential environmental organization. Debates about conservation versus preservation were central to the early environmental movement in the United States. These debates centered on how best to ensure the continued flourishing of ecosystems, and the role of humans in the sustainability and protection of the environment.

Many voices claim that sustainability can be achieved through increased "eco-efficiency" in the use of natural resources. This instrumentalist view sees changing social practices and technologies as key to ensuring these efficiencies. Technological solutions in particular are frequently seen as the key to achieving sustainability. A critique of this perspective is that technological approaches would also need to confront any potential risks that accompany new technologies, which may have unanticipated or unwanted consequences for ecosystems. What many scholars call for is reflection on how we balance technology, human needs, and environmental sustainability (Lipschutz 2009). This perspective cautions us to think through the consequences of our interactions with natural systems. What may lead to reducing environmental damage in one respect might not offer a long-term path to sustainability. What is good for one facet of human life – economic development, for example – might not be compatible with a strong sustainability ethic.

The concept of sustainable development

Like sustainability, sustainable development is a concept with a relatively long and complex history in GEP. It was introduced in the 1980s as a compromise position between those that wanted to draw attention to global environmental damage and those that wanted to ensure that economically marginalized states could continue to develop their economies in ways consistent with the development process of economically powerful states (Happaerts and Bruyninckx 2014). The term was first introduced globally in 1980 in the World Conservation Strategy (IUCN 1980). The most commonly cited definition of sustainable development comes from the World Commission on Environment and Development's[4] (1987: 8) report, *Our Common Future*, which defined sustainable development as "development that meets the needs of the present without compromising the ability of future generations to meet their own needs." The report's title signals the opinion of the Commission that humanity had reached a point where global problems required global solutions (Happaerts and Bruyninckx 2014).

Commitment to the idea of sustainable development was witnessed during the 1992 Earth Summit. The conference, featuring 171 state delegations, endorsed a particular version of sustainable development through *Agenda 21*, a follow-up to *Our Common Future*. The international community met again in Johannesburg in 2002 for the World Summit on Sustainable Development. Throughout each of these global efforts to solidify the concept of sustainable development into workable policy goals, it largely "remained very much a discourse, rather than a plan of action" (Dryzek 2005: 149). Despite this lack of an agreed-upon definition, narratives associated with sustainable development have been adopted by states, NGOs, intergovernmental organizations (IGOs), and multinational corporations (Dryzek 2005; Happaerts and Bruyninckx 2014).[5]

Sustainable development implies a sometimes delicate balance between the needs of humans to improve their well-being, and preserving ecosystems and natural resources in the interest of future generations. This intergenerational component of sustainable development can be understood as the "conservation of options" for future generations (Brown Weiss 1989). It acknowledges that the development choices that we make today can impact, either positively or negatively, the available options for generations to come. There is a critique of sustainable development, however, that says it has become an international buzzword that has come to mean almost everything and nothing.[6] Actors used the term with a focus on either the "sustainable" or the "development" part of the concept to mean very different things. Nonetheless, it remains an often-used concept within discussions of environmental change. Sustainable development is frequently understood as an anthropocentric concept, meaning that it is oriented toward the needs of humans first and foremost (Dryzek 2005). While the policy translation of sustainable development in places like Sweden and Finland has had a strong environmental bias (Happaerts and Bruyninckx 2014), for many actors sustainable development has meant a focus on economic development for present and future generations with a recognition that this is difficult or impossible in a thoroughly degraded environment.

In this way, sustainable development often tends to work with a relatively weak notion of sustainability. It has often been conceptualized as sustainability within the confines of economic growth. This approach has been roundly criticized by environmental NGOs and members of the scientific community for failing to focus more attention on the limits of economic growth that is likely associated with sustainability. At the same time, many NGOs and states from the global South have pushed for development-focused conceptualizations as a means to reduce poverty. Early environmentalism across the regions of the global South was often connected to the concerns and narratives of the environmentalism of the global North – including conservation and/or preservation of wilderness and species. As it became clear that societies in Southern states sought a balance between environmental protection and economic and social well-being, NGOs responded by taking social justice and economic livelihood issues more seriously. This helped feed into the idea of sustainable development (Wapner 2012). Adil Najam (2005: 117) explains that the notion of sustainable development "has been a direct consequence of Southern unease with giving a primacy to 'environmental' politics." Marrying environmental concerns with economic concerns "has been the price that needed to be paid for gaining the active participation of developing countries." A transformation of dominant approaches to sustainable development occurred through a Southern desire, and Northern promise, that sustainable development could foster "a more just and fair international order and of more balanced North–South relations" (Najam 2005: 117). These differing conceptualizations and levels of support for the concept hint at the complexity under which environmental issues intersect with issues of power, incentives, responsibilities, and gender (which will be discussed later).

Poverty in/and sustainable development Global poverty has been a prominent feature in debates about both the need for and path to sustainable development, and the causes of environmental change. *Our Common Future* pointed to poverty as a core cause of unsustainable development. It argued that the best way forward was to stimulate sustainable economic growth. The authors encouraged "developed states" to increase transfers of both economic assistance and technology to "developing states" as a path toward development that was sustainable for the future. It was premised on the belief in "the possibility for a new era of economic growth, one that must be based on policies that sustain and expand the environmental resource base," which is "absolutely essential to relieve the great poverty that is deepening in much of the developing world" (World Commission on Environment and Development 1987: 1). The authors called poverty "an evil in itself," but also declared that "a world in which poverty is endemic will always be prone to ecological and other catastrophes" (World Commission on Environment and Development 1987: 8). This notion of poverty resulting in unsustainable behavior is a widespread one. It is linked to narratives of people acting unsustainably out of a lack of alternative options.

For many, sustainable development is an attempt to marry environmental issues with poverty issues (Jackson 2009). While it is true that "development" goes beyond reducing poverty, that has been regarded by many as an essential first step to development. Some global approaches to sustainable development also contain a focus on poverty. For instance, the 2015 United Nations General Assembly (UNGA) plan for sustainable development includes a commitment to poverty reduction in its very first paragraph. The document states that "[w]e recognize that eradicating poverty in all its forms and dimensions, including extreme poverty, is the greatest global challenge and an indispensable requirement for sustainable development" (UNGA 2015: 1). Ending poverty is the first of the seventeen goals that the document sets out for the global community.

Sustainable development in practice: ecological modernization
Ecological modernization is an influential policy-based discourse related to sustainable development. First identified in the early 1980s by Joseph Huber and Martin Jänicke, German social scientists, ecological modernization has been particularly prominent in Europe (Mol 2003). Hajer (1995: 25) defines ecological modernization as a discourse "that recognizes the structural character of the environmental problematique but none the less assumes that existing

political, economic, and social institutions can internalize the care for the environment." Since modernization and degradation of the environment are linked to the development of a market-driven mode of production, businesses in particular are at the core of the concept. It is largely oriented toward maintaining the neoliberal status quo, albeit with some particular reforms. Advocates support a partnership, founded on workings of the market and technology, comprised of business, government, moderate environmentalists, and scientists. Companies and industry see incentives in participating in reforms, as there are benefits if they are far-sighted rather than interested primarily in hasty profits. Beyond this, the subject matter of ecological modernization includes approaches for capitalist society to move toward greater environmental sustainability through commitments from multiple sectors of the society. These commitments include "foresight, attacking problems at their origins, holism, greater valuation of scarce nature, and the precautionary principle" (Dryzek 2005: 169). Governments perform tasks like setting standards and providing incentives to businesses. Ecological modernization is built on the assumption that environmental protection and economic prosperity can be achieved simultaneously (Hajer 1995). While it has direct implications for power relations and other global processes, there is not a central concern for equity, or justice (Hopwood et al. 2005). There has also been very limited, if any, attention on gender in this and most other notions of sustainable development or environmental sustainability.

Gender and sustainability debates

This book is premised on the argument that gender lenses offer an essential perspective on GEP. In particular, gender lenses aid in rethinking central goals like sustainability and justice, which are deeply influential in most environmental debates. Environmental practices and governance are gendered. The challenge is revealing the areas of complement and contradiction between the various perspectives on gender and the environment, and the important GEP scholarship already being done. Gender lenses challenge existing notions of sustainability and sustainable development by probing power relations, contesting dominant discourses, and offering alternative insights into both the processes of (un)sustainability and how these might be altered in positive ways. While there is no single feminist perspective on sustainability or sustainable development, incorporating feminist insights into debates about these influential concepts can aid in renewing essential discussions, which are important for both scholarly pursuits and policymaking.

In 1995, the Fourth World Conference on Women was held in Beijing, China. Nearly 180 government delegations from countries around the world, along with around 2,500 NGOs, met to discuss a broad range of issues concerning women. The resulting Beijing Declaration committed to the "[e]radication of poverty based on sustained economic growth, social development, environmental protection and social justice." The Declaration also argued that this progress "requires the involvement of women in economic and social development, equal opportunities and the full and equal participation of women and men as agents and beneficiaries of people-centred sustainable development" (UN 1995: 3). The Beijing Declaration and Platform for Action highlighted the connections between gender and the environment in a visible way, but what does this mean for our understanding of the practices of gender and sustainability/sustainable development?[7]

Sustainable relationships   A starting point in discussions of sustainability is reflecting on the place of human beings in processes of environmental change. Many of the discourses that have guided our understandings of "environment" over the years have treated ecosystems as something for humans (or "man") to conquer and harness. This has not always been the case. Throughout history, many societies perceived the Earth as a living, intelligent being (Litfin 2012). For the past several hundred years, on the other hand, the environment has been seen in the global North primarily as external to humanity – something to be utilized for human benefit, with a few designated areas preserved as wilderness or parks. The relationship between humans and ecosystem became conceptualized through domination and triumph. This perspective was connected to the development of capitalism, the Industrial Revolution, and modern science. Karen Litfin (2012: 420) explains that "after Descartes, Western science and philosophy generally understood the world as a machine, a view that has been increasingly globalized in recent decades. Yet, in the larger context of human thought, including the West, the mechanistic view of nature is an aberration." Speaking as a representative of the mechanistic view, Francis Bacon claimed that "the world is made for man, not man for the world" (quoted in Hopwood et al. 2005: 38–9).

Feminist scholars have long expressed their unease with these domination narratives (Harcourt 1994; Merchant 1996; Plumwood 1993). Conceptualizing the environment as an external entity that is subject to first discovery and then mastery serves to mentally sever humanity's deep connection to the ecosystems that give us food, clothing, shelter – life. It also justifies prioritizing human needs over the needs of ecosystems in ways that can lead to unsustainable practices. Val Plumwood (2002: 1) cautions us that "the often-invoked term 'sustainability' tends to obscure the seriousness of the situation; clearly no culture which sets in motion massive processes of biospheric degradation which it has normalised, and which it cannot respond to or correct, can hope to survive for very long." Using gender lenses to understand sustainability allows us to reflect on the ways that domination narratives contribute to both environmental *unsustainability* and the normalization of various forms of inequality in society.

One potential path to overcoming both unsustainability and inequality is to challenge existing values and norms within society. Scholars have put forth concepts like "a sustainability ethic" or "sustainability-oriented values" to denote a normative shift toward privileging environmental protection (Princen 2012). An inclusive sustainability ethic would require considering global power relations that simultaneously contribute to environmental destruction and systematic discrimination based on gender, class, ethnicity, sexuality, etc. It is important to reflect on the likelihood that the domination of humans over other species is potentially detrimental to the sustainability of each. While feminist intersectionality debates have rarely challenged human domination over their environment, they do call attention to the complex ways that difference influences power relations, which in turn inform our understanding of anthropocentricism (Lykke 2009). Feminist environmental scholars have long cautioned that the normalization of domination in one sphere is frequently tied to the normalization of domination in other spheres (Merchant 1996; Warren 2000). It is therefore essential to question the long-term implications of thinking and doing GEP within a mindset that regularizes a view of the environment as something to dominate or master.

Rethinking sustainability through gender lenses also requires examining gendered differences in environmental behavior, and what might account for these differences. This means examining the relationships we have with the environment that are shaped by societal expectations. Studies from around the world have found that men and women often exhibit different environmental behavior and concerns (Sundström and McCright 2014; Xiao and McCright 2014). For instance, there is evidence that white males in the United States are the group that tends to express the least concern about climate change effects (McCright 2010; McCright and Dunlap 2011). Another study finds that after controlling for education, women in China were more likely than men to engage in "private" environmentally friendly behaviors like recycling and bringing reusable shopping bags to stores; however, men on average possessed more environmental knowledge than women, and in urban China, men were more concerned with environmental issues than women (Xiao and Hong 2010). Within both the Swedish general public and local government, women report greater environmental concern than men (Sundström and McCright 2014). Finally, a study from the UK finds that men are less environmentally friendly than women in both beliefs and self-reported consumer behavior (Clements 2012). These results from multiple countries suggest that gendered patterns of life influence environmental behavior. Gendered patterns of behavior in these areas likely relate to gendered roles in households and society. It is important, therefore, for studies to provide information about the ways that gender expectations influence behaviors which have connections to sustainability. Studies like these shed light on the fact that if we are to truly understand human behavior that is either sustainable or unsustainable, we have to understand the social, economic, and political processes that shape those behaviors. To date, there has been much more attention on the various ways that class contributes to sustainability than gender, despite the fact that both are essential to the story of how patterns of behavior are shaped by our societies.

Gender and environmental knowledge   Concern about the future of ecosystems has motivated various forms of environmentalism across the globe. Most of the figures in the US that are centrally associated with foundational environmental concepts like sustainability, conservation, and preservation are men. The group of central figures that are typically taught in US classes on the environment, including John Muir, Gifford Pinchot, Aldo Leopold, and others, is lacking in racial or gender diversity. In general, the early conservation and preservation movements of the global North were generally led by middle- and upper-class white men. Several historical accounts highlight how gender norms played a role in the framing of the movements, as well as the members' understanding of their place within them (Gottlieb 2005; Nash 2001). In the late nineteenth century, concerns about masculinity were heightened as social and economic shifts (e.g., industrialization and urbanization) resulted in new types of white-collar employment. These jobs were regarded as "soft" and incompatible with dominant standards of masculinity for the time (Mann 2011). Wealthy men of this era therefore looked to wilderness adventures to foster "toughness" and "virility" (Nash 2001). Ecosystems provided realms within which to (re)connect with masculinity.

None of this is to say that women were not present as either leaders or members of early environmental movements. Quite the contrary. Women were actively involved in organizations like the Audubon Society from their start. One of the few women typically mentioned in the list of early US environmentalists is Rachel Carson. Carson's (1962) *Silent Spring* is widely credited with helping to usher in a new era of environmental awareness within the US and more broadly. *Silent Spring* sounded an alarm about the harmful effects of pesticides and herbicides, the usage of which increased dramatically during the "chemical revolution" of the 1950s (Wapner 2010a). Carson was trained as a marine biologist and worked at the US Fish and Wildlife Service. She had a distinct ability to convey complex scientific and medical information in understandable arguments about health and environmental sustainability. Her contributions to current environmentalism were vast. Her environmental knowledge challenged scientific assumptions, but was also given legitimacy, at least to some extent, because of her scientific training.

Feminist scholars have often been critical of the ways in which our societies approach science, and the automatic authority bestowed on "scientific information." This includes a critique of contemporary understandings of power and objectivity in scientific inquiry. There is often an assumption that environmental knowledge comes from "experts," rather than other sources. This is a problematic assumption, because it presumes that the scientific community is always an objective source of knowledge that merely needs to be inserted into political discussions. Research indicates that some research questions or issues are not given the same levels of attention as others (Karlsson et al. 2007). Additionally, scientific attention or expertise is not always evenly distributed across the globe (Paasi 2005; Pasgaard and Strange 2013). In a review of over 15,000 scholarly publications about climate change, Maya Pasgaard et al. (2015) found that research production was fairly limited to a select group of states, and the authors tended to speak to other researchers within their own networks rather than there being a large degree of knowledge exchange between networks. These authors concluded that there is a publication bias toward richer and less vulnerable states, which have stronger institutions and more press freedom. The authors claim that a number of factors influence these trends, including the standards and requirements for scientific publishing as well as the tendency to stick to close networks within academia. These findings suggest that scientific knowledge that may be useful to policy debates might be limited due to network trends in knowledge production.

Feminists and other critical scholars challenge the idea that knowledge and expertise on environmental issues should be based on "hard science" alone. Some feminist scholars question the privileging of science in areas like sustainability, and problematize the idea of the "sacredness" of science. For instance, Sandra Harding (1993: 39) claims that "[t]he project that science's sacredness makes taboo is the examination of science in just the ways any other institution or set of social practices can be examined." She argues that scientific knowledge, which is supposed to be objective, is often the subjective knowledge of privileged voices. This is not to say that there is a fundamental problem with scientific objectivity, but rather that we must also critically evaluate the place of the marginalized in the methodological and substantive concept of science (Harding 1993). Science is often assumed to be correct and beyond questioning in today's society. Relying on an institution that both is dominated by males and is a part of the patriarchal social structure of society may be questioned by those that wish to call attention to its potential problems as well as benefits (King 1995). This is not to suggest that feminist environmental scholars advocate for a rejection of scientific knowledge. Rather, they call attention to the need to critically evaluate the societal processes that assign "expertise," and the contributions that local gendered knowledge can also make toward understanding environmental problems and processes of sustainability.

Local knowledge is knowledge that is situated in context.[8] It results from lived experiences. This local ecological knowledge

> can reveal counter-intuitive outcomes and help resolve apparent contradictions through its strengths in situations of high variability, ability to integrate over a range of variables and time scales, and operation outside of Western scientific logic. This suggests local knowledge does not exist to be confirmed or disproved by Western science, but rather can also advance Western science and help contribute to its debates. (Klein et al. 2014: 141)

While scientific knowledge is also situated, it is often regarded as being separate from, and has historically been regarded as more legitimate than, local knowledge, though many environmental scholars and policymakers reject this last point (Ascher et al. 2010).

Concepts like "street science" (i.e., using local knowledge to understand and challenge perceptions of environmental issues) or "citizen science" (i.e., active participation by non-scientists in scientific research) illustrate alternative forms of knowledge, beyond strictly scientific knowledge, that are sometimes used in environmental understanding and policy-making (Johnson et al. 2014). Scholars of environmental science and policy have considered the potential benefits of broad engagement in knowledge production for many years. It is thought to be an important way to gather data and to make science more inclusive (Johnson et al. 2014; Klein et al. 2014). Again, these alternative forms of knowledge genera-tion do not devalue science, but rather provide opportunities to create knowledge through different sources that may make it more reliable, while also making the process of knowledge generation more inclusive. Knowledge may increase in reliability due to the fact that first-hand accounts of environmental change are beneficial to spotting long-term trends as well as understanding the experiences and impacts of environmental change. Local knowledge, like all knowl-edge, is gendered. It is influenced by societal expectations of the roles and responsibilities that people are expected to fulfill. It is shaped by the same social, economic, and political structures that assign greater value to characteristics associ-ated with masculinity than with femininity (Runyan and Peterson 2013).

Gender and sustainable development debates

Sustainable development has become a central narrative in discussions of sustainability. Because it has achieved such a key place in environmental debates over time, it is essential that gender be incorporated in our understanding of sustain-able development. *Agenda 21* was the international commu-nity's attempt to gain momentum on plans for achieving sustainable development. This document stressed the need for gender to be incorporated into our understanding of sustain-able development, since "women are a particularly disadvan-taged group" (UNDSD 1992: 17).[9] Victim and vulnerability of women narratives are rather typical in documents like these. At the same time, however, many women *have* experienced a disproportionate share of environmental burden. It is important to reflect on the numerous experiences that women have with environmental change and benefits. While many women struggle with marginalized environments, women have also expressed their agency during the course of environmental debates. Women have a long history of organizing for environmental sustainability and sustainable development. For example, 1,500 women from eighty-three countries assembled in Miami for the first World Women's Congress for a Healthy Planet in 1991. This event was organized in preparation for the UN Conference on Environment and Development (the Rio Conference), and the resulting *Women's Action Agenda 21* served as an important lobbying document in subsequent global meetings about sustainability (Dankelman 2002). Likewise, the Beijing Platform for Action contained an entire section on "women and the environment," which placed women in essential roles relating to promoting a sustainable future (UN 1995). There is not a single path toward sustainability, but rather multiple paths that pay attention to local context, local perspectives, and diverse power relations (Harcourt 1994). Feminist perspectives intersect with debates about sustainable development in various ways, including challenging expectations about where environmental expertise comes from, providing a critique of mainstream development politics, and providing a critique of mainstream notions of equity.

Gender in policy documents   Gender issues, albeit often in relatively limited form, have appeared in sustainable development debates within the UN. The UN adopted the strategy of "gender mainstreaming" in the 1995 Beijing Platform for Action. Since then, numerous UN branches have included a specific goal of gender mainstreaming in the way they approach their target issue. The UN (2002: v) has defined gender mainstreaming as

> the process of assessing the implications for women and men of any planned action, including legislation, policies or programmes in all areas and at all levels. It is a strategy for

making women's as well as men's concerns and experiences an integral dimension of design, implementation, monitoring and evaluation of policies and programmes in all political, economic and societal spheres so that women and men benefit equally and inequality is not perpetuated. The ultimate goal is to achieve gender equality.

This states that gender equality is the ultimate goal, and gender mainstreaming is conceptualized as a strategy to achieve that goal. The term "mainstreaming" is intended to stress that a simple count of men and women in UN branches is not enough to ensure that the particular needs and perspectives of both men and women are being incorporated into UN policymaking.

UNEP is one of the many UN branches that has instituted gender mainstreaming in its processes. A 2012 assessment of gender mainstreaming practices across UNEP found that the institution has taken multiple concrete steps to mainstream gender across the organization; however, there are some significant areas for improvement. "Mechanisms for gender mainstreaming have been put in place in some of the core areas of UNEP's work, but these are not yet robust enough to ensure compliance and a meaningful integration of gender perspectives into operational or programmatic areas of work." The report found low levels of resource allocation from core funds as well as low levels of awareness of gender mainstreaming practices among staff. Additionally, the "insufficient commitment by management and staff to promote meaningful gender mainstreaming, and inadequate mechanisms for ensuring results suggest that gender mainstreaming in UNEP is not yet sustainable" (Mantilla 2012: 1). These findings are consistent with reviews of gender mainstreaming practices in other UN areas, like peacekeeping (Puechguirbal 2010).

It is important to assess gender practices and understanding within the UN because its branches continue to shape global debates about environmental issues. While the UN is by no means the only important actor that performs this role, its reports have high visibility within the international community. To date, gender has been at least tangentially a part of global environmental debates over sustainable development. When gender has appeared, however, it has tended to be restricted to a focus on women (Dankelman 2002). This is problematic because it makes men invisible. The dominant role of men in making policies regarding sustainable development, as well as the tendency for men to have greater social resources to avoid many forms of environmental vulnerability, are hidden. We are therefore not forced to confront the larger gender structures that shape our daily lives. This focus exclusively on women also has the potential to essentialize across a large array of lived experiences. Women's and men's knowledge of and relationship to environmental change are influenced by not only gender, but also race, class, sexuality, political power, economic position, and social status (Harcourt and Nelson 2015). While it is helpful to identify regularized patterns of experience that can contribute to our understanding of where (un)sustainability lies, it is unconstructive to make broad generalizations that assume lived experiences in one set of circumstances will look the same as those in another. It is therefore necessary to examine power relations in general and how these contribute to knowledge about and solutions to unsustainability.

What development?   A major critique of sustainable development is that it has often been conceptualized in ways that allow change to come in the form of minimal adjustments to current structures of society rather than calling for substantial change. Feminists join other critics who challenge the belief that seeking incremental changes, typically within the boundaries of the existing global processes and power relations, will be able to bring about the real transformations that would be required to realize a sustainable society (Happaerts and Bruyninckx 2014). There is a fear that sustainable development policies are often focused on the "development" side of the coin, with neoliberal development approaches ruling the day (Harcourt 1994). For many, the push for sustainable development is little more than "a vehicle to legitimize further industrial growth by transforming environmental problems into developmental issues, which then could be tackled by means of more money, more technology, and more management" (Park et al. 2008: 4). In particular, many feminist environmental scholars view environmental problems as grounded in fundamental characteristics of our current society – including how humans relate to ecosystems. This perspective argues that reform is not enough, since many of the central causes of environmental problems are located within the very structures of society. Economic and political processes that are not primarily concerned with environmental sustainability or even human well-being cannot just be reformed. They must be transformed in order to avoid a mounting environmental and social crisis. This transformation is typically conceptualized as including a larger role for those who currently find themselves outside of the main centers of power: women, indigenous communities, the poor, etc. (Hopwood et al. 2005). Critiques of neoliberal development come in a range of shapes and sizes, a topic that will be further explored in Chapter 5. Feminist critiques often feature a concern that policy paths toward development tend to favor those who are already powerful (Benería 2003). The costs and benefits of development are usually spread unevenly, and these differences are gendered.

Early attempts to conceptualize the connections between gender and development manifested in a campaign known as Women in Development (WID). The WID perspective emerged in the 1970s as a way to call attention to women's needs in economic development approaches. It argued that women were productive members of economies, and therefore central to development ideas (Bradshaw 2015). Policies associated with this approach were oriented toward removing barriers to women accessing economic resources.[10] Over time, this perspective was critiqued as failing to challenge where those barriers to resources came from and how they were gendered (Sturgeon 1997). The approach was also viewed by some as containing rather simplistic assumptions about "Third World women" that were not very helpful in assessing policy or contributing to alternative development narratives.

The gender and development approach (GAD) emerged as a reaction against the perceived essentialist narratives of WID surrounding women from the global South.[11] There were a few important differences between these perspectives. First, a shift from "women" to "gender" indicates that it is unequal power relations between men and women that are the problem for development – not women. Second, the use of "and" rather than "in" suggests that it is necessary to examine both gender and development, and the various ways that these two fit together. It is not enough to add women to the current discourses and processes of development, but rather it is crucial that those discourses and processes be problematized (Bradshaw 2015).

An additional shift has emerged in the form of perspectives that incorporate women, environment, and development (WED) that begins by questioning whether development processes are sustainable and/or desirable for much of the world (Harcourt 1994; Mellor 2003). WED challenges the traditional approach to development with the claim that its "biases and assumptions exclude both women and nature from its understanding of development, and in so doing, has contributed to the current economic and ecological crisis" (Harcourt 1994: 3). For example, Vandana Shiva has popularized the idea of "maldevelopment" to refer to perspectives on development and modernization that are built on Western ideas of reductionism, duality, and linearity. She argues that maldevelopment is "the violation of the integrity of organic, interconnected and interdependent systems, that sets in motion a process of exploitation, inequality, injustice and violence. It is blind to the fact that a recognition of nature's harmony and action to maintain it are preconditions for distributive justice" (Shiva 1989: 5–6). Those concerned with women's frequent situation of being on the fringes of development are not satisfied with the traditional conceptualization of the term "sustainable development" (Harcourt 1994; Mies and Shiva 1993). Since different paths to development often have survival implications for a population, a feminist approach to sustainable development that takes into account the needs of women alongside men, the ecosystem, and future generations within a particular setting is necessary.

The feminist sustainable development approach taken by this book includes elements of empowerment and agency. It is built on a notion of development as empowering people to make choices. These choices deal not only with economic factors like livelihood, but also with personal reflections on "the good life," while recognizing that these are fluid ideas that are rooted in social understanding. In this way, a feminist sustainable development challenges the power relations embedded in many previous versions of the concept (Di Chiro 2015). Feminist and other scholars critical of the imperialistic undertones of influential sustainable development narratives reject the idea that ideas of sustainability come only from experts. Catriona Sandilands (1999: 128), for instance, claims that sustainable development narratives, like those of *Agenda 21*, are "clearly intended as a way for countries of the North to better hold countries of the South as environmental hostages to particular economic agendas." While not all critics would use language this strong, the sentiment behind it is shared by those who are skeptical of ideas of development that require few changes to the lives and lifestyles of those who are already powerful, and who benefit from economic and political systems that pollute our environment and discriminate against the marginalized.

Gender, poverty, and equity in sustainable development

Two aspects of reworked ideas of development are critical perspectives on poverty and equity. As mentioned previously, poverty has been at the forefront of debates about sustainable development since the earliest days of the concept. For decades, scholars and policymakers have considered factors like differences in poverty levels between states in the global North and global South, and the impacts of these differences for environmental protection (Torras and Boyce 1998). What has frequently been missing from these discussions, however, is the ways in which vulnerabilities and social processes that contribute to poverty are gendered. There have been several global studies noting the overrepresentation of women among the world's poor (UNEP 2005; World Bank 2012).[12] Gender norms result in women often being excluded from opportunities, in a way that includes reduced access to education, livelihood security, political power, and many others, which in turn increases their likelihood of living with poverty and vulnerability (Elborgh-Woytek et al. 2013).[13]

It is important, however, to critically evaluate the links between gender and poverty. There have been many debates within feminist scholarship on the essentializing nature of claims about the "feminization of poverty." It is accurate to say that women are overrepresented within the ranks of the poor in most states. What is necessary is critical reflection on the various ways that this happens across societies. For instance, female-headed households are often regarded as being at great risk for poverty. We know that they often struggle to receive aid in the aftermath of disasters (Enarson 2012), and often suffer disproportionately during times of drought (Fisher and Carr 2015). What is dangerous, however, is only focusing on female-headed households and their relationship to poverty. It is also necessary to examine the "secondary poverty" of women and children in male-headed households, where the household itself is not poor but certain members within the household are (Bradshaw 2015; Chant 2008). The roles of men and women should be assessed for the ways that they intersect with sources and experiences of poverty.

These connections have been incorporated into some policy debates in which ideas about poverty have been broadened beyond income to encompass factors like lack of empowerment, capacity, opportunity, and security (UNEP 2005). Feminist approaches to sustainable development focus on both the sustainability part of the concept and the development part. They recognize that poverty acts as a limit to choice and the ability to live in dignity. A report from the Democratic Republic of the Congo (DRC) reveals that insecurity and poverty have pushed many people into jobs like artisanal and small-scale mining. It is estimated that between 500,000 and 2 million people work formally or informally in mining in the DRC. NGOs and other entities have documented a range of labor and social problems with this employment, including sexual violence. While sexual violence at the hands of soldiers during wartime has a long-documented history, the DRC report revealed that the perpetrators were most commonly civilians who were taking advantage of populations in poverty and vulnerability due to livelihood insecurity and lack of education (Harvard Humanitarian Initiative 2015). Examples like these illustrate that while the international community has long been concerned with the sustainability of mining throughout the globe, there has been very little attention to gendered patterns of vulnerability associated with forms of resource extraction. Poverty connects to both social and environmental vulnerability and unsustainability in ways that are deeply gendered (UNEP 2005).

Feminist approaches to sustainable development reject policy solutions that put additional time burdens on women around the world when their existing contributions to society go unnoticed and uncompensated (Federici 2009). Academics from various disciplines have critiqued essentialist conceptualizations of both indigenous peoples and women, particularly rural women (Dove 2006). These groups are simultaneously cast as resource users who contribute to environmental degradation due to poverty and livelihoods that rely on environmental change and extraction, and as groups with close ties to the environment who can reverse environmental damage (Detraz 2014; Sapra 2009). It is a great burden to place on the shoulders of marginalized populations. Sustainable development should proceed from arguments based on sustainability and equity rather than on romanticized notions of marginalized communities as automatically better stewards of the environment.

Conclusions

In an assessment of sustainability, Leslie Paul Thiele (2013: 13) argues that if current tendencies continue, "future inhabitants of Planet Earth will face a hotter and more disruptive climate, rising oceans, vastly diminished biodiversity, and natural resources in short supply. It will also be a more crowded world, more polluted, and prone to greater social and political instability. Life will be more precarious." As I said earlier, a very basic definition of sustainability is survival. This idea of sustainability, therefore, holds a self-interest imperative for humans. If we alter ecosystems beyond their ability to recover, we all suffer. However, this chapter suggests that we will not all suffer equally.

Using gender lenses to understand sustainability debates leads us to question domination narratives that have become quite popular in discourses about environmental change. They call for a recognition of the deep connections between humans and ecosystems. Gender lenses also challenge the idea that knowledge about sustainability and sustainable paths for the future relies exclusively on the perspectives of the scientific community. While GEP books and articles rarely, if ever, reject alternative sources of knowledge, it is often the case that a reliance on scientific knowledge goes unspoken (and potentially uncontested). Scientific bodies are cited as legitimate voices without the source or implications of that legitimacy being questioned. Feminist perspectives frequently contest what is taken for granted in other areas of scholarship, and this is no less true in debates about knowledge. Women and men have unique perspectives on environmental change and sustainability due to the various roles that they play in society. Scholars and policymakers are likely to miss out by failing to include these varied perspectives.

Gender lenses contribute to notions of sustainable development through problematizing discourses that continue to see development as neoliberal-oriented economic growth. Approaches to sustainable development have often failed to live up to their promises by watering down the concept of sustainability to the point of referring vaguely to "green" initiatives, and limiting the concept of development to a reinforcement of standard growth-oriented economics. Development as a form of empowerment is more closely associated with feminist goals of equity. Development as facilitating agency and livelihood security while reducing vulnerability is more in keeping with goals of both equity and sustainability for current and future generations, a notion that sits at the root of feminist sustainable development discourses. Sustainability is necessary for ecosystem survival, which includes human survival. Gender lenses offer a perspective on sustainability that encourages widespread participation and critical conceptualizations of sustainable relationships, poverty, and development. This approach is beneficial both because it gives us a clearer picture of the practices and processes that contribute to unsustainability, and because it is a more just approach to environmental politics.

3
Revealing Gender in Environmental Justice

Warren County is located in the eastern part of North Carolina, which is in the southeastern part of the United States. The principally rural county has historically been among the poorest in the region, with a large percentage of African-American residents.[1] In 1978, oil laced with polychlorinated biphenyl (PCB) was illegally dumped along roadways in North Carolina. PCB is part of a group of human-made organic chemicals that were produced in the US from 1929 to 1979. Their production was banned in 1979. There is evidence that PCBs cause cancer, as well as have a variety of other adverse health effects on the reproductive system, immune system, nervous system, and endocrine system (EPA 2014). In order to address the PCB contamination, in 1982 the state government of North Carolina ordered that the contaminated soil be dug up and removed. It chose to build a landfill to house the PCB-laced soil in the city of Afton in Warren County (Bullard 2005).[2] The term "environmental racism" was coined by Benjamin Chavis at a protest over the siting of the landfill in a predominately African-American, poor neighborhood. Chavis, the head of the United Church of Christ (UCC)'s Commission on Racial Justice and a trained chemist, defined "environmental racism" as "racial discrimination in the siting of toxic waste dumps and polluting industries, unequal enforcement of environmental laws, and the exclusion of people of color from environmental decision-making" (Schlosberg and Carruthers 2010: 13). This concept of environmental racism highlighted oppression, political disenfranchisement, and poor health as a result of environmental change and the governance strategies to address it. Environmental racism, environmental justice, and ecological justice have become related but distinct ideas that connect a normative commitment to fairness and equity with environmental change. Along with sustainability, normative concerns about justice and fairness have motivated a great deal of environmental activism and GEP scholarship.

Normative concerns   Fairness, inequality, and justice: all of these terms have many definitions that reflect varying perspectives, interests, and contexts. For instance, John Rawls (1971) developed a theory of fairness in distribution based in part on self-interest. It is a moral idea that specifies that when one does not know whether one will end up in a marginalized group, it may be individually as well as socially advantageous to set policy before the outcome is known to ensure that the least well-off member of an affected group is as well off as possible. For Rawls, acting under a "veil of ignorance" means that you act in this way even if you are unsure whether you will occupy the marginalized group. The resulting equity rule says that we act fairly by ensuring equitable distribution of cost and benefit before a negative event has taken place. This rule will assure you receive adequate or acceptable treatment even if you occupy the most disadvantaged role in society. In reality, however, there are regularized patterns of experience that make it relatively simple to determine which groups are likely to fall within the environmentally marginalized category. Those groups who are most likely to bear the burden of environmental change while being excluded from its benefits are those in society who face other disproportionate discrimination: those in racial and ethnic minorities, those in lower classes, women, and other marginalized groups. Focusing specifically on the US, Robert Bullard (2005: 4), a prominent environmental justice activist and scholar, claims that fair treatment "means that no group of people, including racial, ethnic, or socioeconomic groups, should bear a disproportionate share of the negative environmental consequences resulting from industrial, municipal, and commercial operations or the execution of federal, state, local, and tribal programs and policies." The chapters in this book make the argument that gender is an essential, but often neglected aspect of environmental (un)fairness.

Inequality is a concept related to environmental justice that refers to uneven distribution or experience of something between different groups of people. This "something" can be power, influence, opportunity, access to and/or consumption of natural resources, creation of and/or experience of environmental ills, among others. Assessments of climate change disproportionately negatively impacting the global South make us reflect on the inequality of climate change experiences (IPCC 2014). Analysis of fresh-water consumption and access across the globe calls into question the inequality of consumption of and access to natural resources (UN 2014). So, why is inequality bad? This is a complex question that has motivated a huge amount of philosophical discussion. I claim that inequality is something to reflect on and correct because it does not happen by accident. Feminist scholarship, along with many other critical perspectives, clearly outlines systematic patterns of unequal distributions and manifestations of power. These perspectives highlight global and local processes whereby those who find themselves on the beneficial side of inequality do so at the expense of other groups, and *because of* the marginalized position of the other groups. Communities of color face increased exposure to hazardous materials because companies site toxic facilities in their neighborhoods (Bullard 1990, 2005). These same communities are likely to be economically marginalized and have a small role in decision-making. Decades of research show us that inequalities (intentional or otherwise) exist in certain communities with regard to siting decisions, enforcement of environmental regulations, clean-up of environmental problems, standard setting, and opportunities for participating in policymaking (Lekhi and Newell 2006). The idea of justice that motivates this book says that these inequalities should be removed, and reducing environmental damage is the best way to ensure that there are fewer environmental ills to be distributed.

Making sense of environmental justice   Environmental justice is a concept that has become central to understanding the numerous ways that the issues of environmental change, fairness, inequality, vulnerability, and marginalization are intertwined. The widely used concept traces its roots to multiple topics in the international community – including environmental racism. The early focus on environmental racism is still felt in discourses of environmental justice, with concern about race and racist dualisms represented as a prominent feature of many environmental justice ideas (Sturgeon 2009). However, scholars and activists who use the concept of environmental justice utilize a variety of perceptions about the nature of justice.

Most versions of environmental justice have a fairly broad conceptualization of "environment." An often-used definition used within the environmental justice movement is the environment as "where we live, work and play" (Lekhi and Newell 2006: 187). This definition illustrates an expansive notion of what "counts" as the environment. Environment is not restricted to pristine locations untouched by human influence or stocks of natural resources. Environment is that which surrounds us, can nurture us, and can threaten us.

Early versions of environmental justice within the US focused heavily on the notion of the distribution of environmental "bads" (Schlosberg and Carruthers 2010). The story of Warren County, North Carolina, is an example of activists and scholars raising questions about how we decide who has to live with the negatives of environmental change. Race has been a central feature of many such early environmental justice discourses. In 1987 the UCC, an organization that championed the cause of environmental justice in the US, issued a report on "Toxic Wastes and Race in the United States." The report found that race was the strongest variable in predicting where waste facility sites would be located. It explained the siting of facilities better than other variables like poverty, land values, and home ownership (Bullard 2005). Additionally, Marianne Lavelle and Marcia Coyle (1992) found that there was unequal protection and enforcement of environmental law by the US EPA, with predominantly white communities favored over communities of color. Since this time, many additional reports have reached similar conclusions in different countries (Bullard 1990; Mitchell and Dorling 2003; Varga et al. 2002).

Discourses of environmental justice are now found in many regions of the world (Agyeman and Evans 2004). Within GEP scholarship and activism, environmental justice's focus has been broadened to include concerns about unequal exposure by class and ethnicity alongside race. In particular, there has been reflection on the ways that poverty factors into environmental injustice. Since the late 1980s, some environmental justice organizations have used the term "environmentalism of the poor" to describe the struggles of marginalized communities in the defense of their livelihoods against resource extraction (Martinez-Alier et al. 2014).[3] Since that time, academics have adopted the concept in their work, particularly in studies in India and Latin America (Guha and Martinez-Alier 1997; Martinez-Alier 2002). Joan Martinez-Alier (2014) explains that "environmentalism of the poor" responds to and emerges from the tendency of marginalized peoples to advocate for the preservation of nature because it is often in their interest to do so. Since many within these communities might rely on environmental processes for their livelihood, they have an incentive to see ecosystems protected. This environmentalism is therefore about social justice as well as environmentalism.[4]

The marginalization and experiences of indigenous peoples have also taken a central place in environmental justice discussions. There are over 370 million indigenous people in regions around the globe (Martinez-Alier et al. 2014). These communities frequently enter into environmental justice debates through a concern about the extraction of minerals, biomass, fossil fuels, and other natural resources in indigenous lands. Activists, scholars, and some governing bodies have deemed it unjust for indigenous peoples to bear the costs of resource extraction and/or protection without their consent, while frequently being excluded from the full benefits of these processes. David Schlosberg and David Carruthers (2010: 12) explain that threats to indigenous peoples "have been a powerful catalyst to mobilization, as native communities fight against the companies, governments, policies, and other forces that threaten to fragment, displace, assimilate, or drive them toward cultural disintegration." Justice for indigenous peoples has been a rallying cry for activism around environmental issues, but it has also been a frequently occurring narrative within environmental politics scholarship (Schlosberg and Carruthers 2010).

The focus of environmental justice discourses has also been expanded to consider cross-border relationships of equity and environmental change. While early conceptualizations of justice–environment connections are traced to the United States, activists, scholars, and policymakers from the global South have increasingly put forth their own ideas about environmental justice. While there is some overlap in the discourses used in different regions, there are several key elements that have been found in environmental justice discourses from the South, including a concern with corrective or compensatory justice (i.e., the idea that the past should play a fundamental role in addressing present entitlements); a concern with distributive justice (i.e., the idea that equal rights to resources should be accorded to each individual in the world); and a concern with procedural justice (i.e., the adoption of fair procedures and an inclusive framework in the process of reaching decisions) (Ikeme 2003).

Ecological debt, transnational harm, and human rights

Ideas related to justice–environment connections include ecological debt (Warlenius et al. 2015), the distribution of transnational harm (Elliott 2006; Mason 2008), and environmental human rights (Agyeman et al. 2003).[5] Each of these concepts is contested; however, they provide a brief glimpse into some of the prominent debates about justice–environment connections that take place among multiple actors. Transnational harm, according to Michael Mason (2008: 9), refers to "the ways in which environmental harm (defined in relation to publicly justifiable needs or interests) is experienced as a result of material transactions across borders entailing inputs (e.g. extraction of resources and ecological services) and/or outputs (e.g. wastes and other pollutants) associated with production and consumption processes." This environmental harm is "transnational" in that the interactions cross borders as well as involve both state and non-state actors as producers or recipients of harm. Transnational harm is characterized by forms of inequality in which those most acutely impacted are often excluded from participating in environmental governance and denied consent (Elliott 2006). It manifests in normative connections across borders, and raises questions of rights, obligations, and duties.

A related concept, ecological debt, refers to the idea that "wealthy nations have been running up a huge debt over centuries by exploiting the raw materials and ecosystems of poor nations. The debt includes the historical and modern exploitation of non-Western natural resources and the excessive use of 'environmental space' for dumping waste (e.g. the expropriation of global atmospheric resources)" (Roberts and Parks 2009: 392–3).The notion of ecological debt is traced to social movements in the early 1990s, who used the term during a period of increasing awareness of environmental change and rising attention to Western responsibility for past colonial actions (Warlenius et al. 2015). Since its inception in the activist sphere, it has filtered into both academic work and global negotiations on environmental issues. In particular, delegates from the global South have used the associated concept of a climate debt in global climate change negotiations over the past few years (Roberts and Parks 2009).

Finally, the concept of environmental human rights identifies environmental rights as essential human rights that all people should have access to. Rights-based approaches have entered into discussions of various issues, including international development, water management, and biodiversity conservation. A discourse of rights is frequently used strategically in order to make a strong moral and legal claim. To frame a discussion in a rights discourse is to register a particularly strong kind of moral claim. It is further argued by some that claims are strengthened if they are framed in the language of human rights, as this lends them an "essential status that must be respected universally" (Sikor and Newell 2014: 153).[6]

There are various ways that environmental issues have been considered to be human rights issues, including (1) if people who experience environmental change are unable to enjoy basic rights like the right to life, health, or food; (2) if people are denied participation in environmental decision-making; (3) if the costs of environmental change or environmental protection are distributed unfairly; and (4) if the benefits of nature or natural resources are distributed unfairly

(Conca 2012). An example of this concept informing international law is the 1998 Aarhus Convention on "Access to Information, Public Participation in Environmental Decision-Making and Access to Justice in Environmental Matters."[7] It was the first to ensure citizens' rights in the area of the environment. It highlights the importance of substantive rights to a cleaner environment, as well as procedural rights, or the right to participate (Agyeman et al. 2003). These rights arguments have tended to center on humans as the focus of concern, with the environment often conceptualized as either a source of benefits that need to be fairly distributed, or a source of devastation that needs to be mitigated evenly. Environmental rights, ecological debt, and transnational harm all illustrate some of the ways that actors have understood justice–environment links. Each calls attention to the distributional aspects of the sources and experiences of environmental change.

Ecological justice   The notion of ecological justice is another concept that involves a link between justice and environmental issues. This concept is closely associated with the work of Nicholas Low and Brendan Gleeson (1998: 2). They claim that environmental justice is "the justice of the distribution of environments among peoples," while ecological justice is "the justice of the relationship between humans and the rest of the natural world." This ecocentric (i.e., environment-focused) concept calls attention to, and provides a critique of, a tendency to treat humans as dominant over ecosystems, and highlights the negative ramifications that can stem from this assumption. "The question of ecological justice arises from our treatment of the non-human world which is in turn derived from a view about how we are connected with it" (Low and Gleeson 1998: 139). These scholars see a close, and necessary, connection between the concepts of environmental justice and ecological justice.

Ecological justice discourses call into question the anthropocentric nature of most environmental justice concepts, including most of those already discussed. It is primarily concerned with the quality of ecosystems, which are viewed by many as having intrinsic value. One narrative claims that non-human species deserve to live without losing their habitat or facing abuse (White 2008). An ecological justice discourse raises the question of whether we can effectively solve environmental issues by focusing primarily on human needs, as well as the question of whether such a value structure is just or ethical (Baxter 2000). An "interspecies justice" component of ecological justice calls attention to the distribution of environmental harms among various species (i.e., humans versus others) that currently exist across the global community (Cooper and Palmer 1995).[8] These notions critique the assumption frequently asserted in policy and other discussions that humans are dominant over "nature." Movements like those for animal rights use these arguments to claim that animals have intrinsic value (Cooper and Palmer 1995; Okereke and Charlesworth 2014). The ecological justice discourse has helped to challenge some key assumptions about how we conceptualize fairness and equity. It challenges some of the foundational elements of human–nature connections in ways that make it compatible with some other critical approaches to environmental politics. What this and other discussions of justice frequently lack, however, is a focus on the ways that the current patriarchal structures contribute to both environmental and ecological injustice. These structures normalize the domination of humans over other species, and justify an unequal distribution of environmental ills among human communities. For this reason, gender lenses offer essential insight into the various ways that GEP intersects with ideas of justice, fairness, and equity.

Gender and environmental justice

The previous sections illustrate the wealth of thinking about how environmental change and environmental benefits intersect with normative concerns about justice. To date, however, there has been a lack of attention on gendered inequality within GEP scholarship on environmental justice (Buckingham and Kulcur 2009; Buckingham et al. 2005; Gaard 2011). Gender has been much less frequently discussed as a component of environmental (in)justice than has race or class. This is despite the existence of numerous feminist works that explore the gendered differences of experience of environmental change and participation in environmental decision-making (Harcourt 1994; Harcourt and Nelson 2015; Rocheleau et al. 1996; Salleh 2009). Bringing gender more squarely into GEP offers an alternative, complementary perspective on justice that is often missing in current debates. The remainder of this chapter argues that gender must be a central element of the ways in which we think about and create policy surrounding the environment. It claims that environmental injustice and unfairness are gendered – meaning that the processes that contribute to them are deeply connected to social experiences of and expectations about gender. The challenge for us is to reveal these manifestations of gender in order to acquire a more comprehensive picture of justice–environment connections.

What justice? Whose justice?   As mentioned before, inequality does not happen by accident. Gender is a central factor in how inequality and injustice "work" with regard to environmental issues. The fact that the international system is marked by patriarchy means that there are systematic forces influencing who gets what, when, and how.[9] Patriarchy works through feminizing and marginalizing (Enloe 2004). That which is associated with the perceived characteristics of femininity is regarded as "less than" and "not as worthy as" that which is associated with masculinity. These perceptions are reinforced by, as well as serve to reinforce, the distribution of power within and across states in the international system. Until fairly recently, gender has not had a central place in how we talk about justice at the international level. For example, it has only been in the last few decades that gendered experiences of war have been on the radar of scholars and policymakers who use justice and rights frameworks to assess and/or address security issues broadly defined (Bensouda 2014). Likewise, gendered experiences of environmental change and the distribution of environmental benefits have only lately been on the international agenda in a visible fashion (Cutter 1995; MacGregor 2009).

Key questions related to justice discourses are who or what gets included and excluded in calculations of justice and what these decisions are based on. Distinctions between environmental justice and ecological justice raise questions about whether policymaking should be guided by an anthropocentric or ecocentric justice discourse. Concerns over intragenerational and intergenerational justice largely fall into the anthropocentric category, but reflect different conversations about equity relationships. In simple terms, intragenerational environmental justice refers to the distribution of environmental costs and benefits across groups within the same generation, while intergenerational environmental justice refers to the distribution of environmental costs and benefits across generations.

Intragenerational justice concerns revolve around the observation that environmental costs and benefits are distributed in such a way that those who already suffer marginalization tend to bear the greatest burden. These arguments often center on issues like justice between the global North and global South on environmental change, or environmental marginalization based on race or class. An example of these concerns is North–South debates about who is most responsible for causing climate change and who suffers most from climate change (Roberts and Parks 2009; Sikor and Newell 2014). We see these debates play out in GEP scholarship as well as policy negotiations. While these are absolutely essential debates at the policy and scholarly levels, gender is often left out of our assessments of responsibility for environmental damage (Gaard 2011). Multiple studies illustrate that there are gendered differences in transportation uses, which relate to individual greenhouse gas emissions contribution (Best and Lanzendorf 2005). For instance, a 2008 study of transportation greenhouse gas emissions in the UK found that men made up 100 percent of motorcycle users and two-thirds of respondents in the highest emissions category for car users, while equally two-thirds of respondents in the lowest emissions category were female (Brand and Boardman 2008). Studies like these reflect the fact that gendered patterns of employment as well as differences in the occupation of public and private space influence how much a person contributes to environmental change. While a full evaluation of the causes of environmental damage must go beyond individual-level assessments of greenhouse gas emissions or consumption patterns, it is a part of larger gendered patterns of behavior that are typically left off the radar of policymakers as well as scholars. These issues should be a central part of justice debates, just as North–South discussions are becoming more visible.

A second key element of environmental justice is intergenerational justice, which has been the subject of debate for decades. As discussed in chapter 2, the Brundtland Report, *Our Common Future* (World Commission on Environment and Development 1987), conceived of sustainable development as being about the ability of current generations to meet their needs without compromising the ability of future generations to meet their own needs. A few years later, Edith Brown Weiss (1992: 20) proclaimed that

> The theory of intergenerational equity states that we, the human species, hold the natural environment of our planet in common with other species, other people, and with past, present and future generations. As members of the present generation, we are both trustees, responsible for the robustness and integrity of our planet, and beneficiaries, with the right to use and benefit from it for ourselves.

While the idea of justice between generations has had its critics (Beckerman and Pasek 2001), there are many others who argue that there are moral and even legal responsibilities between generations (Brown Weiss 1989; Weston 2012). The "indirect reciprocity thesis," for instance, says that the current generation owes something to the next generation because it received something from the previous one (Okereke and Charlesworth 2014). These ideas have informed activism and scholarship on a number of environmental issues. For example, climate justice narratives suggest that the current generation of decision-makers and polluters must be held to account now for failing to act and for imposing on future generations risks and dangers for which they are not responsible. Additionally, activism on nuclear or toxic waste has articulated justice demands by calling attention to the legacies of pollution caused now for future generations (Sikor and Newell 2014).

Much feminist work acknowledges that considerations of intergenerational justice are an important component of larger debates about equity, fairness, and responsibility, as they relate to not only relations between generations, but also relations among people within generations. Brown Weiss (1992: 22) explains that "no single country or group of countries has the power to ensure a healthy environment for the future. Thus, even when each country cares only about its own people, all nations must cooperate in order to guarantee a robust planet in the future."[10] More explicitly bringing in gender justice, Vandana Shiva (1993: 84) claims that "much has been written on the issue of sustainability, as 'intergenerational equity', but what is often overlooked is that the issue of justice between generations can only be realized through justice between sexes." The positions of Shiva and Brown Weiss, among many others, speak to the position that both intergenerational and intragenerational justice require changes to the dominant economic and political order. Our existing economic and political processes have allowed injustice to thrive. Dominant conceptions of "national interest" and considerations of "the good life," particularly among states in the global North, have fostered overconsumption, unequal distributions of environmental burdens, and the marginalization of many voices, among other ills (Plumwood 2002). For these reasons, approaches to both environmental and ecological justice must consider large-scale changes to the dominant structures that contribute to both unsustainability and injustice.

What is important to remember in each of these discussions is that there are multiple conceptualizations of justice at play. This is not unusual, as there are different perceptions about which aspects of justice should take precedence over others. There are different experiences of (in)justice, even within traditionally marginalized groups. Too often, our narratives about environmental injustice treat marginalized communities as homogeneous groups (Fan 2006). We know that there is, in fact, a great deal of diversity of experience among marginalized groups. Wealthy women will usually experience environmental change differently than poor women, women who live in urban settings tend to have different experiences than rural women, indigenous women often face increased vulnerability as compared to non-indigenous women, etc. (Alston 2010; Leach et al. 2015). This is where intersectional analysis offers us the tools to explore how multiple and sometimes overlapping forms of marginalization shape experiences of environmental change.

Examining environmental issues through gender lenses gives us the opportunity to understand how experiences and perceptions of environmental change and benefits intersect with socially constructed notions of acceptable and appropriate behavior and roles in society. Rather than treat unequal experiences of environmental issues as inevitable or standard for the social context, gender lenses reveal that gender norms are linked to institutional structures that directly influence power relations and distribution of social benefits. Gender justice, in the most basic terms, involves seeking to achieve equality of experiences and opportunity. According to Alison Jaggar (2014: 10), scholars concerned with global justice have traced "the ways in which contemporary transnational institutions and recent global policies, most of them facially gender-neutral, have had systemically disparate and often burdensome consequences for specific groups of women in both the global North and the global South." Gender justice requires reflecting on the sources of gendered disparities and vulnerability and offering fair ways to remove these. In the area of environmental politics, it involves considering the sources of environmental change and the experiences of environmental change and environmental benefits, and coming up with potential ways to achieve fair distributions of these.

I acknowledge that this is a fairly restricted idea of justice as largely focused on equity. While there is a great deal of debate about whether justice goes beyond equity, I feel that this is a good starting point for larger reflections on gender and environmental issues. At present, we do not even meet a very basic standard of equity in many areas. Globally, women tend to be overrepresented in low or unpaid labor, women are at greater risk of facing specific forms of violence than men, women tend to be underrepresented in various forms of decision-making, and the list goes on (Benería 2003; Elson 2014; True 2012; UNDP 2015). While each of these examples requires careful understandings of context-specific social conditions and the various experiences of women (i.e., reflecting on the fact that women are not a single category), regularized patterns of experience exist that intersect with gender norms. None of this is to say that men do not experience injustice based on gender norms. Gender lenses allow us to examine the ways that both women and men are affected by the ways that gender "works" in societies. While there are plenty of examples of men experiencing negative consequences of societal expectations of masculinity, the previous list is intended to illustrate that women frequently experience gender expectations in ways that can be detrimental to their livelihoods, dignity, and security. This book is one slice of some of the larger debates about the very nature of justice.

Gender, vulnerability, and risk   Environmental justice specifically intersects with gender when we consider issues of vulnerability to environmental harm and distribution of environmental risk. The concept of human vulnerability has long had a position in environmental politics discussions (Liverman 2001). Eakin and Walser (2007) define vulnerability as "a dynamic property emerging from the structure of human relations, the internal attributes of specific populations and places, and the nature of social–environmental interactions." This literature highlights the fact that people will experience environmental change differently depending on multiple related processes, including patterns of resource allocation over time, as well as the complex feedbacks inherent in coupled human–environment systems (O'Brien and Leichenko 2000).

Women, and particularly women who face other forms of marginalization like poverty or class or racial discrimination, frequently face many gender-specific barriers that limit their ability to cope with and adapt to environmental change. Geraldine Terry (2009: 7) contends that

> while poor women's greater vulnerability compared with men is partly due to their relatively limited access to resources and their resulting poverty, this is not the whole story. It also arises from social and cultural norms about, for instance, gendered divisions of labour, physical mobility, and who is entitled to take part in decision making at household and community levels.

These elements of vulnerability indicate that it is not an inevitable condition. There are social structures that shape who will be most vulnerable and who will be least vulnerable. This means that women are not naturally vulnerable beings. Rather, women often face particular vulnerabilities because of the ways in which power is distributed in society. Economic power is one aspect of these processes, but vulnerability also connects to political power and other forms of social power.

According to many risk scholars, a risk is an event or scenario located in the future that is linked to policy proposals offering a method of prevention (Corry 2012). A risk makes harmful events possible or more likely. For example, when calculating "safe" chemical loads, the risk is the likelihood that people will get sick after being exposed at given levels. Decision-making about what constitutes safe chemical loads has tended to be calculated on the basis of men's body tolerance to exposure over an eight-hour period, or an estimated average working day (Buckingham 2004). This means that assessments about vulnerability and risk are being made without attention to the specific experiences or needs of many women. Feminist theorists and other critical scholars see risk as "strongly influenced by socially constructed categories – e.g., gender, class and racial categories – that are taken-for-granted as 'natural'" (McLaughlin and Dietz 2008: 103). Past research has found that risk assessments and subsequent decisions are frequently influenced by powerful actors, so we cannot assume that such assessments are objective calculations of vulnerability (Reid 2013).

Additionally, many studies have found that women frequently have different perceptions of risk when compared to men (Arora-Jonsson 2011; Norgaard and York 2005). According to the "vulnerability thesis," white men feel less vulnerable to many risks than do women and people of color, and are more accepting of such risks. This is thought to be due to their dominant position in social structures. This leads to what has been termed the "white male effect" of white males being more accepting of a wide range of risks than are other adults (McCright and Dunlap 2011). These assumptions have been illustrated in work that indicates that women perceive various hazards as more risky than do men (Slovic et al. 1997; Smith and Leiserowitz 2013) and that women are less willing than men to impose health and environmental risks on others (Barke et al. 1997). Several of these studies specifically included members of the scientific community, thereby eliminating the claim that the differences in perception are only due to men being more educated about the expected severity or likelihood of risk (Barke et al. 1997; Slovic et al. 1997).[11] However, some studies do indicate that women may suffer from a lack of adequate information about environmental risks and burdens when compared to men, but this is frequently due to gendered patterns of public–private roles influencing access to primary sources of information about environmental issues (Ali and Ackley 2011).[12]

In studies on climate change perceptions, for example, conservative men were the most likely to downplay the risks of climate change, or deny its existence altogether. Aaron McCright and Riley Dunlap (2011) find that conservative white males are more likely than are other adults to express climate change denial. These authors also find that those conservative white males who self-report understanding global warming very well express an even greater degree of climate change denial. Additionally, a study of US Evangelical Christians found that while Evangelicals in general tended to perceive climate change as less of a risk than non-Evangelicals, the Evangelical women in their study tended to assess climate change as a risk more frequently than men, as did individuals with lower incomes than individuals with higher incomes (Smith and Leiserowitz 2013). These findings suggest that people who have experienced some form of marginalization, be it based on gender or on class, may be more cautious in their assessment of risk. Risks are typically conceptualized as something that cannot be eliminated, but only managed. Differing perceptions of risk may be tied to differing expectations about how well potential insecurity will be managed in the future. Members of groups that tend to be marginalized, including women, may have lower expectations about the likelihood that a risk that will result in their insecurity will be met with adequate policy responses, therefore they view the risk as "real." This relates to larger patterns of inequity in how communities experience social and environmental ills. Additionally, there are studies that find that men are willing to accept higher levels of discrimination than women (Kuran and McCaffery 2008).[13] This is not to say that there is anything essentialized about the experiences of men or women, but rather that the fact that men are more likely to be in dominant categories than women shapes their response to issues like tolerance for inflicting risk and discrimination on others.

In order to understand where risks lie, it is essential to reflect on questions about the processes of marginalization and vulnerability, as well as assessments of specific policy options geared toward improving resilience and security. For these reasons, a notion of justice that takes gender seriously is one that is oriented toward promoting empowerment. The concept of empowerment inspires a good deal of debate among feminist scholars. Empowerment is one of those ideas that has been championed by many, but often lacks clear definition. Empowerment, for the purposes of the current discussion, involves enabling actors to cope with the long-term impacts of environment change. This includes strengthening their general ability to react, as well as enhance their flexibility and resilience (Terry and Sweetman 2009). Empowerment also involves reflecting on the causes of powerlessness and "acting both individually and collectively to change the conditions of our lives" (Lather 1991: 4). We can explore the condition of vulnerability while still recognizing agency. In fact, many feminist scholars and gender NGOs highlight how women are not "victims" or inactive political agents, but often display creative adaptation tendencies in the face of environmental damage. That being said, it is important to understand that because vulnerable women often find themselves on the margins of society, they will sometimes experience environmental problems differently from and more severely than non-marginalized groups. Therefore, it is important to think about empowerment in ways that include a critical, gendered account of the processes that create and sustain vulnerability, and a focus on the ways that people devise ways to overcome vulnerability.

Women in environmental justice movements   A central challenge of identifying gendered patterns of environmental injustice is calling attention to regularized patterns of marginalization that influence how humans experience environmental degradation, while simultaneously avoiding depicting those people as merely victims. Early work on gender–environment connections tended to examine women as individuals, which often resulted in rather essentialist ideas of women as victims of environmental change in need of rescue. Currently, there is more attention to gender as a system structuring power relations that influence drivers and experiences of environmental change (Gaard 2015). In the context of this book in particular, it is important to note the agency displayed by women around the world in the face of environmental change (Wilson 2012). One of the most frequently mentioned connections between environmental justice and gender has been considerations of women's involvement in environmental movements in general, and environmental justice movements in particular. Women have had a central place in environmental activism for decades. Going as far back as the late nineteenth and early twentieth centuries, women participated in protests surrounding air and water pollution, food safety, garbage and sanitation issues, and industrial health and safety. Justification for involvement in these activities often included gendered narratives, like protecting the health of families or even upholding standards of cleanliness. For example, many women involved in early anti-smoke campaigns claimed that coal smoke and soot negatively impacted the health of their communities and made doing laundry and other household tasks difficult (Mann 2011).

More recently, women have been active in a huge array of environmental causes, from climate change to animal rights (Gaarder 2011; Rocheleau et al. 1996). Women have also been active specifically in environmental justice campaigns around the globe (Bullard and Smith 2005; Di Chiro 2015). In the US, women lead many prominent grassroots environmental justice organizations. While men make up a considerable percentage of large-scale, mainstream environmental and conservation groups, women, and particularly women of color, are heavily represented as the heads of environmental justice associations (Buckingham and Kulcur 2009; Bullard and Smith 2005; Di Chiro 2015). In other states in the global North and the global South, women play active roles in highlighting the unequal burden that they bear in the face of environmental change. Some advocate on behalf of themselves, some for their communities, some for the environment, and many for each of these simultaneously (Buckingham and Kulcur 2009; Di Chiro 2015).

One reason for the high proportion of women who participate in environmental justice movements might be a sense of dissatisfaction with the way that environmental issues are framed in many mainstream environmental organizations. Noël Sturgeon (2009) specifically analyzes the ways that mainstream culture and environmental movements develop and utilize a "politics of the natural" that does little to challenge the inequities that reinforce and continue injustice and marginalization. She advances a global feminist environmental justice analysis that sees an interactive relationship among inequalities of gender, race, sexuality, class, and states. This analysis is concerned with uncovering the systems of power that generate complex problems connected to social inequalities and environmental change. She argues that since the 1980s, a mainstream environmentalism has dominated the US; this uses a distinct narrative framework to understand, and in some instances legitimate, particular aspects of American history, US consumerism, global military power, and family values. Those that use this narrative framework often fail to critically assess the implications of painting certain relationships or processes as "natural." This perspective, like many larger discourses of environmental justice, is predicated on the notion that social inequalities and environmental problems are connected. This reinforces the idea that environmental justice and ecological justice are intimately related. It also reinforces the necessity of reflecting on the gendered sources of environmental marginalization and vulnerability, as well as the potential solutions to effectively and justly address these.

Knowledge and participation   Power relations in a society determine who has the authority to speak about environmental issues and whose perception of those issues influences policymaking. Procedural justice relates to the justice of who makes decisions – whose voice is heard, either because they are invited to the decision-making table or because they are regarded as a legitimate actor to speak about the issue at hand. The composition of a decision-making body has implications for the outcome of the decision-making process. A study of European municipal waste management found that the gendered organization and decision-making of municipal waste management in the EU made a difference in the waste strategies adopted as well as the amount of waste disposed of. Recycling performance was strongest under bodies that employed women from diverse backgrounds. Those waste management bodies under the control of older men from engineering backgrounds often favored strategies like incineration, which frequently provoke local protests against environmental unsustainability and injustice. It is interesting to note that many of these protests are led by women (Buckingham et al. 2005).

Likewise, in decision-making about water issues in Western Australia there appear to be connections between trends of commodification of water and the heavy presence of men on decision-making boards.[14] Declining availability of water has been met by proposals for economic measures and technological solutions instead of discussions of local social and community interests. Water boards tend to be dominated by older men, while women and indigenous people have little representation (Alston 2010). Who makes environmental decisions matters. People bring their own perspectives and lived experiences with them to the decision-making table. This means that ensuring procedural justice is not only important because it ensures equity of representation; it is also imperative because it increases the perspectives and options that may be discussed as solutions to environmental problems. This perspective influences the approach of several environmental NGOs around the globe. WaterAid, an international NGO focusing on water, sanitation, and hygiene education, argues that "women's knowledge about water sources is particularly valuable. Because they usually collect the water, women will know where the best water sources are and in which month they usually dry up" (WaterAid 2016). WaterAid also claims that women tend to place a high priority on water projects because they understand how valuable they are to their community. This example illustrates the importance of rethinking environmental governance through gender lenses. When we recognize the various ways that environmental experiences and policies are gendered, we are in a better position to find solutions to environmental problems that are effective and just.

The perceived legitimacy of the scientific community has resulted in its central place within discussions of risk and how it should be managed (Keller 2009), but what are the gendered implications of this relationship? While the environmental justice movement has made strides in its critique of expert-led processes in areas like risk assessment and research, women activists or volunteers "are less likely to receive credit as experts, even though they have important insights and analyses to offer" (MacGregor 2006: 195). It is essential that these gendered perceptions of authority are critically analyzed and problematized if we are to achieve a multifaceted understanding of environmental vulnerability and risks. As discussed in the previous chapter, incorporating multiple forms of knowledge can help with this goal. Bringing in local knowledge can make environmental decision-making more inclusive. Street science or citizen science may be more inclusive because it incorporates additional voices and can be guided by their concerns. It is also seen as beneficial for its potential to advocate for environmental justice or other forms of social change, and to highlight social-ecological links (Johnson et al. 2014; Klein et al. 2014).

Gender, sustainability, and justice as guiding concepts

A review of GEP and policymaking shows that both justice and sustainability have been influential goals within contemporary environmental politics. These ideas have shaped our debates on what environmental concerns should be on the global agenda as well as the proposals we entertain for how we might address them. As discussed in the previous chapter, sustainability at its most basic level refers to acting toward the environment in ways that allow ecosystems to maintain their resilience. It recognizes that humans have great capacity to alter ecosystems. Some technologically optimistic approaches to sustainability argue that humans will likely find ways to help ecosystems maintain their resilience in the face of environmental change. Other perspectives caution against humans altering ecosystems beyond their ability to recover due to the fact that this has negative consequences both for the environment itself and for the humans who depend on it.

Justice can be defined as the equity of the distribution of goods and bads across the international system. This concept contains concerns about who does or does not benefit from certain activities or policies, as well as who is involved in decision-making processes. It is well documented across issue areas that those who find themselves as part of marginalized communities are likely to be passed over for benefits but get a larger share of most burdens. There have been some environmentalists who question whether including justice in environmental discourses is a good move. Some ask whether they should attempt to address justice issues or should continue campaigning on sustainability issues that may be "easier" for global actors to address (Mohai et al. 2009). This thinking says that fixing injustice is hard, so why don't we leave that for later? Calling attention to environmental injustice leads to calls for the removal of that injustice. In the case of injustice based on gender, race, class, and other systems of marginalization, there are no quick and easy remedies. Potential solutions require highlighting and working to dismantle the processes that lead some communities to experience environmental ills while often losing out on environmental benefits.

For this reason, many actors argue that justice and sustainability are reinforcing. There is an ethical obligation to current and future generations for society to practice sustainability (Dresner 2008; Thiele 2013). Some definitions of sustainability and sustainable development have justice elements at their core. For instance, scholars like Julian Agyeman (2013) encourage us to think in terms of "just sustainabilities," which focus on quality of life, present and future generations, justice and equity in resource allocation, and living within ecological limits. Likewise, Agyeman, Robert Bullard, and Bob Evans (2003: 2) define sustainability as involving "the need to ensure a better quality of life for all, now, and into the future, in a just and equitable manner, while living within the limits of supporting ecosystems."[15] The picture of the environment that informs most environmental justice movements is one that is situated and deeply connected to lived experiences. It is not an abstract "elsewhere" (Di Chiro

2015). Unsustainable environments mean unsustainable communities. Sustainability and justice work together to ensure that humans and ecosystems are not merely surviving, but all have the capacity to thrive and flourish.

Experiences of (in)justice and rights abuses are gendered, just as they are classed, raced, etc. Making gender a central component of environmental politics debates offers important insights into how we might understand the sustainability and justice of environmental change. Gender lenses complement some existing critical approaches to environmental politics. They offer conceptualizations of sustainability and justice that avoid thinking only in abstracts, and instead understand what unsustainability and injustice mean for particular communities. These approaches allow us to reflect on the benefits of challenging existing gendered patterns of environmental decision-making and environmental knowledge. They challenge us to critically engage with dominant approaches to poverty and development, which are profoundly connected to sustainability.

So far, GEP scholarship and policymaking have been quiet on the gendered nature of environmental issues. Building on the important existing work on environmental justice, feminist insights enable us to apply the idea that "the personal is political" to GEP. It encourages us to reflect on the sources of environmental change, the distribution of environmental ills and benefits, and the processes that exist for solving environmental problems in ways that challenge unequal power distribution and dominant social structures, which contribute to both environmental unsustainability and systematic marginalization of many groups. A gender-focused approach to sustainability and justice requires reflecting on the various ways that processes of environmental change and the solutions to them are gendered. It also requires being proactive in approaches to the fair distribution of environmental benefits, along with being reactive to the distribution of environmental ills. GEP scholarship has witnessed tremendous strides in developing complex versions of sustainability and justice discourses. The challenge now is to incorporate gender into these important debates in order to reflect on the ways that gender inequity contributes to unsustainability and injustice.

4

Too Many People? Gender and Population Debates

The topic of population has been on the radar of policymakers and scholars for decades. Thomas Malthus warned about human population growth overwhelming our capacity to feed ourselves in the late 1700s. He feared that patterns of population growth meant that human numbers would outstrip the global food supply. More recently, we hear news stories about "too many people" in some areas, and "too few people" in others. Headlines from global media sources proclaim, "Europe needs many more babies to avert a population disaster" (Madrid et al. 2015), "Australia's population growth rate reaches lowest point in almost 10 years" (Evershed 2015), but also ask, "Can the planet handle China's new two-child policy?" (Winston 2015). While it is true that many demographers and policymakers are genuinely anxious about the challenges presented by too few people within a country, this chapter focuses on the opposite concern: too many people. A common narrative within environmental debates has claimed that human populations put pressure on resources, and as we add more people to the equation we further strain resources (Hartmann et al. 2015). Stephen Emmott (2015) uses this narrative to claim that "[c]limate change, extreme weather events, pollution, ecosystem degradation – the fundamental alteration of every component of the complex system we rely upon for our survival – are due to the activities of the rising human population." There continue to be calls to put population concerns higher on the global environmental agenda (Coole 2013), but what does it mean to link human population with environmental change? International debates about population are complex, ethically fraught, and frequently tied to other issues – like environmental sustainability or economic and national security.

A relatively stable population is one component of many definitions of a "state" in IR.[1] States care about population because it matters for questions of availability/provision of social services, potential military force, and potential size of an economic workforce, among others. Policymakers are concerned about too many people, too few people, too many people past working age, and too many young people for the supply of jobs. Policymakers also pay attention to population levels as they connect to environmental stress and damage. Along with scholars, IGOs, and NGOs, policymakers have contributed to the issue of population being on the international agenda for decades. This chapter examines debates about population through gender lenses in order to better understand how this issue connects to the goals of both sustainability and justice. It explores ways to rethink narratives of overpopulation and population movement specifically in ways that contribute both to justice and to environmental sustainability.

Global debates about population

Global population has increased dramatically over time. World population reached one billion sometime between 1800 and 1830. Two billion people was reached around 100 years later in 1930, three billion around 1960, four billion in the mid-1970s, five billion by the late 1980s, six billion by 1999, and seven billion by 2011. According to the Population Division of the UN Department of Economic and Social Affairs (UN DESA), world population reached 7.3 billion as of mid-2015, meaning the world added approximately one billion people in the span of twelve years.[2] While these figures might appear to be very high, current global population growth rates are slower than in the recent past. In 2005, world population grew by 1.24 percent. In 2015, it grew by 1.18 percent. This results in around 83 million people added to the planet annually. The world population is projected to hit the 8 billion mark around 2030, though there are disagreements about how accurately we can predict these numbers (UN DESA 2015).

Future population trajectories depend on future trends in fertility, mortality, and migration. Countries have tended to transition from patterns of high mortality and high fertility to patterns of low mortality and low fertility. In the interim, rapid population growth often takes place because mortality decline typically begins before fertility decline. The states that are still in the beginning or in the middle of the shift to low mortality and low fertility are expected to complete their transitions over the next several decades. Both fertility and mortality levels in these countries are projected to decline (UN DESA 2013). In states where this shift has already occurred, mortality is still assumed to be declining but fertility is expected to remain around or below a level of two children per woman. Migration enters population calculations as overall numbers vary when people migrate either in or out of a state. Patterns of migration particularly influence the population estimates in countries with natural growth close to zero (i.e., when the number of deaths is close to equal to the number of births) (UN DESA 2013).

There has been a concern about the implications of population growth for the extraction or use of resources and species since the mid-1940s to 1950s within early GEP scholarship (Stevis 2014). Population enters GEP debates in multiple ways. Some scholars have been optimistic about population growth and the environment. For instance, economist Julian Simon has been an outspoken critic of over-population narratives. Simon, and others skeptical of these narratives, instead view population growth as a source of human intelligence and ingenuity (Wapner 2010a). Simon (1990: 2) argued that rising incomes along with population growth, through both increased births and immigration, drive up demand and cost of natural resources in an area. These factors motivate individuals to seek new sources and innovative substitutes. "Eventually, these new discoveries lead to natural resources that are cheaper than before this process begins, leaving humanity better off than if the shortages had not appeared." Likewise, agricultural economist Ester Boserup (1992) found that population density results in agricultural intensification, which can create more efficient crop production. What most population optimists have in common is their view that increased numbers or density of humans will result in more efficient use of resources rather than an automatic overuse of resources.

Other voices link overpopulation to environmental damage and human suffering. As mentioned earlier, Thomas Malthus adopted pessimistic population narratives centuries ago. Malthus was doubtful about technology or human ingenuity overcoming what he feared would be decline and disaster brought on by an overwhelming throng of people – the poor in particular (Robertson 2012). He advocated sexual abstinence and late marriages as individual-level changes necessary to reduce population growth. He also suggested revisions to public welfare as a way to discourage large families (Malthus 2007).

Malthusian fears about population impacts declined during the course of the nineteenth century as birthrates in Europe dropped (Wilson 2012). Despite this, concerns about overpopulation and its ills reappeared over time in the works of several prominent scholars like Garrett Hardin, Paul Ehrlich, and the Club of Rome (Bandarage 1997).[3] Many of these concerns were drawn from biological sciences "that emphasized carrying capacity, ecological interconnection, overconsumption, degradation, and hard limits to growth" (Robertson 2012: 2). In "The Tragedy of the Commons," Hardin (1968: 1248) claimed, "the most important aspect of necessity that we must now recognize is the necessity of abandoning the commons in breeding... Freedom to breed will bring ruin to all." He argued that we cannot rely on technical fixes to the "problem" of overpopulation, nor can we rely on appeals to conscience or morality to get people to freely give up their right or desire to have children. Instead, "mutual coercion mutually agreed upon" is necessary. Hardin and other neo-Malthusians writing in the 1960s and 1970s shifted focus from population rates of the poor in the global North to population rates in the global South. Stanford biologist Paul Ehrlich, for example, warned that population growth levels across the world pose a threat to ecosystems and human well-being.[4] These population pessimists theorized that there were limits that humans dare not cross without confronting extreme consequences (Wapner 2010b).

An additional population narrative is the potential for population growth to contribute to insecurity, a topic that will be covered in more detail in chapter 6. These concerns range from population growth overwhelming state capacity for the provision of basic services, to lack of economic opportunities – particularly for young people – leading to social unrest, to conflicts over access to scarce resources (Choucri 1974; Homer-Dixon 1999; Kaplan 1994). Jack Goldstone (1991) has argued that population growth leading to large-scale rural–urban migration has influenced diverse cases of revolution and rebellion over the years, including the English and French Revolutions, rebellions in the Ottoman empire in the late sixteenth century, and the fall of the Ming dynasty in the mid-seventeenth century. These population and migration patterns are argued to result in declining real wages and in opportunities for revolutionary movements.

A final element of population debates is scholarship that focuses on issues like population growth and/or density interacting with environmental stress to negatively affect resource availability (e.g., Döös 2002; Pricope et al. 2013). For instance, Narcisa Pricope et al. (2013) examine the links between population and degradation patterns in rangeland and pastoral livelihood zones in East Africa in order to understand how population growth, primarily among pastoralists, interacts with trends of environmental degradation and food insecurity. Other work has explored issues like the connections between population growth, disease, and environmental degradation (Pimentel et al. 2007). These works treat population "pressure" as a variable that interacts with others to influence both causes and experiences of environmental damage. This scholarship tends to approach the issue of population in a clinical way, avoiding the alarmist tone of strictly neo-Malthusian work while still pointing to population growth as a potential challenge for environmental sustainability. These studies, along with the other dominant threads of population debates, rarely, if ever, consider the myriad ways that population growth and movement are deeply gendered.

Connecting gender and population debates

Population debates continue to be very contentious. There are voices calling on humanity to reduce its numbers in order to avoid unsustainable resource extraction and consumption. There are other voices that view increased numbers of humans as a source of innovation and hope. There are still others that caution us to adopt a critical perspective on these debates which assesses ways that population debates are not gender- (nor class-, nor racially) neutral. This final category will be the subject of the following section.

As already discussed, there is a long history of policymakers and scholars expressing fears about "clouds of Barbarians" or a "human tide" overwhelming us (Christian Aid 2007; Malthus 2007). These fears have led to forceful birth control policies and, in some cases, the sterilization of individuals who were classified as "unfit" to reproduce. For example, estimates from the US in the late 1960s/early 1970s suggest that thousands of women a year underwent forced sterilization. A large number of these women were Native American, Hispanic, and African-American (Nelson 2003). Policies in states around the world that attempt to address "overpopulation" have frequently targeted poor women or women who are members of minority or marginalized groups. There have been very few examples of population control measures, including coercive ones, which target men (Bandarage 1997; Hartmann 1995). These policy battles have largely played out at the level of women's bodies. The gendered, classed, and racialized nature of population control means that it is absolutely essential to consider how issues of population connect to both sustainability and justice.

Critical approaches, like feminism, are helpful in evaluating why the population storyline has continued to be so popular in mainstream environmental discourse. Andil Gosine (2005: 78) argues that in order to do this, we must consider the composition of environmentalism in the global North for much of its history. The environmental movement, particularly in the US, was largely white, middle- to upper-class, and relatively uncritical of neoliberalism for the past fifty years at least. Because of these characteristics, many of the issues that dominated green agendas tended to also be uncritical of status quo economic processes. "Overpopulation, which reduced the complex social, political, economic, and cultural dimensions of environmental degradation, and, more important, posed little challenge to capitalist industrialization and consumption, thus became a highly preferred bogeyman for greens" (Gosine 2005: 78). This assessment suggests that shining a light on population is often done without simultaneously (or alternatively) spotlighting the connections between patriarchal economic processes, consumption levels, lifestyle choices, and environmental change. There are sustainability and justice implications of these frames. The following sections address each of these in turn.

Population and sustainability   It is essential to consider the gendered nature of sustainability debates as they link to population. Gender lenses allow us to rethink sustainability and sustainable development by probing power relations, contesting dominant discourses, and offering alternative insights into both the processes of unsustainability and how these might be overcome. As discussed at length earlier, alarmist voices highlight the challenges to environmental sustainability that come from current human population numbers and future population growth. Narratives about population and environmental harm frequently conceptualize human well-being in ways that pit it against environmental sustainability. It is, however, more accurate to say that the connections between human behaviors, including population numbers, and environmental sustainability are context-specific and fundamentally linked to economic, political, social, and cultural factors (Hartmann et al. 2015). Gender lenses offer alternatives to simplistic and deterministic population narratives. While feminist approaches acknowledge the large toll that human activities have taken on ecosystems, they reject approaches built on relationships of human domination over the environment. These approaches also call attention to the need to inspect the consequences of sustainability-oriented policies.

Challenging simplistic assumptions   Defining sustainability as ensuring resilience, which this book does, might appear to justify prioritizing concerns about sustainability above all else. The feminist approach also guiding these chapters, however, illustrates that policies aimed at sustainability have often been built on assumptions of unquestioned scientific expertise and gender- (and class-, race-, ethnicity-, etc.) neutral approaches to achieving it. At a minimum, this can serve to silence important perspectives on environmental sustainability, but it can also result in policies that are unequal and discriminatory.

"When it comes down to cutting the population to the 'ideal level' of 1 billion people, it will not be the rich and powerful who will 'go,' but the poor, Black and Brown people, and women who are manipulated, sterilized, chemically poisoned, murdered, etc." This quote is from a flyer distributed at one of Paul Ehrlich's speaking appearances in the early 1970s by a group called Women Against Genocide (Robertson 2012: 193). It highlights the dangers of discussing sustainability in clinical and gender-neutral terms. The organization spoke out forcefully against the power relations that sit at the heart of population narratives. Still today, power dynamics of population growth are rarely discussed in either mainstream GEP scholarship or environmental policymaking. Women have frequently been depicted as either dangerous breeders or passive victims in need of a strong institution to empower them with reproductive rights, all while men remain invisible. A more effective way to take steps toward sustainability is to understand the complex social, economic, and political conditions and processes that influence population numbers. Betsy Hartmann (1999: 10) explains that "high infant mortality rates, children as a vital source of labor and support for the elderly in peasant societies, son preference, lack of education and opportunity, and discrimination against women are all factors that can contribute to high birth rates." These pressures and processes must be evaluated if we are to understand how population growth might contribute to environmental damage in some areas.

Poverty narratives   One step toward challenging simplistic assumptions in population debates is to critically examine poverty and population. Environmental scholars and policymakers frequently make connections between poverty and unsustainability. This is similar to arguments for why population growth rates have been high among poor communities. For example, the Brundtland Report, which thoroughly shaped discussions of sustainability and sustainable development among scholars and policymakers, claimed that policies geared toward reducing fertility rates should aim to improve women's position in society. "Poverty breeds high rates of population growth" (World Commission on Environment and Development 1987: 106). However, the report also uses "urgent" language to say that "time is short and developing countries will...have to promote direct measures to reduce fertility, to avoid going radically beyond the productive potential to support their populations" (World Commission on Environment and Development 1987: 51). While some policymakers have used population pressure arguments as a call for women's empowerment, these have also been used as justification for population reduction measures being targeted at the poor in countries across the world.

Neo-Malthusians have connected both environmental destruction and women's poverty to women's fertility (Bandarage 1997). For instance, in 1973, at the height of renewed Malthusian discourses in the US, legislation to require women on welfare to undergo sterilization was being considered in no fewer than fourteen states (Robertson 2012). Outspoken critics of these policy prescriptions called attention to the fact that when population control policies blame the poor for their own poverty and fail to consider political economic structures, capitalist interests are served and women's interests often suffer (Robertson 2012; Wilson 2012). Going all the way back to Malthus, narratives that the poor are responsible for making their own bad choices disguise the reality that poverty constrains the choices of those who experience it. Unsustainable behaviors cannot be analyzed without recognition of the structural conditions under which those choices are made.[5]

Gender lenses challenge us to think through population debates with an eye to revealing the power dynamics that shape global capitalist relations and result in predictable patterns of poverty among marginalized groups. It also pushes our analysis beyond growth-oriented conceptualizations of sustainable development to a recognition that capitalist-oriented growth frequently bypasses those who are marginalized in society. Unfortunately, this often includes large numbers of women. Manifestations of poverty are an essential facet of population dynamics, and should more firmly inform population debates at the global level.

Feminist scholars have suggested that alternative ways of thinking about population are possible. Betsy Hartmann, Anne Hendrixson, and Jade Sasser (2015: 57) call for the creation of a new sustainable development framework focused on an inclusive platform for sexual and reproductive health and rights. "Such a framework would be rooted in a non-negotiable commitment to bodily integrity, including freedom from all forms of violence, and equal access to decent work, secure livelihoods, a clean and safe environment, education, health, and other social services and public goods." This kind of approach to population seeks to marry commitments to sustainability and justice in ways that are consistent with the goals of feminist environmentalism. It is also more likely to accurately assess the complex ways that human behaviors can lead to environmental unsustainability. Simplistic, alarmist approaches to population growth, on the other hand, do little to aid in assessing how and why individuals decide to increase family size or relocate to or from environmentally fragile areas. It is essential to think through individualism, rights, and justice as they relate to population. Choice is important, but we cannot assess choice without first understanding the complexity and justice components of obstacles to choice.

The (In)justice of population control   Justice narratives most frequently appear in critiques of existing population discourses. It is noteworthy that the language of "reproductive rights" is a relatively recent addition to population debates. It was not until the 1990s that population policies were widely discussed in terms of rights and choices (Coole 2013; Wilson 2012).[6] Failure to recognize the gendered consequences of population policies risks dehumanizing women. Kalpana Wilson (2012: 90) claims that "population control discourse reduces 'Third World' women to their reproductive organs, and specifically their wombs, pathologised as 'excessively reproductive' and requiring intervention."

Alarmist population growth narratives were given new life in the early 1990s with the rise of security–environment connections (Ford and Adamson 1995; Sturgeon 2009). Simplistic narratives about overpopulation in "Africa"[7] and other uncontextualized or undifferentiated parts of the global South were used to caution against the dangers of unchecked human behaviors (Ford and Adamson 1995). For the most part, scholars, policymakers, and the media have discussed the connections between insecurity, population growth, and migration as if these are gender-neutral phenomena (Detraz 2014). A lack of reflection on gender in discussions of population growth is a huge oversight. By identifying population increase as a contributor to environmental damage, these actors are automatically making women the potential target of policy "solutions" because of their role as child-bearers (Hartmann 1995).

Securitized narratives suggest that it is appropriate and desirable to prioritize establishing and maintaining security for the primary referent object of the discourse. As will be discussed in chapter 6, in the case of environmental debates this can mean focusing on the security of the state while ignoring the security needs of both human communities and ecosystems (Detraz 2014). Recent popular-press books about population feature titles like *Man Swarm: How Overpopulation is Killing the Wild World* (Foreman and Carroll 2015) and *Life on the Brink: Environmentalists Confront Overpopulation* (Crist and Cafaro 2012). Crisis narratives, like securitized discourses, have been effective in raising attention to environmental concerns, on the one hand, but the hysterical nature of these frames appears to leave little room for critical analysis of issues like population policymaking resulting in injustice, or the responsibilities and consequences of population control being unevenly distributed. How are we to make space for considerations of justice for marginalized women who are most at risk of detrimental population control measures? Sources of this injustice include the overly alarmist narratives that have served to justify repressive measures. While it is true that mainstream GEP scholarship has avoided the hysteria of many population debates, the field is still situated in a context in which overpopulation is regarded by many as one of the biggest environmental challenges we face. It is important to establish alternative population narratives that challenge or replace existing alarmist ones.

Sources and experiences of unjust population policies

Using gender lenses to consider justice in debates about population forces us to seek out sources and experiences of injustice. It is also crucial to avoid essentializing women or assuming that all women view population issues the same way. Indian Prime Minister Indira Gandhi administered one of the most coercive population control attempts in that country's history. In 1976 she claimed, "we should not hesitate to take steps which might be described as drastic. Some personal rights have to be kept in abeyance for the human rights of the nation" (Chawla 2014). The "steps" that the Indian government undertook included enlisting various governmental agencies in the campaign, as well as involving high levels of coercion. It is estimated that around eight million Indians underwent sterilization in the span of a single year. Unlike many other population reduction campaigns, the 1976 Indian population limitation program targeted men. What is also noteworthy is that the campaign resulted in large-scale protests, and some even attribute it to being one of the causes for Gandhi being voted out of office (Robertson 2012; Wilson 2012). It is difficult to identify similar instances of massive protest when women have been the focus of coercive population reduction schemes. Governments do not tend to fall when women are subjected to dangerous population control measures.

When groups have petitioned states to undertake population control strategies, these measures have frequently had both gendered and racist overtones. They are rarely envisioned to reduce the numbers of children born in predominantly white countries where consumption levels tend to be disproportionately high (Gosine 2005). Critical environmental scholars have called attention to negative examples like coalitions being built between environmental organizations and anti-immigration organizations, many of which rely on problematic narratives to paint women of color as a root of environmental ills (Hultgren 2015; Sturgeon 2009).[8] John Hultgren (2015: 128) explains that "immigration 'restrictionists' place incredible emphasis on women's fertility... Whether done out of genuine environmental concerns or anxieties related to a declining Anglo-European majority, critics point out that this practice ignores the gendered nature of transnational neoliberal structures." This desire to restrict immigration in the name of environmental protection echoes previous tendencies to target the fertility of black women in places like the US, the UK, and South Africa for the goals of poverty reduction or resource control. It was marginalized women who were most frequently targeted for population control measures like sterilization – first poor white women, then women of color (Wilson 2012).

Coercive population control around the world Many scholars criticize population limitation development strategies that otherwise ignore or exploit poor women, yet make them the main target of population programs (Bandarage 1997; Hartmann 1995, 1999; Seager 2003; Sen 2004). They feel that population control should not be made a substitute for directly addressing the poor economic situation that many of the world's women face (Urban 2007). Seager (2003: 967) claims that "blaming women without ever actually paying attention to them is a standard patriarchal analytical feat, but it seems particularly pernicious in population environment debates." Rather, population policies should be critically assessed in order to expose why they are introduced, and who benefits from them (Hartmann 1995).

It is undeniably true that in some cases the health of women may benefit from family planning measures or other population-related policies. Additionally, some women may welcome these programs, as they offer them some control over family size. What is essential in assessing this, however, is to remember that many marginalized women in the past and present have been the target of forced sterilization or compulsory or dishonest use of contraceptives, some of which are unsafe. Even widely used birth control methods like "the pill" have a history that highlights the connections between discourses of women's fertility (particularly poor women) and political goals. Women in Puerto Rico, for instance, were used in drug trials of contraceptive pills in the 1950s without being told that the medicine they were taking was a trial. These women, most of whom were poor or otherwise marginalized, had their desire to reduce family size used to recruit them into a drug trial without their knowledge. The health risk to these women was justified by politicians and researchers because of their goals of reducing poverty and the threat of Communism (Briggs 2010).

Many women in the global South have been subjected to "the violence of population control policies," which left them denied access to safe contraceptive methods that were under their control (Wilson 2012: 91). Countries as diverse as India, China, Bangladesh, Indonesia, Brazil, Mexico, and the US have targeted poor women along with racial and ethnic minorities for population control (Connelly 2006; Hartmann 1995; Hartmann et al. 2015). Some feminist scholars also highlight the unequal negative ramifications that population-reduction policies have on women and girls, including high levels of female child abandonment or abortion. Preference for sons over daughters means that families may choose to keep male children over female children, leading to the potential for skewed populations with more men than women, as has been the case in India and China over time (Hartmann 1995, 1999; Human Rights Watch 2012).

Forced sterilization made international headlines when fourteen women died in the Indian state of Chhattisgarh after undergoing sterilization procedures in 2014 (Wilson 2014). Some scholars claim that Western-led "family planning" programs make such deaths more likely. Despite being advocated in the name of female empowerment and choice, they are critiqued as deeply rooted in dangerous discourses of controlling excessive population growth in the global South. While donors and policymakers explicitly claim to reject coercive measures, charges have been made that focusing resources on population control unintentionally results in a reduction of agency and options for poor women around the world. Payment in exchange for undergoing the sterilization procedure amounts to coercion for marginalized women. This extends to the practice of making population control a condition for international food relief to poor countries. For example, there are reports that sterilization has been a condition for food relief in Bangladesh in some cases in the past (Hartmann and Standing 1985). Because of the fact that male sterilization is frequently regarded as socially unacceptable, more recent sterilization policies in India have been aimed at women (Hartmann 1995; Oum 2003). Sterilization has been a controversial topic for many years.[9] Reports of doctors and officials receiving compensation for each operation performed,[10] as well as claims that poor and uneducated men and women are sometimes coerced into compliance have resulted in claims that population control policies are deeply unjust (Chamberlain 2012; Human Rights Watch 2012). Sterilization is often implemented over other population management techniques, like providing birth control pills and/or condoms and education about how to use them (Burke 2014).

This relates to environmental concerns because policymakers in some instances have specifically identified environmental motivations for funding or implementing population control policies. For example, a working paper published by the UK's Department for International Development in 2010 cited climate change as one of the key reasons for supporting population control programs through international aid. The authors claimed that reducing population numbers would cut greenhouse gases. Despite the fact that the document warned of "complex human rights and ethical issues" involved in population control, it still outlined reasons to support these kinds of policies with aid (Chamberlain 2012).

How freely are population decisions made?   Rather than treat population control as a simplistic matter, it is essential to understand how existing policies that marginalize women and make it more difficult to pay for children or care for elderly relatives reduce options and agency. In India, for example, many have pointed out that preference for larger families may be tied to a lack of social services to help provide for the elderly (Human Rights Watch 2012). Neoliberal policies that reduce social spending while implicitly relying on increases in women's unpaid labor become an essential part of the story once we treat population as an issue with fundamental ties to economic, political, and social processes. In many societies men are expected to financially support elderly relatives while women do the home-based care work. Women are caught between making decisions about having children, but forced to also weigh how that decision is regarded by society, and how it will impact them into the future. Also, there are cases in which women have no choice in whether and how they conceive. A 2012 Human Rights Watch report highlights the fact that "India's family planning program focuses predominantly on women, with little interaction and engagement with men. At the same time, it is men who often decide when to have sex and how many children to produce. For India to be successful in its renewed efforts at family planning, it should engage effectively with men too." While most feminist population scholars would likely agree with the idea that both men and women should be included in discussions of reproductive health and choice, it would be problematic if this were done in a way that allowed the pattern of men making these decisions for a family to continue. This is contrary to the goal of increasing equity that many feminists share.

These examples remind us that the results of population debates can have profound impacts on women's bodies and futures. This is true if the policy concern is about the dangers of having too many people, or too few people. The two newspaper articles mentioned at the beginning of the chapter indicate that population is now on the mind of some policymakers due to concerns about stagnating or negative levels of population growth in some states. China's decision in October 2015 to shift from a one-child policy to a two-child policy is understood to have little to do with reproductive rights and women's empowerment, but everything to do with national calculations about demographics and economics (Phillips 2015). At the same time, there is a well-established history of policymaking encouraging families to have more children. This has been the case under conditions of populations feeling threatened by higher birthrates of "outside" communities, as in Israel, as well as in the aftermath of some wars or disasters (Portugese 1998). These kinds of policies, however, have come under fire as making gendered assumptions about "women's roles." For instance, lawmakers from Japan, a state with a negative birthrate, have come under fire repeatedly in the last several years for calling on women to have more babies. Media reports from 2007 explained that

Hakuo Yanagisawa, the Japanese health minister, described women as "birth-giving machines" and asked them to "do their best" to halt the country's declining birthrate (McCurry 2007). In 2015, chief cabinet secretary Yoshihide Suga was heavily critiqued after calling on women to contribute to their country's well-being by having more babies (McCurry 2015). Both of these cases of men urging women to have more children received negative public attention for using simplistic narratives about women's role in society. They also reflect the very reasons why discussions of population that ignore gender are deeply flawed. Our assumptions about population are already gendered. What is essential is that we critically engage with the gendered nature of population discourses and policies in order to promote justice.

Population decisions must be recognized as complex choices that are made with economic, social, and political constraints. In some cases there are no choices at all, only a path that one's family or society sets. A justice-based approach to population works to remove obstacles to choice for women. For instance,

> in 2015, the use of modern contraceptive methods in the least developed countries was estimated at around 34 per cent among women of reproductive age who were married or in union, and a further 22 per cent of such women had an unmet need for family planning, meaning that they were not using any method of contraception despite a stated desire or intention to avoid or delay childbearing. (UN DESA 2015: 5)

This indicates that many women lack sufficient choice in whether to expand their family size or not. By "choice" I mean actual control over the decision of whether or not to increase the size of a family. I do not have in mind aggressive, coercive, dangerous population control, like sterilization, that has often been given legitimacy by using narratives of "female empowerment" while paying little actual attention to the wants of women and the constraints on achieving them (Wilson 2012). Advocating for choice looks very different from conservative movements across the globe that routinely seek to limit women's choices over their bodies by advocating limitations to contraceptives and family planning policies.

Instead, a focus on reproductive rights that has justice as a central goal is oriented toward identifying and removing those economic, political, and social challenges that have resulted in women being targeted for coercive population control measures. I do not mean to suggest that this is easy. Nor does it imply a simplistic picture of a victimized woman and a coercive state.

Feminist scholars have advocated analyses that view "women as agents making rational choices rather than objects of mobilization by the patriarchal state or victims oppressed by patriarchal tradition" (Oum 2003: 421). Women from countries across the world have reacted to population pressures (either state or social pressure to have more or fewer children) with agency. Recognizing the negatives associated with aggressive or coercive population control discourses does not diminish this agency. Calling on scholars and policymakers to rethink population growth narratives also does not mean ignoring the damage that human communities can do and have done to ecosystems. It does mean, however, prioritizing just approaches to reducing the likelihood of ecosystem damage in ways that do not further marginalize individuals who are already living under difficult conditions. It also means realizing that unsustainability is driven by multiple factors, and population is likely much less responsible for environmental problems like climate change than is consumption, the subject of the next chapter (GenderCC 2011).

Case study: the impacts of natural disasters

The city of Chennai, India, experienced the highest level of rainfall for 100 years in late 2015. This abnormal precipitation, along with human encroachment on river banks, clogged river mouths, blocked natural drainage pathways, and a lack of early flood-warning systems, contributed to massive levels of flooding in the city (Ravishankar 2016). Flooding like this is just one example of hundreds of natural hazards experienced across the globe each year. The case of natural disasters allows us to explore conceptualizations of human population growth and movement as contributing to a potential increase in the number or severity of natural disasters, as well as humans experiencing negative consequences of disasters. The term "natural disasters" refers to the degree of suffering that citizens endure following natural shocks. Humans have to contend with a range of natural disasters, some of which are rapid-onset while others are slow-onset.[11] According to the Centre for Research on the Epidemiology of Disasters (CRED), 2014 witnessed 324 natural disasters, in which 7,823 people were killed; 140.8 million felt some adverse consequences of the events. China, the United States, the Philippines, Indonesia, and India were the top five countries for frequency of natural disasters between 2004 and 2013 (Guha-Sapir et al. 2015). China, India, and the US were also the three states with the largest population sizes in 2014. Additionally, of the nine countries expected to account for more than half of the world's projected population increase over the period 2015–50,[12] three are also included in the list of states with high frequencies of disasters over the decade up to 2014 (UN DESA 2015).

The most frequent narratives linking population to natural disasters are (1) population growth contributing to processes like global climate change, which increase disasters; (2) population growth leading to more people negatively impacted by natural disasters; (3) population movement leading to larger numbers of people living in areas most prone to natural disasters; and (4) experiences of natural disasters leading to population movement as people flee the impacts of disasters. The first narrative links human population growth to global processes like climate change, which are predicted to increase the frequency and severity of natural disasters. For instance, climate change, which is connected to human behavior, is predicted to result in natural disasters that are more frequent and more severe than those we have seen in the past (IPCC 2012). This argument will be discussed further in chapter 7. Second, there are claims that increased numbers of people lead to higher numbers of deaths and other negatives associated with disasters (Donner and Rodríguez 2008). Population pressures, in other words, make natural disaster impacts more extreme, resulting in greater numbers of deaths, economic costs, or other outcomes. For instance, a 2005 issue of NASA's *Earth Observatory* claimed that population growth and the landscape changes that go with it may make some disasters more severe. When a swath of trees becomes a neighborhood or an office building, the ground changes from spongy, water-absorbing soil to impervious pavement. Rain that would otherwise have soaked into the ground now has nowhere to go, and runs off as flood water. When land is deforested and remains bare or sparsely vegetated, soil erosion can worsen flooding. (Riebeek 2005)

Additionally, a 2013 report by the Asian Development Bank suggests a link between rising population exposure, greater population vulnerability, and increasing climate-related hazards in the region. Their findings suggest that densely populated areas are at a greater risk of experiencing intense natural hazards (Thomas et al. 2013: 16).

There are additional narratives about population and natural disaster, which include a specific focus on population movement either before, during, or after disasters. Herbert Huppert and Stephen Sparks claim that a consensus is emerging that the key causes of increasing natural hazards are directly linked to human behavior. These causes include population growth and urbanization, and environmental damage caused by human activities. "The world's population is becoming more concentrated in urban areas rather than in the less densely populated rural areas. In 2007, for the first time in human history, more people will live in urban centres than in the countryside. Taken together, these changes make communities much more vulnerable to natural hazards" (Huppert and Sparks 2006: 1878). This leads to the prediction that humans who have the option and resources to flee disasters will do so, at least in the short term (Hunter 2005).

Gender and natural disasters Thinking about sustainability and the justice of natural disaster impacts through gender lenses requires critically examining the roles of humans in influencing the likelihood and experiences of natural hazards. First, it is important to consider how "natural" natural disasters are. While ecosystems experience shocks as part of their natural functioning, the ways that humans experience natural disasters, as well as the extent or intensity of natural disasters, are influenced by human behavior (Blaikie et al. 1994). This speaks to the population-making-disasters-worse narrative discussed earlier. It is essential that we evaluate human behaviors that exacerbate natural hazards, yet are cognizant of the gendered conditions that lead to those behaviors. If populations are moving from rural or urban areas, who are these populations and what are the roots of those decisions? If people are moving into floodplains or drought-prone regions, what accounts for these patterns?

While the 2014 figures for natural disasters are below average, they still suggest that these hazards result in large-scale human suffering (Guha-Sapir et al. 2015).[13] Natural disasters are gendered phenomena (Enarson and Meyreles 2004). This is not to suggest that disasters only hit men or only hit women, but rather that our experiences of natural disasters are gendered. Natural hazards are not felt evenly by social class or gender. The poor tend to be more frequently exposed to disasters, as well as more vulnerable to these when they transpire. Those who are economically marginalized are more likely to live in poorly sited and poorly built housing that is likely to be destroyed during a disaster. At the same time, they likely have few resources to pay for rescue or rehabilitation in the aftermath (UNEP 2005). To date, research and policymaking on natural disasters are frequently silent on gender. There has been important work in the field documenting the experiences of men and women; however, gender is still infrequently mainstreamed in humanitarian relief, integrated into research and field projects undertaken by major disaster centers, or included in disaster training courses (Bradshaw 2015; Enarson 2012).

Elaine Enarson (2012) argues that even in economically powerful states like the US, women are more likely than men to experience forms of vulnerability in the aftermath of disasters, like loss of economic security. She adds that women of color, poor women, and older women are more likely than their male counterparts to experience these vulnerabilities. Forms of marginalization and discrimination translate into greater vulnerability to the dangers of natural disasters. Women are more likely than men to experience food insecurity, physical abuse, and loss of economic opportunity in the aftermath of disasters. Preexisting patterns of gendered marginalization determine where disaster aid is distributed, which job sectors recover fastest, and who is most vulnerable in shelters. These instances of vulnerability are connected to larger patterns of power and privilege in the international system. Jacqui True (2012: 161) explains that "[w]omen are generally poorer than men, they do not own land, they are less likely than men to have an education or access to health care, they are often less mobile due to cultural constraints, and they have less of a political voice in environmental planning and decision making." This means that many women begin a natural disaster experience at a higher level of vulnerability, and with lower levels of adaptive capacity than most men (Alston 2014).

One manifestation of this with ties to population discussions is that, on average, women tend to die more frequently than men in natural disasters (Neumayer and Plümper 2007). Examples from a range of natural disasters that have struck around the world indicate a pattern of these uneven experiences. These patterns can be witnessed in significantly different countries and types of disasters. For instance, five times more women than men died during the 1991 floods that hit Bangladesh. One and a half times more women died in the 1995 earthquake that hit Kobe, Japan. The 2004 South Asian tsunami killed on average three to four times more women than men (Seager 2006; UNEP 2005). The reasons for women dying in larger numbers are multiple and varied. Women tend to lack the same access to early-warning systems as well as being less likely to know how to swim. Social expectations about caregiving in many societies mean that women are more likely to be responsible for caring for children or elderly relatives, so their evacuation may be slowed. A case study of flood-warning systems in Bangladesh illustrates that men and women have different access to information about natural disasters due to expectations about gender roles. Men who spent time in public spaces a great deal had access to flood warnings, while women who largely operated in private spaces did not (Gender and Water Alliance 2006; Thompson and Sultana 1996). This has motivated organizations like Oxfam to work toward improving women's access to early-warning systems in places like Bangladesh, which frequently experience disasters (Oxfam 2010).

Poverty, caste, and ethnicity are also important parts of this story. For instance, minority communities may lack forms of economic, political, or social capital, which can result in them being more vulnerable to disasters. William Donner and Havidán Rodríguez (2008: 1096) point out that "many Hispanic immigrants may lack a crucial form of capital conferred by language, which continues to be problematic in tornado-prone areas where authorities may or will not issue warnings in Spanish." Additionally, research shows that poverty influences risk perception, preparedness, warning communication, psychological and physical impacts of disasters, state response, recovery, and reconstruction after disasters (Fothergill 2004). These examples illustrate the need for intersectional analysis of natural disasters that probes the various ways that forms of marginalization can reinforce each other in experiences of natural hazards.

Women are often portrayed as tearful victims of natural disasters, while men are depicted as stoic and resourceful (Enarson and Meyreles 2004). Men are frequently denied the space or ability to be emotional in the aftermath of natural hazards. Men who have lost family or friends, who feel the stress of worrying about livelihood security or of simply being overwhelmed, are often denied the chance to grieve publicly. Bradshaw (2015: 64) points to the idea of a "crisis of masculinity," which can be exacerbated by an occurrence in which men cannot fulfill their socially expected role. "The losses sustained during a disaster demonstrate that men could not protect their families and goods, and the need for aid demonstrates that they cannot provide for their families." This perspective reinforces the necessity of thinking about the composition of "populations" who experience disasters. The members of these populations experience natural hazards in ways that are influenced by multiple factors, including gender. It is just as essential to understand how gender "works" for men during disasters as it is to understand women's experiences. However, the fact that women's marginalization tends to exist at greater levels than men's means that they are more frequently the subject of feminist analysis.

An example of this is attention paid to how population pressures in the aftermath of natural disasters impact women's choices and bodies. There were reports of women being pressured to have children soon after the 2004 Indian Ocean tsunami in Tamil Nadu in order to replace children lost in the storm (Juran 2012). An Oxfam report a few months after the tsunami cited a greater likelihood that women would be pressured to get married and have children at younger ages than in the past (MacDonald 2005). This would have long-term impacts on the health, education, and livelihood futures of these women. At an extreme, "some women were blamed for the death of the family's children and some were strongly influenced – if not forced – to undergo reverse sterilization in hopes of having children, irrespective of their age, trauma-tized state and physical health" (Juran 2012: 23). This is a dramatic example of an environmental challenge manifesting in gendered experiences. While working toward sustainability is an essential policy goal so that the impacts of natural disasters are reduced, it is paramount that we assess the gen-dered impacts of natural hazards that influence women's bodies and choices about the future.

In sum, there are various narratives that connect human population growth and movement with natural disaster impacts. What is needed, however, is greater understanding of which populations are most at risk of experiencing the negatives of disasters and how this intersects with larger pat-terns of marginalization. Once again, rather than see poor or otherwise marginalized human populations as responsible for their own poor conditions, it is more helpful to reflect on how those at the greatest risk during and after disasters can be aided and empowered. Just as larger environmental debates about population that simplistically link human behavior with environmental ills are problematic for reasons already outlined, discussions of natural disaster impacts that fail to consider gender will focus our attention in ways that do little to highlight overall sustainability and justice.

Conclusions

A few years ago I was at a workshop on environmental change where a participant asked, "Can we put population back on the agenda now?" His question was met with very mixed responses. Some around the table thought that current levels of environmental unsustainability meant that we as scholars had a duty to discuss all contributing factors, including human population growth. A smaller number of participants claimed that putting population "back on the agenda" amounted to opening Pandora's box. Just raising the issue might serve to justify oppressive and dangerous policies that might have positive intentions, but a host of unintended consequences. This chapter has argued that population has never really left the agenda of scholars and policymakers, so it is best to critically engage with population debates rather than ignore them. While debates about population are not solely dominated by harsh neo-Malthusian alarmism, they could move in that direction if alternative narratives are not available in public debates. For instance, a 2015 survey found that respondents in the UK ranked population growth as a greater concern than climate change (Cuff 2016). It is essential that these kinds of population fears do not lead to repressive policies that target those who already face marginalization.

Calls to critically reflect on sustainability and justice in population debates should not be read as outright rejection of concerns about the environmental impact of adding people to the planet. Rather, this should be understood as an opportunity to assess the gendered, classed, and racialized concerns of those who are skeptical of alarmist or simplistic narratives about population growth and unsustainability. Fears about population growth and movement have contributed to gendered, classed, and racialized discourses of exclusion. If fear motivates us to adopt population control policies that are dangerous and unjust, what have we really saved? Is this the world we necessarily want to survive within? Instead, we can look for alternative ways to assess human contribution to environmental harm while recognizing the rights of marginalized communities to live with agency and dignity.

5
Too Much Stuff? Gender and Debates about Consumption

While population has been on the global agenda for centuries, the issue of consumption is a newer addition to the list of environmental concerns. A 2012 publication from the European Environment Agency asked whether unsustainable consumption is "the mother of all environmental issues." This reaction might be understandable given the sheer size of the global challenge of waste, one of the central narratives linking consumption with environmental damage. The EU report explains that the average amount of household waste generated was 444 kg per EU citizen in 2008. Specifically, food waste is estimated at 89 million tons per year in the EU. In the UK alone 25 percent of food purchased is thrown out, much of which (nearly two-thirds) could have been eaten (European Environment Agency 2012).

A 2016 study, however, found that the amount of material consumed in the UK, including metals, building materials, fuel, and food, had fallen from a peak of 889.9 million tons in 2001, which amounts to 15.1 tons per person, to 659.1 million tons in 2013, or 10.3 tons per person (UK Office for National Statistics 2016). There are different interpretations of these findings and how they relate to larger concerns about the many impacts of global consumption. On one hand, it may be that consumers are pushing back against pressure to consume more and more due to a desire to live more simply or more environmentally sound lifestyles. On the other hand, trends like the reduction of metals used in modern appliances or the digitization of books and movies mean that we are not necessarily consuming less, but we are consuming differently (Collinson and Vaughan 2016). The following chapter evaluates debates about consumption as an issue of GEP. It highlights discussions of the role of consumption in dominant economic processes as well as alternatives put forth with an eye to sustainability. It argues that although gender has not featured strongly in GEP discussion of consumption to this point, gender lenses offer essential perspective on why communities consume what, how, and when they do.

Why the focus on consumption?

"Consumption" refers to using something up. If I consume an apple, I eat the apple and it becomes unusable to someone else. If I consume a pair of shoes, I buy those shoes and they are unavailable for someone else to purchase. All organisms consume, utilize, or degrade resources in order to survive. "Background consumption" refers to "the normal, biological functioning of all organisms, humans included" (Princen 2002: 32). These acts of background consumption alter the environment, some only a bit and others a great deal. The total environmental impact is related to the total consumption of the population. When consumption enters discussions about global environmental change, we are not talking about background consumption per se. Instead, we are talking about issues like "overconsumption" or "misconsumption." Thomas Princen (2002: 33) explains that *overconsumption* is "the level or quality of consumption that undermines a species' own life-support system and for which individuals and collectivities have choices in their consuming patterns," while *misconsumption* is the practice of individuals consuming in a way that undermines their well-being "even if there are no aggregate effects on the population or species." As this distinction suggests, there are several themes present in GEP scholarship connecting consumption to environmental issues (Princen et al. 2002). Many scholars have called attention to the environmental consequences of overconsumption specifically, including the environmental impact of resource extraction, and generation of pollution and waste, among others.

A great deal of the debate about consumption revolves around patterns of consumption within our global capitalist economic system. "This is a political economy hailed as one that provides abundance for all, that promotes freedom of choice, that serves the consumer" (Princen 2005: 143). The notion of the "sovereign consumer" refers to markets serving the needs/wants of those with money to spend (Princen 2005). Over time, the growth-oriented and resource-intensive nature of capitalism came under fire for contributing to environmental change. For example, Paul Erhlich and John Holdren famously developed a model of the sources of environmental change. Their IPAT model suggested that environmental impact (I) is a function of population (P), affluence (A), and technology (T). Consumption relates to the affluence component of the model (Holdren and Ehrlich 1974). Affluence within global capitalism refers to those who can afford to consume. Some have expressed concern over the long-term environmental impacts not only of the global North, but also of "new consumers" or people newly economically able to mimic consumption patterns that have been well established in the global North.

However, the globalized nature of capitalism has led to the "blame" for the destructiveness of consumption being difficult to pinpoint. Supply chains are often quite long, and there is disagreement over whether blame should lie with those who supply raw materials, those who produce goods, those who consume goods, those who fail to sustainably dispose of goods, or some combination of these (Dauvergne 2005; Plumwood 2002). Additionally, these lengthy and complex supply chains serve to hide many of the consequences of consumer society away from consumers, as the negative consequences of consumption are felt by communities thousands of miles away (Dauvergne 2008, 2010).

Some scholarship has asked whether we can think of capitalism as a positive force for sustainability. These analyses typically start by recognizing that capitalism is the economic structure that our political economy is built on. They then ask whether there are positive forces of capitalism in addition to the negatives that have already been outlined. Peter Dauvergne and Jane Lister (2013: 2), for instance, use the concept of "eco-business" to highlight the ways that global corporations are adopting the language of sustainability and implementing their own version of the concept through their operations and supply chains. Eco-business refers to "taking over the idea of sustainability and turning it into a tool of business control and growth that projects an image of corporate social responsibility." These authors conclude that rather than a strong version of sustainability that has long-term ecosystem health at its core, the sustainability that is promoted by eco-business is fundamentally about the sustainability of big business and its increased ability to efficiently control supply chains and project a positive image to consumers. These efforts are more about changing what consumers buy, and how they feel about the process, than reducing what they buy.

These issues have led some scholars to ask whether capitalism can be significantly transformed in ways that lessen environmental change (Fuchs and Lorek 2005; Newell 2012; Parr 2012). There have been very mixed responses to this question. Some, like Peter Newell and Matthew Paterson (2010: 1), have suggested that "climate capitalism" – "a model which squares capitalism's need for continual economic growth with substantial shifts away from carbon-based industrial development" – might offer solutions to one of the most pressing issues of our age. Locating the target of policymaking in capitalism recognizes that the origins of climate change are rooted in the development of the global capitalist economy. These authors claim that rethinking and revising capitalism by decarbonizing it is a monumental task, but one that is necessary if we are to adequately, effectively, and justly address climate change.

Alternative voices bring the concepts of "sacrifice" and "sufficiency" to the debates on overconsumption (Maniates and Meyer 2010; Princen 2003, 2005). An approach guided by either of these concepts requires asking questions about how actors conceptualize their relationships to the goods and services they utilize, both at the level of the individual and at the level of the state. Thinking about consumption through the lens of either sacrifice or sufficiency would likely require significant changes to business-as-usual economic processes. Princen (2005: 7) claims that sufficiency in the context of environmental sustainability "compels decision makers to ask when too much resource use or too little regeneration jeopardizes important values such as ecological integrity and social cohesion; when material gains now preclude material gains in the future; when consumer gratification or investor reward threatens economic security; when benefits internalized depend on costs externalized." Rather than marvel at the efficiencies of major societal institutions like "the factory, the laboratory, [and] the market," each of which has contributed greatly to current patterns of environmental change, a logic of sufficiency asks *how much is enough* to achieve both short-term and long-term goals without exposing our community and other communities to undue risk (Princen 2005: 8).

Each of these examples illustrates that there has been quite a bit of scholarly and policy attention paid to issues like overconsumption and misconsumption in recent years; however, questions about consumption were not asked, at least not loudly, in GEP scholarship and policymaking for a good deal of its history. An examination of the journal *Global Environmental Politics* from 2000 to 2015 shows that "consumption" and "ecological critiques of economic growth" made up less than 5 percent of articles published (Dauvergne and Clapp 2016). While there have been many important contributions to GEP scholarship on consumption over the years, it has still remained a less visible topic than others like the general form and nature of environmental governance.

As far as policymaking goes, questioning the environmental impacts of consumption requires thinking about issues of power relations, lifestyle choices, and personal responsibility, among others, which require uncomfortable soul-searching for many in the international community. The 1992 Rio Earth Summit, which popularized the concepts of sustainability and sustainable development, also witnessed participants from the global South, activists and government officials alike, challenge the consumption patterns of the global North. These participants questioned the tendency of Northern voices to focus on their "overpopulation," which they claimed was not as detrimental to environmental sustainability as Northern consumption. They urged their Northern colleagues to tackle consumption rather than simply pass the blame to processes more typical to the South. These challenges to confront consumption were taken up by some individuals, environmental organizations, and municipalities in the wake of the summit, including the decision to make Chapter Four of Agenda 21 focus on "Changing Consumption Patterns" (UNDSD 1992). Despite this, discussions of consumption (and overconsumption and/or misconsumption) are still often missing from global policy debates about major environmental challenges (Maniates and Meyer 2010; Princen et al. 2002).

As with each of the chapters in this book, it is impossible to draw firm boundary lines between debates. Concern about consumption is tied to concern about population in many ways. Consumption is frequently conceptualized as a double-edged sword. High consumption levels often accompany advances in health and material comfort. Simultaneously, however, they also have high environmental costs. Over time, improvements in education, health, and opportunities result in demographic transitions toward slower population growth. These improvements also, however, result in longer lifespans over which people consume goods and services. There are fears that as more communities develop economically, they will begin to mimic the consumption patterns of the global North (UNDSD 1992). Consumption is regarded as a worrying companion to development in the global South. While it has increasingly been discussed as a component that is necessary to understand for strategies of sustainability, it has overwhelmingly been discussed as a phenomenon that is gender-neutral.

The gendered nature of consumption

Despite this general lack of attention to gender in debates about consumption, there has been some scholarly work that examines the nexus between masculinity and femininity on one hand, and consumption patterns on the other. This work finds that socially conditioned roles and responsibilities influence what and how we consume (Ghodsee 2007;

Johnsson-Latham 2006; True 2003). For instance, examinations of consumption patterns in communist and post-communist Bulgaria illustrate that multiple actors actively attempted to shape ideas about femininity in order to influence the consumption of beauty products (e.g., make-up, lotions, etc.) in that state. During the communist era, "ideals of revolutionary femininity" were used to explain and justify the limited supply of many beauty products during the period. The state specifically attempted to convince women that fashion and beauty were not relevant to their identities as women. This changed in the post-communist period, which was marked by large-scale economic shifts. Competition in new labor markets is said to have contributed to new gender roles and beauty standards for women, which featured expectations that consumption of beauty products was an essential component necessary to get highly competitive jobs.[1] A dramatic increase in television and print advertising reinforced these new standards of femininity (Ghodsee 2007). This example illustrates that consumption patterns are not gender-neutral. Companies that spend large sums of money annually on gender-specific advertising know this very well (Casey and Martens 2007). Where once products like soap or body wash were considered to be acceptable for use by everyone, now we have "men's" versions of these packaged in dark-colored wrappers and "women's" versions packaged in light colors. A quick check of the labels shows that they contain much the same ingredients, but we are now encouraged to buy twice as much. Additionally, the "women's" version of many products is more expensive than the "men's" version (Willsher 2014). But what does this mean for thinking through the influence of consumption on sustainability and justice? The next two sections address how gender relates to these two important concepts.

Gendered consumption and sustainability There appears to be at least a tentative consensus that current forms and scales of consumption across the globe are unsustainable. Where there is still a lack of consensus is how to address this. Can capitalism be the great hope? Notions of green consumption, ethical consumption, or sustainable consumption encourage us to use goods and services in ways that enhance current quality of life while not jeopardizing the needs of future generations (Barr et al. 2011; Fuchs and Lorek 2005; Lewis and Potter 2011). For instance, the EU's approach to sustainable consumption encourages the creation of "a virtuous circle: improving the overall environmental performance of products throughout their life-cycle, promoting and stimulating the demand of better products and production technologies and helping consumers to make better choices through a more coherent and simplified labelling" (Commission of the European Communities 2008: 3). These ideas suggest that we just need to consume the right way in order to avoid environmental change.

But who is responsible for making changes to consumption patterns? Much of the rhetoric about "addressing consumption" couches it as an individual-level problem (Barr et al. 2011; Dauvergne 2010; Littler 2011; Maniates 2001). Scholars have noted that this is an individualistic representation of society wherein the responsibility of tackling issues as substantial as poverty and pollution fall to the purchasing decisions of individuals (Barr et al. 2011; Littler 2011). Michael Maniates (2001: 33) refers to this as the "individualization of responsibility." Focusing on recycling, altering everyday behavior like walking more, or changing the kinds of products we buy are all locating responsibility for addressing environmental change at the level of the individual, and often in the person as an individual consumer. This focus does not necessarily entail a wholesale rejection of capitalism, but rather a shift to a kinder, greener capitalism. Maniates (2001) finds this notion to be problematic and dangerous. He argues that an individualization of responsibility narrows our possibilities for policymaking. Individual-level thinking that identifies strategies like recycling as a viable solution to over-consumption treats the symptom without ever asking about the cause. It allows global systems to remain unchanged, or with only minor tweaks. None of this is to say we should all stop recycling; it is rather to say that individual-level solutions to global problems cannot be the final fix.

Changes to global systems Examining these debates through gender lenses allows us to critically reflect on the kinds of changes that are necessary to adequately address environmental degradation. Many feminist approaches high-light the need to remain open to significant changes to global structures in order to achieve multiple goals, including environmental sustainability and justice (MacGregor 2006; Salleh 2009; Seager 1993). For example, feminist environmental scholars have called attention to the mutual accommodation of capitalism and patriarchy (Seager 1993). Each system justifies domination in ways that result in the marginalization of certain groups within society. Women have tended to be heavily represented among the marginalized in each. These complex, overarching systems cannot be altered through individual-level strategies like small-scale shifts in consumption. They reach across the globe and fundamentally shape our lived experiences surrounding environmental change and beyond (Harcourt 1994; Harcourt and Nelson 2015; Plumwood 2002; Rocheleau 2015).

An example of the ineffective status quo approach to environmental sustainability is also seen in the fact that when corporations have taken up the challenge of altering consumption, it has frequently been in rather limited ways that leave them open to the charge of "greenwashing," a term used to describe making environmental friendliness a part of a company's public image whether or not the company adopts a strict commitment to environmental sustainability (Lewis and Potter 2011; Parr 2009). Ecobranding, a "strain of branding committed to showcasing a company's social and environmental responsibility," has been advanced through initiatives like sustainable consumption (Parr 2009: 15). The continuing growth in global consumption patterns may cause some to question the long-term feasibility of approaches to sustainable development that assume a business-as-usual approach to political economy. Positions like ecological modernization underestimate the problematic nature of global consumption. Instead, they sell us on the promise of getting the right mix of green, capitalist-oriented policies in place that require very little alteration to existing economic processes or power dynamics.

Some debates about consumption assume that we can use technology to increase efficient use of resources, and therefore consume less of those resources. For example, Doris Fuchs and Sylvia Lorek (2005) identify technology as one element of sustainable consumption that ultimately results in improvements in the eco-efficiency of consumption. These authors recognize, however, that technologically based efficiency increases will only lead to a "weak" version of sustainability if they are not coupled with overall changes in consumption patterns and reductions in consumption levels. This is due to the fact that gains made in efficiency are often overcompensated for by growth in the total volume of consumption (Dauvergne and Lister 2013). Each of these examples of relatively small-scale changes to global capitalism suggests that sustainable, green, and eco-efficient consumption are unlikely to overcome environmental unsustainability if they are conceptualized in limited ways. Additionally, technological fixes to unsustainability are associated with a masculinized view of environmental policymaking (Plumwood 2002). Data from European states suggests that many men identify culturally with high-powered technologies (Buckingham et al. 2005; Johnsson-Latham 2007; Spitzner 2009). This begs the question of whether technological solutions to overconsumption are being suggested because they are the best hope for enhancing environmental sustainability, or because they are associated with culturally specific, gendered assumptions about progress. Are Promethean options[2] suggested because we truly think they hold the most hope, or because technological solutions allow us to prove mastery over our domain while simultaneously avoiding making significant changes to our lifestyles and approaches to development?

Rather, consumption needs to be assessed as a socially embedded process (Dauvergne 2008; Princen et al. 2002). Gender lenses aid in this rethinking. We cannot effectively identify and hope to halt unsustainable practices associated with consumption if we continue to ignore the ways that patterns of consumption connect to gendered perceptions of "development," social pressure, and dominant economic processes. Just as population issues are deeply related to gendered social pressures, political debates, and economic realities, consumption choices (or lack of choice) relate to much the same processes. Versions of environmentalism that promise the benefits of environmental sustainability without the challenge of reflecting and acting on notions of "sacrifice" or "sufficiency" are likely selling false hope (Wapner 2010b).

Optimism needs to be connected to accurate assessments of the scale of consumption as an environmental problem.

Revising our picture of consumption   Acquiring a more complex picture of consumption can aid in understanding why actors consume the way they do and hopefully how meaningful changes to consumption might be reached. The actors in our analysis must go beyond individuals to include corporations and states, among others. Additionally, these changes should not serve to reduce the livelihood security of marginalized communities – including many women, the poor, ethnic or racial minorities, etc. – but rather must be built on the commitment that we all deserve access to healthy and fulfilling lives. One of the most visible connections between consumption and the environmental concern of bio-diversity loss is the loss of endangered species to illegal activities such as poaching. Demand for illegal wildlife products is understood to be "based on their use in traditional East Asian medicine, the international trade in commercial goods (e.g. timber) and exotic pets, and a desire for status symbols, among other factors" (UNEP 2014: 25). Illegal trade in plants and animals is one of the largest sources of criminal earnings in the world. In 2014, illegal wildlife trade was estimated to be worth US$50–150 billion per year. The global illegal fisheries catch is valued at US$10–23.5 billion a year, while illegal logging reached US$30–100 billion (UNEP 2014).

Feminist and other critical environmental perspectives take issue with how poaching is often framed in global debates. If we want to understand poaching, we must understand the factors that make the practice profitable or desirable and the incentives for the people involved. There are gendered and racialized assumptions at work in media depictions of poachers. They are frequently represented as tough, male, merciless "African" killers who are driven by greed. These depictions can result in policy that ignores the livelihood security motivations for poaching. Peter Newell (2005: 79) argues that in some instances conservationist goals have been "allowed to trump considerations of human welfare. The policy of shoot to kill, applied to poachers in Kenya, was encouraged by conservative conservation groups such as WWF and Conservation International who took the position that 'increasing population was a major threat to the survival of elephants and other wildlife'." While it is unfair to say that global conservation organizations predominantly express these sentiments, it is true that local resource users and wildlife management schemes have often had tensions (Brockington 2002; Swatuk 2005). We must take care to consider illegal wildlife trade and poaching as part of larger global economic patterns and processes.

Hunting wild game, or bush-meat hunting, is considered to be a specific category of poaching (Knapp et al. 2010). Bush-meat hunting is often a strategy for achieving food security or livelihood security for members of local populations. Some communities indicate that wild meat is a cheaper source of protein for them than other alternatives (Knapp et al. 2010).[3] In places like Kenya, where bush-meat hunting has been banned since 1977 due to concerns about biodiversity and tourism revenue loss, it remains a relatively common drought-coping strategy for many. Bush-meat is consumed in the home, sold at the market, and sold to restaurants. This means that while men are mostly involved in the hunting of bush-meat, women are frequently involved in its consumption, preparation, and sale. In this and other illegal coping strategies (e.g., wild-game hunting, home-brewing alcohol, charcoal production, prostitution, forest uses and theft) women's activities tend to be limited due to gender norms, which also limit their financial independence (Mosberg and Eriksen 2015). While biodiversity loss is an extremely important global environmental concern, we are unlikely to fully understand it if we fail to recognize the ways that gender, class, and other systems of marginalization connect with consumption. Thus, despite wild-game hunting being an illegal strategy for coping with poor environmental conditions, communities still engage in it due to livelihood and food-security needs.

Additionally, poachers respond to the incentives of global markets where demand for products from rare or endangered species of plants or animals makes engaging in this illegal activity more lucrative than many legal ones (Brack 2002). This illustrates the complexities involved in understanding environmental unsustainability and the policies enacted to protect against it. Instability in many biodiverse regions contributes to biodiversity loss, but that instability is connected to larger ties of power distribution in the international system (Brack 2002). Likewise, consumption patterns in one part of the world can have implications for the lived experiences of locals and for the health of ecosystems thousands of miles away. Reflecting on environmental justice and equity involves considering the ways in which global consumption patterns contribute to larger patterns of environmental vulnerability and cost. Some poaching is done in order to supply protein to be consumed or sold locally, while some is done to supply global markets with products to be consumed far away.

Links between consumption and marginalization   We can gain a more holistic picture of consumption by reflecting on these power relations, resource access, and forms of marginalization. It is also essential to reflect more closely on gendered trends in consumption. There have been some studies from countries around the world that identify trends of women tending to have consumption patterns that are more sustainable than men (Johnsson-Latham 2006, 2007; Spitzner 2009). For example, more women than men travel by public transportation or on foot in Europe (Spitzner 2009). Reports from Sweden, for instance, suggest that women's unpaid (invisible) house labor means that they are more likely to buy basic household essentials like food and clothing, while men are more likely to purchase expensive capital goods as well as to be the registered owners of things like cars, homes, and electronics (Johnsson-Latham 2006, 2007). The author of the reports, Gerd Johnsson-Latham (2007: 5), argues that "[t]he study points to how a changed behavior among men – notably rich men who are decision-makers – can be crucial in addressing climate change and in enhancing the opportunities of all human beings to enjoy sustainable development." It is noteworthy that these trends of gendered consumption patterns are apparent in states in the global North, where some might expect fewer differences between the behaviors of men and women as gender equity levels increase. Sweden, for instance, typically ranks high on many indicators of gender equity yet we still see clear gendered differences in behavior.

This is not to say that women are necessarily consciously choosing options that are more environmentally sustainable. For some this is a conscious choice, for others it is not. Instead, it is essential to reflect on differences in consumption patterns between men and women, which reflect social expectations and pressures that are deeply connected to gender. Throughout the book, the point has been made that automatically connecting women to essentialized notions of environmental protection is unhelpful. What is necessary, however, is critically engaging with the social, political, and economic reasons that men and women often tend to exhibit different patterns of consumption. Additionally, including both men and women in environmental decision-making on issues like consumption better ensures that a range of experiences and perspectives are incorporated into policymaking. This strategy is likely not only beneficial for getting a better picture of patterns of overconsumption, but also a more just option for decision-making in general.

As discussed in chapter 2, street science and citizen science are concepts in which the process of knowledge production/generation involves people outside of the scientific community. Broadening the circle of people who produce knowledge can potentially have a number of benefits, including making the process of knowledge generation more inclusive and acquiring a more complete picture of environmental change. A study that evaluated the experiences of citizen scientists volunteering with conservation organizations in Bangalore, India, found the practice of having non-scientists engage in scientific research can also contribute to increased environmental awareness among the general public. The volunteers were highly motivated, with a great deal of interest in one or more environmental issues. They gained expertise through their participation with the conservation organizations and passed along these skills and knowledge to peers through social networks (Johnson et al. 2014).

Increasing participation can also be beneficial in other aspects of decision-making. Bina Agarwal (2009) has studied women's participation in forest committees in India and Nepal in particular, and found that the presence of women on these committees, the overall percentage of the committee that is made up of women, and the willingness of women to speak up in meetings are all significantly correlated with improved forest conditions. Similarly, in a cross-national study of women's participation in community forestry, Eric Coleman and Esther Mwangi (2013: 193) found that women's participation is most likely when households have more education, when there are low levels of economic inequality in general and across sexes in particular, and when institutions are inclusive. The study also found that women's participation was found to influence the amount of "disruptive conflict" associated with the group. These studies illustrate that environmental sustainability and the inclusion of women are reinforcing aims. This is particularly important to highlight since women are often underrepresented in biodiversity governance schemes (Deda and Rubian 2004; UNESCO 2010). What these and other studies illustrate is that broad participation can actually aid in sustainability. It is unlikely that we will confront the processes resulting in unsustainable biodiversity loss until we incorporate multiple forms of knowledge as well as confront the underlying reasons that this loss is happening at such fast rates.

The justice of current and future consumption   The procedural justice of including women in decision-making on environmental issues is one element of a consumption–justice nexus. All resource users deserve to be participants in environmental decision-making to the extent possible because they have a stake in the outcome of environmental management. Additionally, gender lenses allow us to critically reflect on questions like these: what are specific patterns of inequality in global capitalism, are capitalist-based solutions to overconsumption just and effective, and why has there been such slow progress in getting consumption on the global agenda when compared to population?

Focusing on consumption necessitates a corresponding focus on the influence of capitalism across the globe. The neoliberal economic thinking that supports the spread of capitalism encourages growth, and grow we have as a global economy. According to the World Bank (2015a), the world's gross domestic product (GDP) in 2000 was US$33.28 trillion. In 2014 the world's GDP was US$77.87 trillion. What these global figures hide, however, is the unequal distribution of economic prosperity across the international community. One of the key consequences of the spread of capitalism has been an increase in inequality in the international system (Newell and Paterson 2010). This inequality is revealed in differences in prosperity and security between the global North and the global South, but it has also resulted in predictable patterns of inequality among various communities. Our global political economy profoundly impacts both sustainability and justice as it relates to global environmental issues and beyond. It provides luxury goods for a wealthy minority, often through degrading the environments of a marginalized majority who bear the unequal burden of environmental costs without benefiting from the exploitation of natural resources in the same fashion as the wealthy (Dauvergne 2005).

These patterns, however, are also deeply gendered. The very neoliberal economic structures that contribute to large-scale levels of consumption and environmental damage also result in reductions in women's economic rights and livelihood security (Benería 2003; Detraz and Peksen 2016; Harcourt and Nelson 2015). They also often treat women's work as supplemental, or worth less than men's (Elson and Warnecke 2011). These structures are built on the assumption that women's unpaid care and domestic work is unproblematic (Leach et al. 2015; UNDP 2015). Global patterns of gendered economic discrimination have meant that women are overrepresented among those in economically precarious positions in most states. Their labor can often be underpaid or in informal sectors. This is not to essentialize all women as underpaid or unpaid caregivers; however, this does characterize a large number of women around the globe. Women are still expected to provide care to children and relatives as part of many societal gender roles. Care relates to environmental change in that environmental stresses can also manifest in greater care burdens. Additionally, women are also often responsible for making consumption choices for families due to socially constructed gender norms (Braun and Traore 2015). Again, it is not the case that women are more moral or necessarily in tune with the ecological consequences of consumption. Their choices are often shaped by social, political, and economic forces. All of this contributes to differences in consumption patterns at individual levels

(Johnsson-Latham 2006). This also means that when states cut spending on services like public transportation or child care, there are consequences for consumption patterns. Reduced public transportation means an increase in personal vehicles for those who can afford them (Spitzner 2009). Each of these factors reinforces the necessity of understanding consumption as a gendered social, political, and economic phenomenon that will only be addressed effectively and ethically if we probe the global structures that fuel and reinforce it.[4]

Consumption within current economic structures   Capitalism is a system that relies on consumption. The costs of consumption are averted by those who benefit the most and forced on those who benefit the least (Dauvergne 2008). While this is often conceptualized in terms of North–South distributions in GEP scholarship, these issues are also felt within the population of a state. It is marginalized peoples who are most likely to be exposed to the hazards of production and disposal of consumer goods. Val Plumwood (2002: 71) cautions that "[r]emoteness allows a high level of dissociation between costs and benefits, between elite consumption benefits and ecological damage." Complex commodity chains and various forms of remoteness associated with current modes of capitalism sever our perceptions of ecological embeddedness. Conceptualizing humans as "outside of nature," or, even worse, the gendered "masters over nature," soothes our guilt and fears by suggesting that small-scale or technological changes can fix a set of problems that are profoundly linked to unequal and unsustainable global structures.

One way to assess the complexity of consumption is through examining global food consumption patterns. Multiple GEP scholars have focused specifically on meat consumption and environmental change (Dauvergne 2008; Paterson 2001). The environmental consequences of feedlots and slaughterhouses are well documented (FAO 2006a). A study of the EU found that cutting consumption of meat, dairy products, and eggs in half would reduce nitrogen emissions by 40 percent, reduce greenhouse gas emissions by 25–40 percent, and reduce per capita use of cropland for food production by 23 percent (Westhoek et al. 2014). Deforestation in the name of agricultural or ranching expansion results in significant losses of biodiversity (Dauvergne 2008; FAO 2006a). Meat consumption, like driving cars, has also become a symbol of modernity and wealth, according to Matthew Paterson (2001). Global consumption of meat has increased as the fast-food industry has grown rapidly over the last few decades (Dauvergne 2008).

Many feminist scholars have challenged us to think about anthropocentricism, meat consumption, and masculinity. Carol Adams (1990) argues that meat is a symbolically masculine food. This association between meat and masculinity reinforces the domination of humans over nature in much the same way that patriarchy reinforces male domination over females. Associating meat-eating with masculinity makes it desirable in a way that practices associated with femininity are not considered to be. This is how patriarchy works. Associations of meat with masculinity coupled with assumptions about meat-eating and status result in global patterns of meat consumption being very difficult to change. In fact, many environmental NGOs choose not to pursue meat-reduction education campaigns because these are seen as issues with limited political and social appeal (Laestadius et al. 2014). This is similar to other individual-level suggestions of how to live more sustainably, including driving more fuel-efficient cars, which are not considered to be "manly" in many societies with large environmental footprints (Reddy 2015). We can think of the politics of meat in similar terms to the politics of technological environmental solutions. Options associated with progress, which are often also associated with masculinity, are regarded as positive and it is therefore difficult for alternatives to shift the dominant discourses. Patterns of global food consumption must be evaluated for their sustainability, but this requires understanding the social forces that reinforce certain choices and limit others, and the justice of these processes.

Why have we discussed population more than consumption? Part of a gender analysis of the justice of consumption debates also requires questioning why narratives about population and environmental harm have been so much more widespread for the history of GEP scholarship and policymaking than narratives about consumption and environmental harm. There have been numerous calls over the past few years to shift our attention from global population to global consumption. For instance, narratives about population and security predict that population growth will result in increased levels of scarcity. However, some scholars argue that pointing the finger at population without simultaneously considering the role of consumption in driving scarcity is incomplete at best, and could result in inefficient policymaking (Deligiannis 2013). As discussed in chapter 4, population is often treated rather simplistically in ways that assume that more people means more consumption, which means more environmental damage. However, it is essential to reflect on agency when assessing the justice of consumption reduction proposals. Focusing on population allows for business as usual in the global economy, as corporate pollution is rarely discussed. When the environmental impact of corporations is discussed, it is often assumed that businesses are only responding to consumer demands, and therefore reducing the number of people will reduce environmental change by reducing demand. This claim ignores the fact that corporations spend huge sums of money each year to manage and create consumer demand. Companies spend trillions of dollars annually trying to convince us to spend money on products and services (Dauvergne 2010). A limited focus also fails to consider that consumers have no control over corporate decisions on extraction, manufacturing, or distribution (Angus and Butler 2011). Rethinking consumption requires powerful people to confront possible changes to the systems from which they benefit. It has, therefore, been much easier to put more emphasis on population across the international community. The following section discusses some of these contentious but important debates as they relate to international concerns about the environmental harm associated with consuming plastics.

Case study: the environmental and social consequences of plastics

Plastic is used in an enormous number of consumer goods. It is used in packaging, electronics, building materials, and a variety of others products, and 10–20 million tons of plastic ends up in the world's oceans each year. UNEP (2014) estimates that this costs approximately US$13 billion per year in environmental damage to marine ecosystems, including financial losses incurred by fisheries and tourism, and time spent cleaning up beaches. One "cost" associated with plastic pollution is the harm that it causes to the species that live in marine ecosystems. Around 99 percent of seabirds are predicted to ingest plastic by 2050. Seabirds are particularly vulnerable to plastic pollution, as they ingest floating plastic. Impacts of plastic pollution on seabirds are found to be greatest at the southern boundary of the Indian, Pacific, and Atlantic Oceans, although the "threat is geographically widespread, pervasive, and rapidly increasing" (Wilcox et al. 2015: 11899). The story of plastic pollution indicates that human consumption can have profound effects on ecosystems, including on the biodiversity that exists within them. Biodiversity refers to diversity at all levels of life, including plants, animals, and microorganisms. Biodiversity loss can occur through "natural" processes, but much recent biodiversity loss has been attributed to human behavior, including population growth and movement, and patterns of consumption.

Policy discussions surrounding microbeads stem from environmental concerns about biodiversity loss and the health of marine life as well as human well-being. Microbeads are tiny beads, typically made of plastic, meant to aid in exfoliation, and are found in body wash, soap, facial scrubs, toothpaste, and other products. These beads get washed down the drain by the billions and are often not biodegradable. The controversy surrounding them stems from the fact that they have been found in waterways as well as the bodies of fish and other marine life after they have passed through water filtration systems. A report by the New York attorney general's office in the US estimates that nearly 19 tons of microbeads may be washing into New York's wastewater every year, and the water treatment plants cannot process it (Nalbone 2015). The plastic acts like a sponge for toxic chemical pollutants and can enter the food chain as fish and other sea life ingest it. The problem is not limited to the US.[5] A study of fish in the English Channel found that one-third of the fish examined contained microbeads and other forms of plastics in their digestive system (Smithers 2013).

The New York attorney general's report on microbeads claims that "the most effective way to address this problem is at the source – the consumer products that contain microbeads" (Nalbone 2015: 1). There have been calls to boycott products that contain microbeads in countries around the world. 5Gyres, an environmental organization that urges action to reduce plastic contamination in waterways, launched an online platform called "Beat the Microbead," which allows consumers to check whether a product contains microbeads, and whether the manufacturer is phasing out microbeads, by scanning the barcode of personal care products (5Gyres 2015). The controversy over microbeads is related to larger debates about the impacts of consumption on the environment. It speaks to the products we buy, why these are available, what the options are for reductions or alternatives, and how all of these issues relate to environmental health and well-being.

The consumption of plastics has important, often ignored gendered components. While gender is fluid and masculinities and femininities shift from community to community, there are regularized patterns that shape the ways that people identified as women and people identified as men experience consumption and environmental change. Failing to understand these patterns makes it difficult to develop an understanding of consumption's environmental impacts as well as successful and equitable policies to address these effects.

Gender and plastic consumption   As already discussed, patterns of consumption are gendered. We can reflect on the influence of gender norms in consumption and biodiversity by considering the negative implications of plastics on species living in many different ecosystems. The production and consumption of plastic goods have a range of negative environmental consequences. In particular, microplastics, or tiny fragments of plastic that result from the breaking down of plastic material, are considered to be a potential source of contamination of the food web through marine ecosystems. Plastic is also a concern for non-marine ecosystems.

One of the most potent symbols of plastic pollution is the plastic bag. Plastic bags were developed and promoted by the US oil and gas industry, and their introduction was initially met with some skepticism by consumers. This early hesitancy was overcome as US shoppers consistently had access to plastic bags in supermarkets and shops by 1977. Western European countries followed in their use of plastic bags by the 1980s, and many countries in the global South by the 1990s. Estimates suggest that between 500 billion and 1.5 trillion plastic bags are used worldwide each year.[6] Plastic bags often end up as garbage or litter. Many states lack recycling or consistent waste management to effectively get them out of landfills or streets. Plastic bags can cause health risks to livestock like cattle or sheep that may ingest them. Plastic bags often wash into rivers, and become microplastic, which both threatens aquatic wildlife and potentially damages crops (Clapp and Swanston 2009).

While the environmental and health consequences of plastic bags have been well documented, less is known about the ways in which gender and consumer behavior intersect around this item. Gendered division of household labor means that women are often the ones doing the food shopping. Chenyang Xiao and Dayong Hong (2010), for instance, found that women in China demonstrated greater participation in environmental behaviors inside of the home, including recycling and bringing reusable bags for shopping. Women's responsibilities vary within and across societies, however. Through participant observation and interviews with women in southern Mali, Yvonne Braun and Assitan Traore (2015) observed that women were the primary consumers of plastic shopping bags because of gendered roles that placed women as the primary caregivers, cooks, and shoppers for their families. Women also use plastic bags in their roles as vendors to package and carry goods. Interviews revealed that many women felt that plastic bags were much more convenient than needing to go home for a shopping basket, enabling them to do their shopping while on their way to do other tasks. The interviews also highlight the connections between globalization and consumption patterns. Before plastic bags became widely available in Mali, people used handmade shopping bags or baskets. Some study participants expressed a desire to go back to reusable shopping bags either to support local people who made them, to avoid adding garbage and litter to the streets, or to return to a more authentic Malian way of doing things. Others claimed that plastic bags are more modern and convenient. This highlights the futility of essentializing women's experiences into a homogeneous group. Analyses of consumption must examine the complex ways in which globalization and consumption play out in people's everyday lives. Finally, these analyses require examining the ways in which policies geared toward improving sustainability related to consumption need to recognize how gender affects consumption and other behaviors that impact sustainability.

At the same time, alterations to consumption patterns must not place unfair burdens on women who hold roles as household resource managers. Braun and Traore (2015: 868) remind us that

> [w]omen who are expected to be the primary consumers for their families make their choices in a constrained context that is limited by both personal and larger structural forces, which can become deeply intertwined at the individual level in potentially patterned ways...Focusing on individual choices alone obscures the larger structural forces and interests that shape this context within and across scales, including political, economic, and corporate actors who influence and benefit from globalization, consumerism, and patriarchy.

While some GEP scholars have also called into question the effectiveness and justice of individualistic narratives within consumption debates (Maniates 2001; Princen 2002), the lack of attention to how these narratives are gendered is a gap that should be filled. Additionally, the very fact that GEP scholars overlook some tough policy issues like plastic consumption should be altered by evaluating policies geared toward sustainability but that also contribute to equal burden and benefit within communities (Dauvergne and Clapp 2016).

Women's typical role as the primary shopper for households is an illustration of the ways in which gendered divisions of household labor can and often do result in an increased "burden of care" for women. Interviews with environmental activists in Canada reinforce that it is often women who initiate and maintain "green" practices at home, and that many women feel guilty about failing to live up to their goals of living sustainably (MacGregor 2006). These kinds of internal and external struggles play out in environmentally focused debates about cloth versus disposable diapers (or nappies as they are known in some states). Disposable diapers typically consist of a plastic outer layer, a core of absorbent materials, and a protective top layer. Studies in several states have assessed the environmental impact of these products, particularly as they contribute greatly to global municipal waste streams (Aumônier et al. 2008). Disposable diapers are widely used in the UK, where they make up around 3 percent of the waste stream. New mothers may be influenced in their decision on which diapers to buy by the distribution of "bounty packs" through the British National Health Service, which contain "disposable nappies and toiletries using artificial chemicals." Susan Buckingham and Rakibe Kulcur (2009: 668) find this problematic due to the fact that

> [n]ew mothers are a vulnerable and impressionable "market" in their anxiety to be "good" mothers, a point which manufacturers of disposable nappies exploit in their advertising and marketing campaigns. On the other hand, these women are urged by women's environmental and health campaigning groups to consider the links between their children's and their environment's wellbeing, and adopt the use of reusable nappies.

This means that the gendered politics of care intersects with global discussions of environmental sustainability in ways that are often underexplored in both policy and scholarly circles.

In sum, the politics of plastic is better understood when we take gender into account. We have substantial evidence that our frequent use of plastic has significant environmental impacts. Likewise, the fact that many states and cities have regulated or outright banned the use of certain forms of plastic, like plastic bags and microbeads, illustrates that there is political attention to this issue. What is still needed, however, is greater reflection on the gendered patterns of consumption as a way of achieving sustainability while also ensuring that policies aimed at this sustainability do not unfairly burden marginalized peoples in society.

Conclusions

The intersection of global consumption and environmental change is complex, important, and ethically fraught. There appears to be growing consensus that current patterns of consumption, particularly overconsumption and misconsumption, are problematic for environmental sustainability. There has been less attention to the ethics of these processes in terms of the distribution of benefits and costs of consumption and environmental damage. There has been even less attention paid to the ways that each of these issues is gendered.

As with debates about population, we cannot understand consumption patterns without understanding societal factors that shape behavior. When corporations spend trillions of dollars on advertising and lobbying, this impacts consumption. When our economic systems normalize growth and suggest that corporate or technological solutions will fix any negative consequences of it, this impacts consumption. When norms influence our expectations about what we "need" in order to be successful or happy, this impacts consumption. It is unhelpful to think of consumption as being primarily about wealthy people being greedy. While this is likely part of the story, patterns of consumption are much more complex.

Gender lenses aid in understanding the multiple, multifaceted processes of consumption, how they connect to sustainability, and how they intersect with debates about fairness and equity. Thinking about gender requires us to reflect on why and how we consume the way we do. It challenges us to question assertions that capitalism and technology are the best options for moderating consumption and the environmental negatives that accompany it. The critical and feminist scholarship that informs this book considers what large-scale shifts to our economic and social systems might look like and whether these might be more amenable to the goals of sustainability and justice. Gender lenses also highlight that an individualization of responsibility is never truly about the individual, but rather about the society – its economic, political, and social structures, which deeply influence not only patterns of consumption, but also our ability to freely make choices (or not) in this area.

6
Too Little Security? Gender and the Securitization of the Environment

Food is one of life's basic necessities. Living things cannot last without access to food. The international community experienced a food crisis when prices spiked dramatically in 2007–8. In 2008 the cereal price index reached a peak 2.8 times higher than in 2000 (UN 2011). Several reasons for the crisis have been put forward, including "rising energy prices, the depreciation of the U.S. dollar, low interest rates, and investment portfolio adjustments in favor of commodities" (Headey and Fan 2010: xiii). Rising energy prices are problematic for the agriculture sector since they are an important supply cost in cereal production. Additionally, rising energy prices encourage the demand for biofuels, resulting in significant changes to the production and consumption of biofuel crops like maize (Headey and Fan 2010). This food crisis resulted in thirty-six states requesting emergency food aid, and contributed to civil unrest in over forty states in the global South. Some estimate that the food crisis contributed to driving over 130 million people into poverty in 2008 (UN 2011). Even in a wealthy state like the US, the number of people living in food-insecure households swelled from 36.2 million in 2007 to 49.1 million in 2008.

The story of the 2007–8 food crisis illustrates, first, how interconnected environmental, political, and economic processes have come to be. Economic activities in one part of the world, like currency depreciation or low interest rates, can lead to a series of events that eventually lead individuals to pay more and more for basic foodstuffs in their local markets or shops. Second, it highlights the connections between environmental issues and security issues. Fears about food security and economic security contributed to domestic unrest across the Caribbean, the Middle East, Africa, Asia, and Latin America. At the same time, fears about energy security and the perceived promise of biofuels were at least partially connected to the spikes in commodities like maize (Koizumi 2014; Shiva 2008). While this is only one piece of a very complicated story, it demonstrates the multiplicity of connections between environmental processes and "security." This chapter traces the various ways security issues and environmental issues have been linked, as well as the important contributions of gender lenses to considerations of which environmental issues are security issues, who or what is the primary referent object of security, and how policymaking can contribute to security for both humans and ecosystems.

Connections between security and the environment

Security has traditionally referred to the study of the threat, use, and control of military force (Nye and Lynn-Jones 1988). Over time, understandings of security have shifted by incorporating various sources of insecurity. These alternatives still include military threats, but go beyond this to consider threats posed by environmental change and other processes. Additionally, ideas of security have moved beyond a narrow focus on the state as the actor whose security we are concerned with (i.e., the primary referent object of security). These shifts in security discourses have been referred to as the broadening and deepening of security (Krause and Williams 1996).[1]

The past few decades have seen numerous actors ponder the connections between security and the environment specifically. As an academic field, environmental security studies (ESS) was largely a response to two events: the end of the Cold War in the late 1980s to early 1990s, and the 1992 Rio

Earth Summit. The first of these necessitated a rethinking of the concept of security by both security establishments and scholars, and the second mobilized evidence of global environmental change into a global policy agenda that became widely regarded as pressing and vital (Floyd and Matthew 2013). Since the early 1990s there has been a flood of academic scholarship on the connections between security and the environment, as well as a tendency for policymakers and the media to increasingly use securitized language to talk about environmental issues. There are three main ways that actors consider the environment–security nexus: concern over resource conflict, concern over human insecurity linked to environmental damage, and concern about the fate of ecosystems (Detraz 2014).[2]

The first of these concerns, the potential for resource conflict, is closely associated with traditional security matters like state security and the potential for actors to engage in violent conflict. When Robert Kaplan (1994) famously called the environment "the national-security issue of the early twenty-first century," he drew on ideas of resource conflict and instability, among others, to make this argument. Since then, there have been many scholars who outline the case that actors will engage in violent conflict over access to natural resources (Baechler 1998; Homer-Dixon 1991, 1999). The focus is on states and their citizens as the primary referent object of security. This is not to say that there is no concern for the environment; however, the environment is chiefly conceptualized in terms of its benefit to human beings. The threat is located in violent conflict over access to resources, and those who are vulnerable are communities at a local level, and the state at a broader level.

Resource conflicts can spring from either scarcity of resources (Homer-Dixon 1999) or abundance of resources (de Soysa 2013), and are understood to contribute to state instability and insecurity. While the explanation of abundance of resources sparking conflict has been popularized with the notion of a "resource curse" (i.e., states with high levels of natural resources suffering from poor economic growth and instability), scarcity concerns have motivated a large portion of the ESS literature. Most scholars do not propose that environmental degradation is usually the sole cause of a conflict. Instead, environmental factors are often conceptualized as "threat multipliers" that exacerbate existing tensions and make violent confrontations over access to resources more likely (Homer-Dixon 1999). Substate actors are expected to be the most likely participants in resource conflict, rather than states (Matthew and Gaulin 2002). Several factors are identified as increasing the likelihood of environmental conflicts, including resource and environmental scarcities, expanding and migrating human populations, economic forces that impact resource use and distribution, and economic and social relations between groups (Barnett 2001; Dalby 2009; Detraz 2014).

A second central way of linking environmental and security issues is a concern about the negative impacts that environmental change has on human communities (Barnett 2001; Dalby 2009; Matthew et al. 2010). The idea of "human security," which was popularized in the mid-1990s, is central in these narratives. A human security discourse rejects the militarized, state-centric nature of traditional security concerns and is concerned instead with the health and well-being of individuals and communities. When this concept is applied to discussions about environment and security, it manifests in a concern that environmental change will cause human populations to experience insecurities like increased exposure to disease, increased experience with natural disasters, food insecurity, and livelihood insecurity, among others (Barnett 2001). The primary referent object of security is humans at the individual or community level rather than the security of states.

Actors who discuss human insecurity caused by environmental factors often focus on human *vulnerability* to global environmental change. As discussed in chapter 3, much has been written about the concept of vulnerability within the literature on environmental politics in general (McLaughlin and Dietz 2008). Typical ideas of vulnerability focus on the "characteristics of a person or group in terms of their capacity to anticipate, cope with, resist and recover from the impact of a natural hazard" (Blaikie et al. 1994: 9). Vulnerable people lack the ability to resist threats associated with environmental change, or may lack the capacity to move away from danger (Liverman 2001). Those who are vulnerable are more easily harmed and recover more slowly than those who are not. Environmental insecurity is directly tied to vulnerability in that it is experienced by those who lack the means to avoid the negative impacts of environment damage, and who either cannot recover, or else take the longest to recover, their well-being and livelihood in the aftermath of environmental change.

Human insecurity can be caused or exacerbated by both naturally occurring sources of environmental change and human damage to ecosystems. Natural disasters or biophysical changes (e.g., changes in precipitation levels), the growth or decline of species populations, or changes in levels of pathogenic microorganisms can also contribute to environmental insecurity for humans (Pirages and DeGeest 2004). Many of these natural processes can also be worsened by human behaviors like population movement, alterations in resource use, and climate change, among others (Dalby 2009). Human communities have always faced danger and vulnerability from naturally occurring phenomena like storms, floods, and fires. Ecosystems are all faced with some type of frequently occurring natural disaster. When human communities aggravate these phenomena, their impacts on human insecurity are increased. The human behavior that is understood to worsen environmental damage and intensify natural disasters then becomes a source of environmental insecurity.

A final concern in the environment–security scholarship is the negative impacts of environmental change for ecosystems (Floyd and Matthew 2013).[3] This ecocentric narrative largely focuses on human contributions to environmental degradation (Litfin 1999). The primary referent object of security is ecosystems and the largest source of threats is human behaviors. A range of human activities are regarded as harmful to the sustainability or security of ecosystems. For those concerned with ecological security, "security is about securing environmental health (within specific ecosystems; or at the level of the planetary biosphere) and, by extension, human well-being for humans are part of the biosphere, not separate from it. To ensure this 'security' requires a holistic understanding of the ways in which humans interact with 'nature'" (Swatuk 2006: 217).

Reflecting on human contributions to ecosystem insecurity involves evaluating the relationship between humans and environment, and challenging "traditional" conceptualizations of security. For those who reflect on ecological insecurity, humans are understood to be a part of many ecosystems but not something that should be regarded as dominant over other species. For this reason, those who adopt this perspective often focus on the environmental impacts of militaries during times of both peace and war. Militaries around the world tend to have large environmental footprints (Jorgenson et al. 2010). Even peaceful military activities take their toll on ecosystems due to sizable amounts of resource extraction and use, greenhouse gas emissions, and other negative environmental impacts. During times of war, these sources of environmental degradation are expanded and intensified (Jorgenson et al. 2010; Matthew and Gaulin 2002; Seager 1999).

There are many who view the linkages between security and environment as fundamental to both scholarship and policymaking. There are others, however, who critique the particular narratives that have been used to understand the environment–security nexus, and still others who critique the trend of discussing the environment in security terms at all. The early 1990s, which was a period of growth for environment–security debates, saw some high-profile critiques of this trend. One of the most famous scholarly pieces decrying the environment–security trend was Daniel Deudney's (1990: 282) plea to keep these areas separate for the sake of both. He argued that "[i]f everything that causes a decline in human well-being is labeled a 'security' threat, the term loses any analytical usefulness and becomes a loose synonym of 'bad'." Deudney warned that state militaries are unlikely to be very helpful in addressing environmental concerns, and that we run the risk of doing more harm than good by linking environmental issues to state security.[4] Similarly, Barry Buzan et al. (1998) warn against moving the environment to the category of high politics, saying this represents an undesirable "securitization" of the environment that limits the range of means available for resolving environmental problems. They argue that, in the long run, environmental conflict is more likely to be avoided if it is made part of the daily political debate (Graeger 1996). Environment–security debates have also been critiqued for having a Northern bias, for the possibility that securitization may lead to the militarization of numerous issues, and for the possibility that the measures[5] proposed to deal with problems that cause environmental insecurity do not follow the logic of securitization (e.g., rule breaking and extraordinary policies) (Barnett 2001; Floyd and Matthew 2013). A more recent critique added to this list is the lack of a strong focus on gender in any of the central environment–security narratives.

Gender, environment, and security

For many scholars, security narratives that included environmental problems held the potential to offer alternatives to the dominant, military-focused and state-centric conceptualization of security. Like human security discourses, environmental security could shift our debates away from being state-centric and reactive (Barnett 2001; Dalby 2009). The environment can open up new possibilities in the realm of security studies by reflecting on the various threats that humans are exposed to. I argue that reflecting on these issues through gender lenses further helps us to open up new possibilities in the areas of both security studies and environmental politics. Gender lenses allow us to see aspects of insecurity that were previously hidden.

In order for us to understand the value-added of gender to environment–security debates, it is first necessary to examine the current place of gender in scholarly and policy discussions of these connections (Detraz 2014). Some feminist scholars have strongly critiqued ESS for failing to consider the implications of using securitized language to point to things like population growth, migration, or globalization as contributors to environmental change while ignoring the gendered aspects of these phenomena (Hartmann 2010; Urban 2007). These scholars argue that securitizing these issues may result in their militarization (i.e., adopting military solutions to a range of domestic and international problems), which has potentially negative implications for both the environment and its human inhabitants. Feminists have long called attention to the gendered and environmentally destructive consequences of militarization (Enloe 2007; Seager 1993, 2003).

In response to these and other critiques, scholars have begun pushing for gender to become a central aspect of environment–security scholarship in ways that reject militarization and reflect on the gendered aspects of human insecurity (Detraz 2012, 2014; Goldsworthy 2010; Oswald Spring 2008). For example, Úrsula Oswald Spring (2008) has advocated thinking about these issues in terms of "human, gender and environmental security" (HUGE). This concept reflects on the ways that understanding gender helps us to reevaluate priorities. Importantly, this means getting away from a focus on maintaining existing social orders, which often contribute to insecurity, and instead focusing on human vulnerabilities. Additionally, I have argued elsewhere in favor of an alternative perspective on environment–security connections that has human security, gender justice, and environmental sustainability at its core (Detraz 2014). This gender-focused approach to security–environment connections illustrates that we miss important gendered aspects of environmental threats, risks, and vulnerabilities when we act as if environmental change is gender-neutral. More scholarship along these lines is needed, particularly work that speaks to the community of ESS scholars and those policymakers who utilize securitized environmental discourses. While there is currently very little integration of gender into the ways that actors combine security and the environment, there is room to reflect on how the goals of sustainability and justice are threatened by environmental and ecological insecurity.

Sustainability as security   Within debates about environment–security connections, threats to sustainability can be understood to constitute threats to security – albeit security in different forms. For example, a "sustainability as survival" narrative would most likely be connected to the survival and security of the state for those who focus on the potential for environmental conflict, whereas sustainability is linked to thriving communities and ecosystems for those who pay attention to environmental and ecological security. Security studies have largely been dominated by perspectives that see the survival of the state as the primary goal. The sustainability envisioned by these perspectives is that of policies or power relations that allow for the maintenance of state survival. The broadening and deepening of security have shifted this focus somewhat to allow for alternative goals, including human health and well-being, the flourishing of cultures, and the health of ecosystems (Buzan and Hansen 2009).

The sustainability envisioned by a gender-focused environmental security perspective, on the other hand, ensures that both human and non-human life can thrive on the planet. It recognizes the interconnectedness of environmental protection and human well-being. Human security is an extreme challenge for many within communities who experience environmental degradation, particularly those whose vulnerability is increased due to societal marginalization. Feminist security scholars claim that gender is an important component of understanding sources and experiences of insecurity, both for human communities and for ecosystems. Gender norms and expectations have an effect on which individuals or communities are most at risk of experiencing insecurity within society.

An additional component of sustainability that directly relates to environment–security connections is the link between sustainability and peace. Koos Neefjes (1999: 250) claims that "peace is an important precondition for social justice and ecological sustainability" and "strong sustainability cannot be pursued in a situation of poverty, rapid population growth, economic decline, and weak systems of governance." This suggests that at the most basic level, sustainability cannot be pursued if governments and communities are burdened with conflict and low levels of capacity. Violent conflict contributes to environmental damage, general human devastation, loss of economic and livelihood security, and increased levels of gendered insecurity for women (Detraz 2012; Seager 1993). The connections between militarism, patriarchy, and environmental damage have been discussed by feminist scholars for decades (Seager 1993, 1999, 2003; Tickner 2001). These structures and processes have a variety of negative consequences for society, including a lack of sustainability. For this reason, having a strong version of sustainability as a policy goal might actually be at odds with traditional ways of practicing security. Simon Dalby (2009: 4) suggests that

> [t]aking environmental change seriously requires us to rethink security quite dramatically. It might even mean that we should abandon it altogether; ecology, science, and history all point to the inevitability of change. Insofar as security is about making things, notably our consumer society, stay the same, it may in fact be part of the problem, rather than a way of thinking that is helpful in dealing with the future.

Feminist scholars have long argued that the security of the existing structures and institutions – including our current state system and dominant economic systems – is unlikely to lead to sustainable outcomes. If the sustainability of state security or even human security is incompatible with ecological sustainability or survival, then fundamental revisions to our approaches to "security" must be considered. State security has tended to be privileged over human security and ecological security by policymakers. Sustainability of political systems has been prioritized over the long-term survival of communities, individuals, and ecosystems.

Health and environmental security   One environmental risk that has garnered a good deal of attention is environmental health (Brown 2007). This concept can have both ecocentric and anthropocentric elements. In environmental sustainability debates, questions of environmental health evoke concerns about the long-term functioning of ecosystems. In environmental security debates, on the other hand, environmental health worries are connected to larger patterns of the negative consequences of environmental change for human well-being. For instance, various environment–security scholars have argued that increases in population as well as increases in the mobilization of populations are central to understanding outbreaks of disease (Pirages and DeGeest 2004). Additionally, environmental change like climate change can worsen the spread of water-borne and vector-borne disease. Infectious vector-borne diseases are typically sensitive to climatic conditions (McMichael 2003). Climate change is predicted to result in an increase in the physical range and seasonality of diseases like dengue fever and malaria. These factors remind us that many of the processes that contribute to environmental unsustainability also contribute to human insecurity.

It is also essential, however, to reflect on the fact that health components of human insecurity are gendered. In a direct sense, women may more immediately experience the consequences of environmental degradation. Rachel Stein (2004: 11) explains that "women's sexed bodies are...particularly vulnerable to environmental ills, due to the way that toxins accumulate in fatty tissues such as breasts, and due to the way that hormones such as estrogen may be affected or mimicked by many of the pesticides and chemicals that we are releasing into the larger environment." For instance, EU policies specifically mention that pregnant women, nursing women, and women who may become pregnant in the future are particularly vulnerable to environmental pollution (Buckingham and Kulcur 2009). Intervening social trends also affect women's health. International organizations like the World Health Organization (WHO 2008) maintain that health issues like spread of disease should be examined through gender lenses. They claim that social processes – including poverty, unequal power relationships, and lack of education – inhibit many women from receiving adequate health care. This reminds us that determinations of sustainability should include not only an assessment of the various ways that environmental damage undermines the health of both ecosystems and the humans that inhabit them, but also the social processes that determine how those health consequences are felt differently within the population. Gender lenses aid in making sense of the complex picture of unsustainability.

Who speaks security?   Moreover, gender shapes our expectations about who is a "legitimate" security actor just as it influences who is most likely to play a primary caregiving role for a family. Within most communities in most societies, men are typically associated with security while women are associated with care – either care for children or elderly relatives, or often care for the environment (MacGregor 2006). While we can all think of important exceptions to these roles, the "naturalness" of these assumptions is so taken for granted in most communities that they come to be regarded as normal

(Sandilands 1999). What is particularly interesting is that despite these care expectations, women are still often excluded from environmental decision-making (Bretherton 2003). Knowledge gleaned from everyday experiences is rarely held in the same esteem as the knowledge of scientific or security "experts." We need to carefully assess multiple facets of these assumptions. First, why does knowledge about security and/ or sustainability from lived experiences tend to be assigned less value? Second, why do men tend to be associated with providing security while women are frequently associated with both peace and care (Tickner 2001)? These gendered assumptions serve to paint women into a category of benevolent mothers who deserve respect, but not as active and informed citizens who have much to contribute to sustainability debates (MacGregor 2006; Sandilands 1999).

As discussed previously, gendered knowledge is an important component of understanding where environmental unsustainability occurs, as well as of some potential solutions to it. The incorporation of multiple forms of knowledge means that environmental debates and policymaking cannot be top-down enterprises. This largely goes against traditional patterns of security policymaking, and is indicative of an important shift that accompanies expanding our notions of insecurity and knowledge. Through the analysis of environmental issues that directly impact people's lives, a gender-focused approach to environment–security connections can determine particular gender-differentiated impacts, responses, and contributions to environmental degradation, as well as call attention to the gendered assumptions in society through which these issues are typically understood.

Authors like Karen O'Brien (2006) claim that the current tendency in society to treat environmental concerns as issues of "science" rather than of human security fails to engage society in creating the transformations necessary to achieve sustainability. Like many others who argue in favor of more inclusivity in environmental politics, O'Brien claims that the framing of an issue shapes the types of questions that are asked, the research that takes precedence, and the solutions and policies that are suggested. When we frame environmental issues as human security concerns rather than scientific puzzles, it forces us to reflect on lived experiences. This is not to belittle the essential place of scientific understanding of environmental issues, but rather to challenge us to go beyond limited understandings of what constitutes science. Science is not something divorced from human experience (Harding 1991, 1993), but rather it requires the input of information that can come from multiple sources and involve multiple voices. The very people who experience insecurity due to environmental change are likely to have important information about where those insecurities come from, and this should inform our assessments of sustainability.

Poverty and insecurity   As noted several times before, poverty in particular has been discussed as a driver of both unsustainability and insecurity. Reflecting on poverty in the context of environment–security linkages requires understanding the various ways that poverty contributes not only to the potential for unsustainable resource use, but also to greater vulnerability to environmental insecurity. This vulnerability has ties to social, political, and economic processes that influence "the differential exposure to risks and capacity to cope with risks systematically attributed to people across space and time" (Neumayer and Plümper 2007: 552). This conceptualization of vulnerability implies that it is not a "natural" or unproblematic condition (Blaikie et al. 1994). It is necessary to understand the condition of vulnerability while still recognizing agency. In fact, many feminist scholars and gender NGOs highlight how women are not "victims" or inactive political agents, but often display creative adaptation tendencies in the face of environmental damage and insecurity (MacGregor 2006). One case of this is the Women's International League for Peace and Freedom (WILPF), an NGO established in 1915, which focuses on fostering peace along with racial, social, and economic justice. WILPF marries an overarching concern with peace and anti-militarization with a dedication to sustainable development and environmental justice in several of their campaigns. The organization's Climate Justice+Women+Peace project illustrates the links between environmental damage, conflict and militarism, and humanitarian crises, with calls for wide participation and education on environmental issues.

An additional example of activism on environmental concerns is the Chipko movement in India. The Chipko movement emerged in the Himalayan region of India in the mid-1970s as a protest against deforestation (Fulfer 2013). Popular depictions of the movement are of local women hugging trees as a way of putting their bodies in the path of machinery to be used in deforestation (Rocheleau 2015; Sturgeon 1997). While there is debate about whether Chipko should be designated as a "women's movement" (Shiva 1989) or rather as a more general livelihood movement (Gaard 1998; MacGregor 2006), one of its central elements of protest was the damage caused by deforestation for ecosystems and the economic security of households and communities.[6] Clearing forests for commercial use in this case was destructive to watersheds, biodiversity, livelihoods, and human health (Fulfer 2013). No matter if we understand this movement as explicitly feminist in nature, it does serve as an example of local communities protesting against what they saw to be the unsustainable use of resources. Women and men actively moved against the forces they saw as undermining their environmental and livelihood security.

Examples like these remind us of the importance of having broad participation in sustainability and human security policymaking and implementation. At the same time, it is important to understand that because many women find themselves on the margins of society, they will sometimes experience environmental problems differently from and more severely than people in non-marginalized groups. While numerous studies have documented gendered aspects of women's environmental vulnerability, these must be assessed with an eye to understanding the social processes that make these vulnerabilities persist, rather than be treated as natural consequences of environmental change (McLaughlin and Dietz 2008). This speaks to the fact that sustainability is impossible to separate from larger concerns of fairness and justice.

Insecurity as injustice　Most scholars and activists for environmental justice argue that inequality is the result of global processes that make it relatively easy to predict which communities are most likely to experience the negatives of environmental damage (Agyeman 2013; Bullard 2005). Using a justice discourse to understand environment–security connections calls attention to the fact that it is unjust that marginalized peoples and communities are at greater risk of experiencing environmental insecurity. Vulnerabilities that are the result of marginalization in society (e.g., poverty, livelihood insecurity, etc.) are likely to manifest in insecurity in the face of environmental damage. This means that it is not just that marginalized groups have to bear greater costs, but that this unjust distribution of ills manifests in various threats to security, including livelihood insecurity, community insecurity, and even personal insecurity. Multiple environmental threats to security can result in loss of life. As discussed in chapter 4, for example, on average women tend to die in larger numbers than men in natural disasters (Neumayer and Plümper 2007). This is a clear example of a threat to personal security that is impacting more women than men. The aim should be not only to focus on reducing the number of people who die in disasters, which is absolutely an essential goal, but also to question why this threat to security is not experienced evenly across society.

Competing ways of thinking security   There are also justice implications to *how* the environment is conceptualized as a security issue. Environment–security scholars as well as policymakers have tended to prioritize threats to state and human security over threats to ecological security (Floyd and Matthew 2013). For example, debates over climate change as a security issue have tended to include concerns about resource conflict as well as fears over human insecurity tied to climate change impacts, but there has been very limited discussion of whether human-induced climate change threatens the security of the environment (Detraz and Betsill 2009; Detraz 2014). This is consistent with environmental justice debates being more prevalent than ecological justice debates, as well as anthropocentric discourses being dominant in general. While it is true that the chapters in this book also tend to focus heavily on human concerns, they argue as well for recognizing the deep human–nature connections that exist. Treating ecosystems as storerooms of resources for human consumption is unjust in the sense of potentially denying the needs of other species, but this mindset of domination likely has deeper connections to other social processes that legitimize marginalization (Merchant 1996; Seager 1993, 1999). It is therefore crucial to ask why we tend to discuss environmental issues in such starkly anthropocentric terms, and what the larger consequences of this practice might be.

Securitized narratives are typically infused with a sense of "urgency" or "crisis" (Hartmann et al. 2005). In a similar way to that in which alarmist population narratives can shut down crucial debate (as discussed in chapter 4), these crisis narratives are not necessarily the most conducive for reflecting on justice and environmental change. Calls for urgency can be used to encourage immediate action without challenging the form or consequences of this action through careful deliberation. This may essentialize people and spaces and reinforce problematic power dynamics (Hawkins and Ojeda 2011). Betsy Hartmann (2010: 239) has claimed that "[p]laying with fear is like playing with fire. You cannot be sure exactly where it will spread." Crisis narratives are salient, but not always effective at achieving long-term justice. For instance, discussions of environmental migrants or refugees are often read as urgent threats to state security rather than as large-scale humanitarian concerns (Detraz and Windsor 2014; White 2011). This frame is more likely to result in policies that reinforce border security rather than ones that welcome migrants fleeing environmental insecurity. These differences in approaches indicate that links between human security issues and environmental issues must be carefully assessed in ways that avoid alarmism, and instead foster reflection on the best means of addressing marginalization as well as human and ecological insecurity.

One of the original motivations for linking environmental issues to security narratives was the desire for increased attention to the former (Floyd and Matthew 2013). The idea was that security issues are typically regarded as being salient for scholars, the general public, the media, and policymakers. If something is identified as a security issue, there is often a corresponding push for a response to that issue. While there are definitely problematic consequences of this set of assumptions, including rushed policymaking and the justification of undemocratic "emergency measures" (Buzan et al. 1998;

Hartmann et al. 2005; Wæver 1995), the goal was to gain attention and resources to combat important environmental issues. In reality, however, many of the debates about environmental issues as security issues have focused on how state security is threatened by things like resource conflict. More rarely asked are questions that focus on equity and environmental security, for instance whether there is an environmental responsibility to protect (R2P) in the international community (Dalby 2013). The R2P doctrine is a humanitarian-oriented principle which claims that "intervention for human protection purposes, including military intervention in extreme cases, is supportable when major harm to civilians is occurring or imminently apprehended, and the state in question is unable or unwilling to end the harm, or is itself the perpetrator" (ICISS 2001: 16). Does the international community have an obligation to provide environmental security for those who lack it?

Some scholars are quite skeptical about the R2P doctrine in general (Mégret 2009), and the idea of an environmental R2P in particular (Eckersley 2007). I share some hesitancy about adopting a doctrine that originally comes from debates about military humanitarian intervention into debates about environmental change, but it does raise some important questions regarding gender, justice, and environmental unsustainability. If we regard large-scale environmental change to be on a par with large-scale instances of human insecurity, like genocides, then this would seem to require that we identify and address the sources of these insecurities. In debates about both R2P and global environmental change, existing securitized narratives have not been very good at sorting through the drivers of insecurity. Quantitative literature on resource conflict, for instance, treats concepts like violence and scarcity as rather simple things (Ross 2004). A good deal of feminist scholarship, on the other hand, evaluates how communities relate to resources beyond a straightforward cost–benefit analysis. For instance, Farhana Sultana (2011: 164) examines emotional aspects of nature–society relationships. Resource conflicts, like those over water, are not only about rational calculations of resource need, but instead they involve emotional responses that shape lived experiences and perceptions of how a society conceptualizes resources. "Such an analysis can provide more nuanced explications of what constitutes resource conflicts and politics, by showing that conflicts over resources are thus as much about property rights and entitlements as they are about embodied emotions, feelings, and lived experiences relating to the resource." Emotions like suffering and pain due to resource shortage are an important component of interpretations of security. Our perspectives on nature–society relations are shaped just as much by these emotional responses and lived experiences as they are by legal definitions of access and ownership. While it is necessary to avoid painting gender lenses as being exclusively focused on stereotypically "feminine" factors like emotion, bringing in this component of lived experiences is essential for getting a fuller picture of why resource conflicts might occur. We can assess "the multiplicity of ways that emotions are not feminine, but are constituted as a result of spaces, places, bodies, and experiences" (Sultana 2011: 164). Most existing approaches to environment–security connections fail to focus on these elements.

Reflecting on sources of insecurity   Gender lenses, on the other hand, help in understanding the sources and manifestations of environmental vulnerabilities that result in insecurity. They highlight the unequal exposure to environmental risks that links to marginalization in society (Enarson 2012). They outline how experiences of environmental insecurity are not gender-neutral, as they appear in most of the existing literature and policy debates (Terry and Sweetman 2009). One case of this is security implications for a community experiencing water shortages. Debates about "water wars" as well as the human insecurity that accompanies shortages of clean water have long been central to environment–security scholarship (MacQuarrie and Wolf 2013). Because women tend to be expected to provide water for household use in societies around the globe, there are gendered experiences of water shortage that must be evaluated (Sultana 2009, 2011). These connections between gender and water have been acknowledged at the international level in documents like the Dublin Principles, which came out of the 1992 International Conference on Water and the Environment, as well as the Convention on the Elimination of All Forms of Discrimination against Women (CEDAW). However, gender is very rarely incorporated into either scholarly debates about water security, or policy approaches to achieving or maintaining water security (Detraz 2014).

If we hope to find just and equitable solutions to environmental insecurity, these are all essential pieces of environmental politics that must be in our analyses. The concept of human security is focused on life and dignity, and is people-centered. Likewise, a gender-focused environmental security discourse is oriented toward the protection of security at the level of individuals and groups. This means paying attention to the various insecurities, vulnerabilities, and risks that humans are daily exposed to. It means exposing the causes and larger consequences of these insecurities, vulnerabilities, and risks. This has been a goal for many ecofeminist scholars and activists for several decades (King 1995; Seager 2003). Women are frequently among those who experience environmental insecurity most acutely because of consistent patterns of marginalization across the international system. The following section evaluates the ways in which gender-focused perspectives on sustainability and justice aid in understanding specific fears of food insecurity.

Case study: food security

Food security is one of the most frequently invoked securitized narratives in environmental discussions. Scholars and policymakers regularly use the language of security when talking about food (McDonald 2010; Shaw 2007). Food is related to state security and stability through concerns about the role of food shortages driving instability within a state, as well as the economic impacts of food shortages (McDonald 2010). Food security is considered to be an important element of environmental security in that access to food is a necessity for human health and security. In fact, more people die from hunger than in wars – the security topic that has tended to dominate security studies for most of its history (Shaw 2007). The ability to achieve food security is directly tied to the health of the environment, and thus environmental damage and unsustainability can be detrimental to food security. In many cases of food insecurity, there is not an overall shortage of food. Rather, the problem is one of distribution and uneven access to food (Fukuda-Parr 2015). A global food network exists, which includes areas of both abundance and scarcity. These areas exist in both economically advanced and economically marginalized regions, meaning that there are undernourished people in the global North as well as overnourished people in the global South (Clapp 2012). The Food and Agriculture Organization (FAO) defines food security as follows: "food security exists when all people, at all times, have physical and economic access to sufficient, safe and nutritious food for a healthy and active life" (FAO 2012). The concept contains four components: adequacy of food supply or availability; stability of supply without fluctuations or shortages from season to season; accessibility or affordability of food; and the quality and safety of food. Debates about how to conceptualize and achieve food security have direct links to the goals of sustainability and justice.

Food security as a gendered phenomenon   Recall from chapter 4 that Thomas Malthus (2007) popularized a focus on human behaviors (i.e., population growth) and environmental unsustainability through a fear about food shortages, meaning that fears about food have a long history (Hartmann et al. 2005). For Malthus, and many neo-Malthusians, human population growth threatens food availability to the point of insecurity. Policymakers are acutely concerned about a lack of food security for their citizens because it is detrimental to both human well-being and state stability. What is important to note, however, is that securitizing food can have unintended consequences. The discourses we use to talk about food as a security issue frequently prioritize human communities without necessarily addressing the long-term environmental consequences of many agricultural policies. This means that in some cases, environmental sustainability might suffer while food security improves.

Agricultural practices can have a variety of impacts on the environment. These include the consequences of fertilizer use, pesticide use, irrigation of cropland, etc. (MEA 2005). Our current food system is also heavily dependent on oil.

According to Karen Litfin (2012: 426), "[o]il is the lifeblood of the world food system." Nearly all farm machinery runs on petroleum. Additionally, most herbicides, fertilizers, and pesticides are petroleum derivatives (Litfin 2012). The use of these additional inputs as well as mechanization have been the hallmarks of agriculture since the time of the Green Revolution (i.e., the series of agricultural reforms that took place between the 1960s and 1980s and that involved introducing technological advancements in agricultural practices).[7] This heavy reliance on oil, along with other characteristics, makes agriculture a contributor to multiple environmental ills, including climate change (FAO 2011; Johnson et al. 2007).[8] The MEA (2005: 6) states that agricultural systems and practices have exerted a wide range of impacts, many of them adverse, on ecosystems globally. "Both the extensive use of water for irrigation (some 70% of water use globally is for irrigation) and excessive nutrient loading associated with the use of nitrogen and phosphorus in fertilizers have resulted in a decline in the delivery of services such as fresh water and some fish species." These negative consequences of agriculture for environmental sustainability suggest that the technology-based solutions to low agricultural yields need to be tempered with careful assessment of their ecological as well as social impacts. As discussed in chapter 5, techno-fixes that are not accompanied by adequate reflection on human–nature connections are not only unlikely to be sustainable, but may also have unintended side effects like encouraging an environmental policy approach that ignores the complex interplay between economic, political, and social processes and the ways in which they influence ecosystem health (Plumwood 2002).

Securitizing food without considering the long-term ecological consequences of agricultural policies is deeply problematic. Critical approaches to GEP, like using gender lenses, encourage us to ask questions about not only whether and how food security is achieved, but also who suffers food insecurity (and who suffers *for* food security) most. There appear to be significant challenges to achieving food security as well as environmental sustainability in the way that global food production currently operates (Clapp 2012). While some measures of hunger and other facets of food insecurity have decreased over time, there are still many communities and individuals across the globe who fail to meet the FAO's definition of having food security (IFPRI 2015).

The politics of food security is a topic with strong connections to gender and environmental justice debates. A number of international organizations have emphasized the connections between gender and food security. These include the FAO, UNEP, WHO, World Bank, and many others. Discussions of food security involve concerns about where the negative impacts of environmental damage are felt most. South Asia and sub-Saharan Africa are the regions that currently experience the highest levels of hunger (IFPRI 2015). Food insecurity is a gendered phenomenon, meaning that it is not felt evenly across a society, or even within a family. Several states report that women specifically face undernourishment and other aspects of food insecurity within their borders (IFPRI 2015). There is a great deal of evidence that during times of food scarcity it is women and children who suffer most (Davidson and Krull 2011; Kerr 2005). Studies of adaptation strategies in the face of food insecurity have shown that women are most likely to go without food in situations of food shortages (Davidson and Krull 2011; Uraguchi 2010). In situations where food insecurity is exacerbated by conflict, women and other marginalized groups tend to feel the effects most (IFPRI 2015).

Gender is also an important part of the story of food security because women are important stakeholders in debates about agriculture and food security. This is due to the fact that they are responsible for producing a large share of the world's food. While it is difficult to get precise, gender-differentiated numbers on percentages of food production, women in countries around the world play roles in growing crops for both subsistence and income, selling food in markets and shops, and preparing food in restaurants and homes (Fukuda-Parr 2015; Sachs and Alston 2010). Many scholars have been quite critical of what they view as a tendency for women's agricultural labor to be exploited, particularly in the context of a globalized, corporate food-production network. According to Carolyn Sachs and Margaret Alston (2010:

280), women are employed in flexible or temporary labor in multiple locations in the global food system and "have become a largely invisible reserve army of labor for corporate agriculture." Agrifood companies frequently pay women less than men, yet benefit from knowledge and training that women bring from previous labor in this field. "Women have become a marginal, cheap, and highly exploited labor force" (Sachs and Alston 2010: 280). Patterns of women's labor in the agrifood system are similar to general patterns of women's labor in the global capitalist system, in which women tend to be overrepresented in informal, low-wage labor (Elson 2014). These labor patterns in food production do not appear to be the most efficient strategy for achieving livelihood security for these women, who can be left in precarious employment situations. The 2007–8 food crisis discussed in the introduction to this chapter resulted in specific hardships for marginalized groups. According to the UN,

> [t]he impact of the food crisis is likely to be much more severe among women and children. Because of gender discrimination and various cultural practices that influence intrahousehold resource allocation, these groups tend to be more vulnerable to chronic and transitory food insecurity...Lack of social protection for female workers in the informal sector compounds their vulnerability to such external shocks. (UN 2011: 63)

While there are important reasons to be wary of lumping women and children together in order to understand marginalization, this passage does reinforce the fact that food insecurity is not a random phenomenon. Rather, it is closely connected to larger societal patterns of social, political, and economic power distribution.

Obstacles to feeding oneself include systematic marginalization, which negatively impacts access to food, livelihood, and security. For example, around the world there is a disproportionate number of landless or land-poor rural households that are headed by women. Land tenure matters for achieving food security. Studies show that women's land ownership is related to the degree of their participation in key decision-making about the land. They are more likely to be able to make decisions aimed at ensuring food security if they have control over the land (Deere et al. 2013). Additionally, women tend to face inequality in access to credit and other financial services, machinery, livestock, and other agricultural inputs (Fukuda-Parr 2015). In a cross-national analysis of nine sub-Saharan African states both men and women reported that "women more than men lack land and have no access to improved technology or equipment, manure or labor. They also have few training opportunities. In general terms, therefore…women have less access than men to productive resources and opportunities" (Perez et al. 2015: 100).[9] An example of this is women's ability to utilize adaptation strategies like planting drought-tolerant crops in order to maintain food and livelihood security in tough conditions. A study from Uganda indicates that compared to men, women have much lower rates of adoption of drought-tolerant maize, largely because of differences in resource availability, like access to land, agricultural information, and credit (Fisher and Carr 2015). These factors overlap with class, race, ethnicity, and other forms of marginalization, and have a direct link to food insecurity (FAO 2011). Marginalization and inequality, therefore, undermine the ability to provide food security.

In sum, global debates about food have been heavily securitized. These debates most frequently involve narratives of human insecurity during conditions of food shortage. Gender lenses help to reveal how food insecurity intersects with power dynamics in society. Food security and gender intersect through the socially constructed norms and responsibilities of women in many societies, making them the primary actor in charge of purchasing, cooking, and in some instances growing food for households. Food security and gender also intersect through the global patterns of women's economic and political marginalization, leading them to often face food insecurity as well as lack a seat at the decision-making table to decide about food policy. It is necessary for ideas of food security to acknowledge the larger, structural contributions of power inequalities and marginalization. This must be done in ways that avoid essentialization, but point out relatively consistent patterns of behavior and experience. Examining food security as an issue of sustainability involves reflecting on how past, current, and future behaviors undermine the health of ecosystems in ways that impair our supply, access, and quality of food supplies. Combining gender, sustainability, and justice requires reflecting on how environmental ills associated with food production become distributional issues due to power relations within and across societies.

Conclusions

Actors have deliberated on the connections between security issues and environmental issues for decades. To date, these debates have largely centered on whether and how human communities might engage in conflict over access to resources, or how human communities experience insecurity due to environmental change. Unsustainability leads to insecurity for humans and ecosystems, and the threats, vulnerabilities, and risks associated with these forms of insecurity are not evenly distributed in the international system. The injustice of insecurity means that approaches to sustainability must reflect these distributional issues if they are to be considered fair. As with debates surrounding population and consumption, discussions of security–environment connections benefit from the inclusion of gender, as none of the processes mentioned here is gender-neutral.

A gender-focused environmental security discourse that is centered on justice and sustainability seeks to identify and find avenues for removing sources of environmental change which threaten the security of humans and ecosystems. This means that this discourse considers the threats and vulnerabilities of human communities as well as ecosystems. It recognizes that the two are intimately and inextricably connected. A gender-focused environmental security discourse focuses on the distribution of power in environmental decision-making, as well as the distribution of environmental benefits and ills. It seeks the health and security of all populations, not just the most powerful. Finally, it recognizes that the way to achieve these goals is to maintain sustainable ecosystems. A gender-focused approach to environmental security strives for environmental sustainability. The sustainability envisioned here ensures that both human and non-human life can thrive on the planet. Feminist scholars have considered the gendered implications of militarization and environmental degradation for decades; however, this narrative has rarely been incorporated into ESS or policymaking circles. What is needed in the future is a greater dialogue between actors who have corresponding goals of equity and environmental sustainability.

7
Conclusion: Gendered Sustainability and Justice in Climate Change Debates

In late 2015, the international community was gearing up for the global climate summit in Paris. Preparations for the 21st Conference of the Parties (COP) to the United Nations Framework Convention on Climate Change (UNFCCC) brought out debates about how much countries were going to be willing to reduce emissions, what are the best strategies to enforce emissions reduction schemes, and whether we can still "afford" to act based on the principle of common but differentiated responsibilities in the realm of climate change. The Paris summit was unique in that many within the international community looked to the meeting as a much-needed turning point toward strong global action to combat climate change; however, it represented one of a large number of annual global discussions about the threats and challenges of climate change.

Climate change is predicted to be one of the widest-ranging environmental problems the international community has ever tried to address. According to the Intergovernmental Panel on Climate Change (IPCC), humans influence climate change through record amounts of anthropogenic emissions of greenhouse gases. The IPCC argue that "[w]arming of the climate system is unequivocal, and since the 1950s, many of the observed changes are unprecedented over decades to millennia. The atmosphere and ocean have warmed, the amounts of snow and ice have diminished, and sea level has risen" (IPCC 2014: 2). These changes are expected to result in climate-related extremes, including "alteration of ecosystems, disruption of food production and water supply, damage to infrastructure and settlements, morbidity and mortality, and consequences for mental health and human well-being" (IPCC 2014: 6). These impacts have negative consequences for ecosystems and the people that live within them. Climate change will pose important challenges to human health and well-being through undermining livelihoods, undermining identity and culture, and undermining the capacity of states to protect and provide for their people (Adger et al. 2014). How is such a huge set of challenges to be managed? The international community's environmental agenda has grown over time to include a varied array of concerns (Stevis 2014). Climate change, biodiversity, deforestation, desertification, resource use and shortages: these are just a small number of the environmental issues that are on the radar of policymakers at all levels of society. Tackling each of these issues is no easy task. Climate change in particular is difficult to govern because it is such a wide-ranging issue involving actors from virtually all regions of the world. It is frequently discussed as urgent, but also difficult because it requires changes to human behaviors – either changes to the behaviors that contribute to climate change (i.e., climate change mitigation), or changes geared toward preparing for the consequences of climate change (i.e., climate change adaptation).[1]

This concluding chapter reflects on the manifestations of gender in climate change debates. In some ways, climate change has come to dominate many facets of GEP scholarship and environmental policymaking (Dauvergne and Clapp 2016). For this reason, it offers a unique lens through which to explore (1) how deeply connected environmental debates are, and (2) the value added when gender becomes a central focus of environmental discussion and decision-making. Global discussions of climate change governance illustrate the connectivity of each of the previous discussions of sustainability, justice, population, consumption, and security.

Gender and climate change

The chapters in this book have argued that altering discourses of environmental issues is important to the goals of sustainability and justice. Why is focusing on discourse helpful to this endeavor? The use of one discourse over another influences the policies we imagine will be effective (Hajer 1995). For instance, if we used reductionist, alarmist population narratives then the policy solution would be to stop having babies. If we used simplistic consumption narratives we would enact policies geared at having us consume the "right" stuff. If we used alarmist security narratives we would seek to "fix" those things that make us unsafe. The problem with each of these sets of narratives is that they may not necessarily help us on the path of sustainability, at least not very effectively, and there are crucial elements of (in)justice, frequently gendered injustice, wrapped up in each of those potential policy options. Discourses matter because they set the tone for how we understand, discuss, and address global issues.

Gender lenses aid in revising the discourses we use in ways that treat environmental issues as extremely complex. To date, neoliberal economic assumptions have had a central place in dominant environmental policymaking discourses (Dryzek 2005). Gender lenses allow us to take a broader look at environmental debates, and therefore facilitate alternative discourses about key environmental problems and how they might be addressed. These alternatives incorporate the opportunities afforded by rethinking global structures. Many of the processes that lead to environmental change, like climate change, have close associations with patriarchy. For instance, capitalism and patriarchy both reinforce domination. Those in power remain in power by marginalizing others. Examining GEP through gender lenses encourages us to challenge each of these systems due to the fact that they contribute to unsustainability and injustice.

As mentioned earlier, climate change is predicted to have a range of negative consequences for ecosystems and human communities across the world. What is important to assess through gender lenses, however, is the fact that these consequences are not felt evenly across society. Many marginalized women feel the impacts of climate change through alterations in their access to water, energy, and food, which in turn influence their education, livelihood, and health. These factors compound existing inequalities within their societies, including reinforcing gendered roles like divisions of household and community labor. Environmental marginalization associated with climate change causes the unpaid care burden to increase for huge numbers of women (Alston 2014; Arora-Jonsson 2011; Dankelman 2010). For example, Jouni Paavola (2006: 216) assesses climate change and gender in Tanzania and concludes that the tasks that are often performed by women – tilling fields and collecting firewood and water – will be adversely affected by changing climate. "More time will be needed for carrying out these activities and less will be left for other activities such as earning cash income. More market-oriented activities of male members of households will be less affected. Predicted climate change impacts could thus increase gender inequality. This is particularly so given the low participation of women in formal labor markets."

Gendered climate change policymaking Despite these gendered patterns of climate change impacts, decision-making about climate change policies has not tended to include the most marginalized voices or concerns. These issues are slowly being incorporated into GEP and policy-making circles. Feminist academics are beginning to pay more attention to gender and climate change issues. In the past, when feminist academics have studied gender and climate change they have tended to be gender, environment, and development (GED) scholars or feminist researchers working for the UN, government ministries, and women's environmental organizations (MacGregor 2009). This is changing, as more feminist IR scholars publish in this area.

At present, the major international climate change agreements contain very little consideration of gender. Neither the UNFCCC nor the 1997 follow-up (the Kyoto Protocol) mentions women or gender (Spitzner 2009). Over time, the issue of gender equity and climate change has been discussed with greater frequency at COP meetings; however, it has not been incorporated into agreements as much as many would like. The Copenhagen Accord, the non-binding resolution that came out of COP-15 in 2009, did not mention either gender or women. There was some excitement about an explicit commitment to gender balance that came out of COP-18 in Doha; however, some had wished for a stronger commitment to gender equity or justice rather than a narrower focus on gender balance (GenderCC 2012).[2] The Paris Agreement, which came out of COP-21, does refer to "gender equality" and "empowerment of women" in a discussion of parties needing to address climate change in ways that are consistent with human rights obligations (UNFCCC 2015: 1–2), but various NGOs argued that there was still very little substantive movement on the recognition of women as key stakeholders in climate change issues. The agreement was also criticized as allowing for business-as-usual approaches to both mitigation and adaptation (Bowser 2015; GenderCC 2015).

Several participants and journalists also noted a dearth of female representation at the Paris talks (Piotrowski 2015). Mary Robinson, the UN special envoy for climate change, pointed out the lack of gender balance among high-level negotiators and argued that this is detrimental to achieving an inclusive final agreement. She claimed that "[t]here is a tendency to think that this is not a place for women, and we have to resist that. I have heard women here saying they feel strange to be here. Women have to be here in large numbers, to have critical mass" (Harvey 2015). In general, women have tended to have a relatively small share in the delegation of parties at climate change conferences and decision-making. Women's representation in bodies and boards in the UNFCCC ranges from 36 percent to 41 percent. Female heads of national delegations make up only 26 percent to 33 percent of total numbers. Eight of thirty-four IPCC chairs, co-chairs, and vice-chairs are women, and only one out of five authors of the 2014 IPCC fifth assessment report was a woman (Ivanova 2015). There has been a slow increase in women's representation over time (Hemmati and Röhr 2009), and while these increases are positive, there is still a long way to go toward increasing women's overall participation in climate change decision-making. The UNFCCC (2013: 47) acknowledged this need at the 2013 Doha conference, in which they recognized "the importance of a balanced representation of women from developing and developed country Parties in the UNFCCC process so that gender-responsive climate policy responds to the differing needs of men and women in national and local contexts." Even media coverage of climate change witnesses gender imbalance, with only a small percentage of those interviewed on climate issues being women (Ivanova 2015).

Some argue that climate change exemplifies "the multi-actor and multi-level nature of global environmental governance" (Andonova et al. 2009: 52). There are many actors that play a role in mitigation efforts and adaptation schemes related to climate change. Having actors who focus on gender issues plays a larger role in climate change policymaking, and other activities may help to change this continuing pattern of gender imbalance. Women have a long history of climate change activism (Gaard 2015).[3] Actors like the Women and Gender Constituency (WGC) push for gender to be a central component of the ways in which we conceptualize climate change. WGC is a civil society observer of the UNFCCC comprised of fifteen women's and environmental NGOs. It was established in 2009 and granted full constituency status in 2011. These groups work together to promote women's voices and rights in all facets of the UNFCCC framework. These kinds of actors publicize it when the international community takes positive steps toward addressing gender and other forms of inequity, as well as when they fall short. This leads into discussions of both sustainability and justice, as the inclusion of a diverse group of people is likely to be beneficial for achieving both goals as they relate to climate change.

Revealing gender in environmental debates

Addressing climate change is no easy task. It is a complex, multidimensional environmental problem that has generated huge amounts of political debate. Previous feminist scholarship can offer suggestions for using critical approaches to understand complex issues, put them in a broader context, and assess possible policy options to address them. For instance, Charlotte Bunch (1987) suggests we ask questions like "what is the problem?, how did it originate?, what do we want?, and, how do we get there?" (Gaard 2015: 23). These questions aid in applying gender lenses to environmental debates, including debates about climate change. We must ask about the costs and consequences of climate change, the sources of climate change, what steps we think should be taken to address climate change and its impacts, and what are the best ways to achieve those steps. The following sections address the goals of sustainability and justice. The chapter then assesses how debates over population, consumption, and security all enter deliberations over the causes and consequences of climate change, as well as the best ways to address it.

Sustainability as a goal of climate change governance
Gender matters for understanding sustainability. The previous chapters have shown that taking gender seriously involves viewing multiple actors as stakeholders who should be included in environmental decision-making. Including multiple perspectives gives a fuller picture of the causes and experiences of unsustainability. Women's perspectives can be different from men's due to the socially conditioned roles that they are expected to play in their communities. When women's voices are left out of major climate change negotiations, it matters for the final outcome of those negotiations. Evaluating the sustainability of ecosystems in the face of climate change is also gendered. As discussed in chapter 2, there are gendered and racialized patterns regarding who is most likely to express concern about climate change effects (McCright 2010; McCright and Dunlap 2011). There are also gendered patterns of behavior that influence greenhouse gas emission patterns (Johnsson-Latham 2006, 2007).

So how do we get to greater sustainability on the climate change front? Multiple chapters have noted feminist concerns about heavy reliance on technological fixes to environmental issues without a thorough examination of the social processes that make these approaches attractive.[4] "Technofix solutions make no attempt to rethink human culture, dominant lifestyles and demands on nature, indeed they tend to assume that these are unchangeable. They aim rather to meet these demands more efficiently through smarter technology" (Plumwood 2002: 8).There is evidence to suggest that women are often skeptical that technical solutions, like carbon capture and storage, or further development of biofuels, are sufficient or the best way to address climate change (Hemmati and Röhr 2009). These gendered patterns need additional study, but they likely relate to larger trends of Promethean approaches being associated with a "masculine" approach to problem-solving. Julie Nelson (2015: 100) argues that we tend to use gendered stories, metaphors, and archetypes to aid in understanding the world around us.

> Consider the archetypal image of the young adult male hero. He is brave, active, adventurous, innovative, knowledgeable, clever, confident, independent, in control, and not constrained by family, tradition, or public opinion...He achieves victory, dominance, status, and reaps his just rewards. The Hero evokes admiration. A heroic policymaker would be brash and fearless. The heroic policymaker might even laugh in the face of danger – especially if the danger seems uncertain, and distant in time or space.

The heroic policymaker would not tend to be concerned about the "potential" impacts of climate change that would only be problematic if heroic scientists or entrepreneurs fail in their quest to provide techno-fixes. Approaches like the "Precautionary Principle" are only for those who lack the confidence to decisively make policy. These gendered assumptions signal that gender lenses are necessary not only for assessing what activities contribute to climate change, but also for assessing the policymaking process itself (Adger et al. 2011).

This leads one to question the role of individual policy-makers as well as the state itself in climate change decision-making. The role of the state in environmental protection has been widely debated within GEP for decades (Dryzek 2003; Eckersley 2004). Some see the state as having a unique position within the international system. The principle of state sovereignty means that states are regarded as ultimately responsible for the policies within their borders. They are the ones who create and enforce domestic environmental regulations, as well as ratify and implement global environmental agreements. States also possess resources that many other, smaller actors lack. At the same time, the state has been critiqued by many as an entity that protects the status quo even when that means that the position of the powerful is maintained at the expense of equity and environmental sustainability. For instance, scholars adopting a political ecology perspective have criticized the measures taken by states in the name of biodiversity protection (Brockington 2002; Peluso and Watts 2001). At times these measures have resulted in human insecurity for local communities, and continued environmental destruction due to ineffective policies. Simultaneously, feminist scholars have called attention to the status quo orientation of the state as a political entity (Enloe 2004; Runyan and Peterson 2013), and challenged whether it is wise to entrust the state alone with environmental protection (Seager 1993, 1999). For these reasons, environmental governance should incorporate a combination of actors into environmental policymaking.

In particular, women have been put forward as a great hope for combating or adapting to climate change. According to Lakshmi Puri (2015), UN Women Deputy Executive Director,

> we have to recognize the power of parity and we have to do it now because we can no longer afford to dismiss and waste the potential of women's agency and their huge role in devising and leading responses to climate impacts...The force multiplier and transformative potential of empowered women and girls should be harnessed to arrest and reverse climate change and adapt sustainably to its impact.

This perspective seeks to channel the various roles and responsibilities that women have in society into improved understandings of drivers of environmental change and how we might combat it. This perspective can potentially contribute to both sustainability and gender equity; however, it is necessary that we approach women's empowerment as a goal in its own right. Women should have their voices included in climate change policymaking not only because it helps us achieve the goals of slowing or adapting to climate change, but because it is just.

The justice of climate change It has been well established that climate change will not impact everyone evenly. Those who experience economic, political, and social marginalization are at greater risk of experiencing climate change ills than are non-marginalized groups (Alston 2014; Arora-Jonsson 2011; Dankelman 2010). This speaks to larger issues of vulnerability and marginalization. Problematizing the concept of vulnerability by using gender lenses can help us understand the complexity inherent in the predicted future impacts of climate change. It can also identify sites of agency to build on in the process of addressing climate change. Highlighting the connections between climate change and vulnerability must be done in ways that acknowledge the coping mechanisms that communities already use. This portrayal will go further toward affirming that these communities should be central parts of environmental governance.

Participation is a central component of notions of procedural justice. Justice arguments suggest that all stakeholders should be incorporated into the policymaking process; however, policymaking often fails to adhere to this standard. Demonstrating the resilience of marginalized communities avoids oversimplification and may help to persuade policymakers to include them in environmental governance. At present, policy documents routinely perceive women primarily as the victims of climate change and not as positive agents of change or people who can actively contribute to mitigation and adaptation strategies (WEDO 2008). Stakeholders in environmental management deserve to have their input in the decision-making process. This is not to say that everyone can have a say in each environmental policy enacted by decision-making bodies, but rather that there are mechanisms for including a range of perspectives and knowledge about environmental matters. Focusing on participation in climate change debates and policymaking reinforces a feminist commitment to active citizenship. Scholars like Sherilyn Mac-Gregor (2004, 2006) have argued that focusing on citizenship over care is a more fruitful way of connecting gender and environmental politics. While early versions of ecofeminism and other feminist environmental thought tended to depict close connections between women and "nature" due to women's caregiving roles, this has been widely critiqued by those who claim that these essentialist ideas of care and women do little to encourage society to view women and men as active participants in environmental protection (Sandilands 1999).

Existing assumptions and discourse on climate change can influence who is included in decision-making processes, as well as what kinds of policies might be introduced to address it. MacGregor (2009) has argued that climate change is becoming a masculinized issue area due to the influence on the expectation that scientific knowledge is the most legitimate form of knowledge on climate change, along with the tendency to securitize climate change debates. Climate change policymaking should therefore be critically assessed for the reinforcement of patriarchal structures, and alternative discourses should influence climate change debates. This book offers alternatives built on not only sustainability but also justice. It suggests that policies designed to address climate change should be evaluated not only for their potential to halt or reverse environmental change, but also for how they are likely to impact the lived experiences of marginalized groups.

It is unjust to expect those in society who bear the least responsibility for causing climate change to pay the highest costs in mitigation and adaptation policies (IPCC 2014). For instance, market-based climate change solutions are likely to take a greater toll on poorer individuals and households. These policies can impact men and women differently due to differing levels of income as well as access to markets and services. If the policies were not designed carefully, they would serve to worsen gender inequality (Hemmati and Röhr 2009). Additionally, these kinds of neoliberal-oriented policies feed into the individualization of responsibility for environmental change.

> The gender division of labour, and stereotypes about women's and men's roles, leads to a disproportionate amount of work in the home being done by women. Requirements that households should use less energy would therefore have most impact on women. In general, private households are the societal institutions with the least influence and representation of their interests in the context of climate negotiations. (Hemmati and Röhr 2009: 21)

One alternative to the individualization of responsibility is the active participation of stakeholders in environmental management. Are there problems with this? Yes. Gender often "works" in ways that reduce the active participation of women in policymaking at multiple levels. Women are under-represented at the top in global environmental negotiations (GenderCC 2011; Bretherton 1998, 2003). Even at grassroots or community levels, gender roles and expectations can result in the silencing of women. Additionally, the unpaid care burden that many women face makes it difficult to even get in the door (Paavola 2006). A United Nations Development Programme (UNDP) report found that women continue to have a large unpaid care burden. The report argues that "[a]cross most countries in all regions, women work more than men. Women are estimated to contribute 52 percent of global work, men 48 percent. But even if women carry more than half the burden, they are disadvantaged in both realms of work – paid as well as unpaid work – in patterns that reinforce each other (UNDP 2015: 11). These patterns result in fewer free hours for women to participate as environmental stakeholders. This results in justice concerns regarding gendered economic patterns as well as the larger ramifications these have on how men and women spend their time. A gender-focused approach to addressing climate change that is informed by the goals of sustainability and justice is sensitive to the manifestations of economic disparity, as well as to challenges associated with fears about population growth, overconsumption, and insecurity as they relate to climate change.

Problematizing population narratives in climate change debates Climate change debates have once again served to bring population concerns to the global agenda (GenderCC 2011; Hartmann et al. 2015). The IPCC (2014: 3) makes a specific connection between human activities and climate change, saying, "[h]uman interference with the climate system is occurring, and climate change poses risks for human and natural systems."[5] Reports have focused on assessing predicted "futures" of climate change that include information on economic growth, energy use and emissions scenarios, and demographic data including population growth. These studies have been critiqued for failing to emphasize differences in resource consumption between rich and poor countries and consumers, however: the link between population growth and rising greenhouse gas emissions is still guiding policymaking in many circles (Guzmán et al. 2009; Hartmann et al. 2015). Family planning is often promoted as a strategy for mitigation and adaptation to climate change.

> While there are scientific and ethical problems with this approach, it is gaining ground through its solution-oriented focus, for two key reasons. First, it frames population–climate interventions as socially just and woman-centered: a "win–win" for women and the environment. Second, it ignores the complex and challenging social-structural forces that determine whether, when and how women access the tools available to support reproductive decision-making, by subsuming them into simplistic solution narratives. (Hartmann et al. 2015: 74)

These narratives employ the language of women's rights and empowerment, yet they do little to encourage critical reflections on whether population growth or other factors are bigger contributors to environmental unsustainability. At the same time, when something is identified as a "problem" by the international community, policymaking tends to follow, and the policies adopted may not be just. The long history of coercive and unsafe population control measures that have been implemented across the world should be reason enough for scholars and policymakers to be careful when linking climate change to population.

Institutions like the IPCC have been criticized for addressing population and environmental change simplistically by including figures on population size and growth in early emissions projections without considering differences in emission levels of different social or demographic groups (GenderCC 2011; Guzmán et al. 2009). All groups are not equally responsible for emissions levels that contribute to increasingly dangerous natural disasters. This becomes clear when we compare total greenhouse gas emissions levels with per capita levels. We must not be seduced by a simplistic policy approach that views family planning programs and population growth reductions as an easy climate change mitigation strategy. We must unpack "population" beyond merely growth levels. The sustainability of population growth must be assessed with an eye to both the numbers of people and where and how they live.

Reflecting on climate change and consumption   Metric tons per capita of CO_2 are very low in many parts of the global South. For instance, estimates for 2011 show that countries like Bangladesh, Benin, Bhutan, Cambodia, Cameroon, Ghana, Guatemala, Haiti, Liberia, Myanmar, Nicaragua, Nigeria, Pakistan, Tajikistan, and Zimbabwe all have less than one metric ton of CO_2 per capita.[6] This is compared with the US at 17.0, Canada at 14.1, and Australia at 16.5 metric tons per capita. The global average is roughly 4.9 metric tons per capita (World Bank 2015b). Most European states also have emissions levels that exceed this global average.[7] While the links between greenhouse gas emissions, levels of consumption, and economic processes are complex, these numbers hint at lifestyles and economic processes in the global North contributing to a large percentage of total CO_2 emissions, while high levels of poverty contribute to the low per capita figures for many states in the global South.

Global consumption patterns have frequently been identified as a driver of climate change. The IPCC (2014: 24) claims that "mitigation scenarios that are likely to limit warming to below 2°C through the 21st century relative to pre-industrial levels entail losses in global consumption." The way that emissions counting has worked in global environmental decision-making, however, has focused much more attention on production processes than on consumption as a source of greenhouse gases. Calculations of greenhouse gas emissions focus on those that come from production processes within states. There is important potential in rethinking approaches to climate governance toward a more central focus on consumption. Paul Harris and Jonathan Symons (2013: 10) explain some of these benefits thus:

> A switch to consumption-based accounting and targets would potentially allow "differentiated responsibility" to be implemented through policies targeting high-consumption lifestyles everywhere. At the level of individual behavior, consumers

who wish to minimize climate impacts require ready access to information about emissions embodied in products. If national consumption-based emissions targets were adopted, policymakers would probably create price signals or point-of-sale labeling schemes to supply this information. Consumption accounting might also change perceptions in ways that could promote international cooperation on border measures, transport emissions, and technology transfer.

Despite these advantages, many policymakers continue to be hesitant to tackle consumption – even from states that have been at the forefront on climate action (Harris and Symons 2013). This reinforces the claim made in chapter 5 that while consumption has made it on to the list of drivers of environmental change, there has been little political will to aggressively tackle it.

Discourses surrounding consumption persist in framing consumption choice as an individual responsibility. This once again raises important questions about the role of the state in environmental governance. While many feminist scholars have been quite critical of state institutions for their tendency to reinforce patriarchal processes (Enloe 2004; Runyan and Peterson 2013), there appear to be few other actors who have the capacity to make large-scale positive changes in global consumption patterns. This is where gender lenses allow us to critically reflect on the role of the state in ways that acknowledge its potential while problematizing existing distributions of power and authority and the ways that these are gendered (and classed, and raced, etc.). To date, most states have been relatively unwilling to govern consumption. It is important to ask why this is the case, what the implications of this hesitancy are for goals of sustainability and justice, and what shifts in this tendency might occur in the future. At the same time, the best chance of achieving consumption that is truly sustainable requires us to understand how and why people consume the way they do. Examining climate change through gender lenses requires reflecting on power relations and economic processes that contribute to both overconsumption/misconsumption environmental change.

Addressing climate change to reduce insecurity   Many actors in the international system discuss climate change as a security issue (Detraz and Betsill 2009; Floyd and Matthew 2013; Trombetta 2008). Actors discuss the possibility that climate change will result in resource shortages, which will contribute to resource conflict and/or environmental migration (Gleditsch 2012). Actors also consider the large-scale threats to human security that come from potential food shortages, more frequent and more dangerous natural disasters, and shifts in vector-borne diseases (Adger et al. 2014). Leaders from the global South have likened climate change to warfare (Detraz and Betsill 2009). For these states, the causes of climate change (greenhouse gas emissions in particular) are understood to be coming mostly from outside, like a line of enemy soldiers advancing toward their borders. In October of 2015, representatives from numerous African and island states met in Paris to discuss the implications of climate change for defense issues. French foreign minister Laurent Fabius claimed that "climate and international security are closely linked." He argued that floods, droughts, and famines force people to migrate and "increase the risk of conflicts." Likewise, the defense ministers of Niger and Chad discussed the growing desertification of Africa's Sahel region as a threat multiplier, particularly in the Lake Chad region, which faces attacks by the extremist group Boko Haram (Associated Press 2015).The casualties of this source of insecurity will largely be marginalized communities in marginalized states who lack the capacity to adapt to climate change's impacts.

As discussed in chapter 6, some scholars wonder whether "security," as it has been traditionally conceptualized, is compatible with sustainability (Dalby 2009). What we are likely to need are new ways of thinking and doing security. The concept of "sustainable security" is one possibility. The Oxford Research Group's (2014) Sustainable Security project "prioritises the resolution of the interconnected underlying drivers of insecurity and conflict, with an emphasis on preventative rather than reactive strategies." This project identifies four main drivers of insecurity: climate change, competition over resources, the marginalization of groups of people connected to processes associated with globalization, and global militarization. Rather than maintain the status quo, this approach would see both the mitigation of and adaptation to climate change as necessary steps toward security (Dalby 2013). There is also space for considerations of gendered justice issues in this kind of approach. The marginalization of people due to globalization, as well as militarization, is a central component of many feminist environmental perspectives. The securitization of climate change through discourses that privilege state security can intentionally or unintentionally reinforce existing structures, including militarization and patriarchy. For many critical scholars, including many feminist security scholars and feminist environmental scholars, this should be avoided due to the fact that both of these structures contribute not only to marginalization and inequity, but also to unsustainability (Seager 1993).

Challenging militarization and patriarchy entails evaluating concepts like citizenship, nationalism, and the role of the state in environmental policymaking. There is quite a bit of overlap between rethinking these concepts in GEP and among feminist scholars. For GEP scholars, these things need to be rethought largely due to the transboundary nature of environmental change, along with the links between the global capitalist system and environmental change (and the fact that many international interactions support the global capitalist system). For feminists, these things need to be rethought because they are a part of the patriarchal system in which socially constructed norms about gender mean that women bear the brunt of not only environmental change, but also other forms of discrimination.

Alternative discourses of connections between security and climate change that highlight the goals of environmental sustainability, human security, and gender justice are necessary. This would represent an important shift in the current securitized discourses on climate security in that it highlights the ways that gendered sources of insecurity intersect with environmental vulnerability. Rather than think of climate change as a threat multiplier, gender lenses reveal it as a vulnerability intensifier that requires reflexive, participatory solutions (Detraz 2014). For climate change policymaking to be effective at removing insecurity linked to unsustainability in ways that are fair and just, these discourses should guide policymaking debates.

Conclusions

Gender lenses offer critical perspectives on climate change. They provoke complex responses to questions about the costs and consequences of climate change, the sources of climate change, what steps we think should be taken to address climate change and its impacts, and what are the best ways to achieve those steps. First, the costs and consequences of climate change include loss of livelihood, health, well-being, and even life. The most vulnerable of society bear a disproportionate share of these insecurities. Climate change offers a clear illustration that when environmental sustainability suffers, the consequences are felt unevenly. Those who experience vulnerability in society through factors like poverty and marginalization are also vulnerable to environmental insecurity. Second, the sources of climate change can be traced to human activities (IPCC 2014). What is important to realize, however, is that these human activities are situated in gendered social, economic, and political processes. Population trends and consumption patterns are highly dependent on societal conceptualizations of acceptable behavior. Those who have full agency to make decisions – and not everyone does – do not make them in a vacuum. Rather, behavior is shaped by assumptions about masculinity and femininity, which also shape power relations. Third, the steps that we should take to address climate change and its impacts are those that are oriented toward both sustainability *and* justice. As human beings who are dependent on functioning ecosystems, we have an incentive to work toward sustainability. But as humans who live, work, and play in communities and societies, we also have obligations to each other and to the environment that sustains us. If we achieve sustainable ecosystems at the expense of the poor, or disenfranchised, or marginalized, then what kind of a world have we really saved? Fourth, the best ways to achieve sustainable and just climate change policies are to reflect on where these are compatible with existing structures, and on where they might need alteration. Current climate change governance has been critiqued for continuing to be status quo oriented (Dryzek 2005; GenderCC 2015; Kronsell 2013). Our existing discourses and modes of operation have, to this point, contributed to the environmental change and global inequities that we currently face (Plumwood 2002). While gender lenses cannot hope to offer a simple solution to correct this path, they do provide space to problematize simplistic and essentializing assumptions about how environmental change occurs, who is responsible for it, and what policies might address it.

One thing that should be clear at this point is that the topics covered in each chapter are all closely tied to the others. For example, poverty can be a driver of environmental unsustainability, but that is not the only reason we should care about it. Poverty is connected to population levels. It constrains choices and options regarding family size. It constrains choices and options related to consumption. It leads to vulnerability to environmental insecurity, and it is often a manifestation of unequal structures in society. One challenge to addressing these overlapping issues is overcoming doom and gloom while also keeping our eyes open to the scale of the problems facing humanity. The perspective outlined in this book is compatible with the idea of sacrifice or sufficiency, but of a particular sort (Wapner 2010a). It is the sacrifice of some groups so that others may have justice and security. It is a sacrifice on the part of those who have been fortunate enough to come out on the winning side of existing power relations and structures. It is their sacrifice of their environmental (and economic and social and political) privilege. This perspective points out inequities, but remains optimistic about the future. Since sustainability and justice are reinforcing goals, and gender is a central component of each of them, there is hope that we can move forward to address environmental change by recognizing and addressing factors that are harmful to ecosystems and all human well-being.

Gender lenses contribute to our understanding of environmental issues by problematizing existing ways of understanding topics like sustainability, justice, population, consumption, and security, and by revealing various ways that each intersects with gender. It is impossible to treat these topics as gender-neutral, just as it is impossible to treat them as separate categories for discussion and policymaking. Some may claim that calling for broad, critical definitions of environmental concepts contributes to muddying the waters of GEP. Environmental issues are often incredibly complicated and involve a large number of factors and actors. While I acknowledge this, I argue that this call is a necessary component of identifying the larger processes that contribute to the related social ills of environmental degradation and discrimination against marginalized populations. Feminist scholars have a great deal to contribute to the ways in which we understand and act on environmental issues. The task at hand is encouraging a dialogue between scholars who have corresponding goals of preserving ecosystems and their inhabitants, including the humans within those ecosystems. Most projections about the future of the international system indicate that environmental concerns, like climate change, will continue to occupy a place on the agenda of scholars and policymakers. Since gender is a fundamental component of the economic, social, and political processes that contribute to environmental change as well as environmental sustainability, we have an obligation to include gender in our environmental deliberations. It not only aids in our self-interested incentives to maintain sustainability, but also forces us to consider just paths to this sustainability.

Notes

Chapter 1

1   The use of discourse analysis has become fairly routine within GEP. Barbara Johnstone (2002: 3) claims that one particular meaning of discourses is that they are "ideas as well as ways of talking that influence and are influenced by the ideas. Discourses, in their linguistic aspect, are conventionalized sets of choices for discourse, or talk."

2   I use the terms "global North" and "global South" to refer to divisions of power between economically and politically powerful states (which tend to be found in the Northern hemisphere, with few exceptions) and the rest of the international community. Other scholars use labels like "minority/majority worlds" to refer to a similar notion of power distribution (e.g., Doyle 2005).

3   IR scholars tend to date the rise of the modern state system to the signing of the Treaty of Westphalia in 1648.

Chapter 2

1   The concept of resilience emerged out of the environmental sciences in the 1970s. Since that time it has migrated into different disciplines, including GEP.

2   The European Union (EU)'s strategy for sustainable development adds a fourth pillar: good governance (EU 2009).

3 There are a few different labels used within GEP scholarship to refer to basically similar categories (weak/soft sustainability or strong/hard sustainability).

4 The World Commission on Environment and Development is sometimes known as the Brundtland Commission after the leader of the commission, Gro Harlem Brundtland.

5 For instance, the EU included "sustainable development" as an overarching objective of EU policies in the Treaty of Amsterdam in 1997. This commitment to sustainable development was strengthened through policy recommendations in the Gothenburg Declaration of 2001 (European Commission 2016).

6 In fact, the Transportation Research Board of the United States National Academy of Sciences spent a million dollars trying to come up with a definition of sustainable development in the early 1990s. The final product was largely a combination of the ideas of its members rather than a succinct definition (Dryzek 2005).

7 The Fourth World Conference on Women produced both the Beijing Declaration and the Beijing Platform for Action. Both contained commitments to women's active involvement in environmental protection and management.

8 Julia Klein et al. (2014: 143) explain that they choose to use the term "local knowledge" in order "to stress that this knowledge is constantly changing, rather than static, as the terms 'traditional' and even 'indigenous' may be taken to imply. Like Western scientific knowledge, local knowledge is always in the making."

9 In particular, *Agenda 21* stressed the need for gender-differentiated data in several places. This is a suggestion still made today.

10 Ester Boserup's 1970 *Women's Role in Economic Development* was influential in shaping the WID perspective on women's productivity in agricultural and commodity production in the global South.

11 An intervening approach between WID and GAD was "women and development" (WAD), which located gender struggle in the structure of capitalism. It focused more heavily on capitalism than patriarchy as the source of undevelopment or underdevelopment (Bradshaw 2015).

12 In addition to women being overrepresented as members of the lowest classes, they are often poorer than men within classes. Gender disparities exist even in countries that have a reputation for being progressive on gender equity issues. For example, in Sweden men earn more than women in all income groups (Johnsson-Latham 2006).

13   Gendered poverty also relates to the fact that much of the labor that women around the world are expected to perform is unpaid (UNDP 2015).

Chapter 3

1   For example in 1980, around the time the county became connected with environmental justice debates, African-Americans constituted 63.7 percent of the population of Warren County, and 24.4 percent of the population of North Carolina (Bullard 2005).
2   Detoxification of the landfill did not begin until 2001, and was completed in 2003 with a price tag of $18 million (Bullard 2005).
3   Former Peruvian senator and activist Hugo Blanco used the term in 1991 in an article about the struggles of poor and indigenous peoples (Martinez-Alier et al. 2014).
4   "Popular environmentalism" is a related concept often used by those who find the term "poor" to be problematic.
5   Many of these concepts originated in environmental justice organizations and were later picked up and expanded on and/ or altered by environmental scholars (Martinez-Alier et al. 2014).
6   At the same time, this strategy will not always be appropriate due to the individualistic and universalizing tendency of human rights frames.
7   The Convention, which entered into force in 2001, is based on Principle 1 of the 1972 Stockholm Declaration on Environment and Development, and Principle 10 of the 1992 Rio Declaration on Environment and Development (Agyeman et al. 2003).
8   See Okereke and Charlesworth (2014) for an overview of some of the different strands of arguments used by philosophers to advance the claim for non-anthropocentric environmental ethics.
9   Harold Lasswell, an influential political science scholar, famously defined politics as who gets what, when, and how.
10   This description of the connections between intergenerational justice and intragenerational justice is similar to those found in *Our Common Future* (World Commission on Environment and Development 1987).
11   The Barke et al. (1997) study involved risk assessments of members of the American Association for the Advancement of

Science, and the Slovic et al. (1997) study involved assessments of members of the British Toxicology Society.

12 In a study of the mining industry in Fiji, Ali and Ackley (2011: 75) find that women "have less access to direct information about mining risks than men do" and that "women tend to receive information about such risks from secondary sources."

13 In their study in the US, Kuran and McCaffery (2008: 228) find "that the willingness to tolerate discrimination varies significantly across domains, with a very high tolerance of discrimination against poorly educated immigrants and a strikingly low tolerance of discrimination against the genetically disadvantaged. Regardless of domain, tolerance is greater among men than among women."

14 Commodification of water has gendered consequences in that men tend to be more likely to have access to economic resources than women. In this way, men have multiple levels of control in the way water is used and distributed (Alston 2010).

15 Furthermore, Agyeman et al. (2003: 2) claim that "a truly sustainable society is one where wider questions of social needs and welfare, and economic opportunity, are integrally connected to environmental concerns."

Chapter 4

1 Other components of states include geographically defined borders, a government that has a relationship with its citizens, and diplomatic recognition by other states.

2 As of 2015, 60 percent of the global population lives in Asia (4.4 billion), 16 percent in Africa (1.2 billion), 10 percent in Europe (738 million), 9 percent in Latin America and the Caribbean (634 million), and the remaining 5 percent in Northern America (358 million) and Oceania (39 million) (UN DESA 2015).

3 The Club of Rome was a collection of individuals who worked on what they considered to be pressing problems of the day, including population growth impacts. Their 1972 *Limits to Growth* was considered to be an example of neo-Malthusian fears about the negative consequences of population growth patterns.

4 In *The Population Bomb* Ehrlich (1968) recommends the US cut off food aid to countries that are overpopulated.

5   It is not only poverty that acts as a constraint to choice. Gender expectation about having children mean that many women who may choose to have no children or limit the size of their family feel social pressure to have children (Hartmann 1995).

6   For example, the language of rights and choice was used more frequently after the 1994 UN International Conference on Population and Development than in the years before (Wilson 2012).

7   Population growth patterns vary across the many states of the African continent. This fact contributes to the frustration of many who critique the tendency to lump regions of the global South together with no context or differentiation.

8   Sturgeon (2009: 143) explains that "a former board member of the Sierra Club, John Tanton, has since the 1970s built a set of anti-immigration organizations (including founding the Federation for American Immigration Reform) that are virulently racist while he simultaneously supported organizations (such as Population-Environment Balance) that claim that immigrants and overpopulation are the source of environmental problems."

9   India has a long history of controversial sterilization policy. Men were often the target of sterilization campaigns in the mid-1970s. As of the mid-2010s, the country has one of the world's highest rates of female sterilizations. The government reports that close to 4.6 million Indian women were sterilized in 2011 and 2012. The UN reports that around 37 percent of women have had the operations, compared with 29 percent in China (Burke 2014).

10 According to Jason Burke (2014), "local officials in Chhattisgarh[, India,] say they were set a target by central government of 220,000 sterilisations a year."

11 There are different categories of natural disasters, including hydro-meteorological (e.g., droughts, floods, slides, waves/surges, extreme temperatures, wildfires and wind storms), geological (e.g., earthquakes, volcanic eruptions), and a third category that does not fit into the other two, often referred to as "other" (e.g., epidemics, famines, insect infestations).

12 India, Nigeria, Pakistan, the DRC, Ethiopia, the United Republic of Tanzania, the US, Indonesia, and Uganda.

13 The annual average frequency of natural disasters between 2004 and 2013 was 384, while 2014 saw 324 – the third lowest number of reported disasters since 2004 (Guha-Sapir et al. 2015).

Chapter 5

1   Jobs among women became increasingly competitive due to the fact that many jobs that had previously employed men (e.g., heavy industrial enterprises) were removed from the labor market, which meant that men increasingly turned to jobs that had previously been associated with women's labor. In this new labor environment, where concern for profits often drove labor decisions, women were seen as more costly since they might require maternity leave or time off to care for family members (Ghodsee 2007).

2   Prometheus is a figure from Greek mythology who stole fire from Zeus. John Dryzek (2005: 51) identifies the Promethean discourse on environmental politics as one that has "unlimited confidence in the ability of humans and their technologies to overcome any problems – including environmental problems."

3   Knapp et al. (2010) studied bush-meat consumption in Tanzania in particular.

4   Additionally, research on topics like the production and consumption of products such as skin lighteners further illustrates the ways that consumption connects to class, gender, and race (Glenn 2008).

5   Several US states have banned or regulated the use of microbeads, including California, Illinois, Maine, New Jersey, Colorado, Indiana, and Maryland. At the federal level, President Obama signed a bill banning microbeads in December 2015.

6   "Estimates suggest that 8 billion plastic shopping bags are used per annum in the United Kingdom, 4.3 billion in Australia, 9.8 billion in Hong Kong, 3.3 billion in Bangladesh, 100 billion in the United States and 300 billion to 1 trillion in China" (Clapp and Swanston 2009: 317).

Chapter 6

1   "Broadening" refers to increasing the number of concerns linked to security, while "deepening" refers to increasing the actors, both above and below the level of the state, whose security is of concern (Krause and Williams 1996).

2   Elsewhere I refer to these as three distinct environment–security discourses labeled environmental conflict, environmental security, and ecological security (Detraz 2014).

3 Rita Floyd and Richard Matthew (2013) refer to this as "biosphere security."

4 One rejoinder to this is the claim that alternative ways of connecting security and the environment do not necessarily rely on exclusively focusing on state security, and would therefore not require a primary, or any, role for the military (Dalby 2009).

5 Scholarship that examines the possibilities of resource conflict in particular has been critiqued on numerous grounds, including definitional ambiguity, selectively excluding political and economic factors in analyses, selecting only cases where environmental conflict occurred rather than those where it did not, and confusion about the appropriate levels of analysis to examine conflict (de Soysa 2013).

6 Scholars like Sherilyn MacGregor (2006) and Greta Gaard (1998) have warned against essentialist depictions of movements like Chipko and others where women from the global South are painted as naturally more caring for the environment than others.

7 Green Revolution shifts included the development of high-yielding varieties of food grains, land consolidation, private tube-well irrigation, mechanization, and the use of fertilizers and pesticides.

8 According to the FAO (2011: 19), "[a]griculture contributes to greenhouse gas emissions through nitrogen fertilizer use, predominantly as nitrous oxide, and through methane, from wet-rice production and at a larger scale, from enteric fermentation in ruminants (cows, sheep and goats)."

9 The study covered the following countries: Burkina Faso, Ethiopia, Ghana, Kenya, Mali, Niger, Senegal, Tanzania, and Uganda (Perez et al. 2015).

Chapter 7

1 Mitigation refers to attempts to halt or reverse climate change, while adaptation refers to adjusting to the impacts of climate change.

2 Gender balance is often associated with liberal feminism's commitment to removing legal and other obstacles to equal participation, but it does not necessarily mean a pledge to address larger, structural gender problems.

3 Women from the global South have frequently pointed out the gender-specific nature of climate change impacts (Spitzner 2009).

4 It is also essential to confront the potential negative environmental consequences of these approaches. For instance, there have been many debates about the potential or pitfalls of geoengineering for addressing climate change, and public perceptions of these (e.g., Cairns and Stirling 2014).

5 The IPCC (2014) also raises the issue of population growth as contributing to greater numbers of people who are vulnerable to climate change impacts.

6 This is not an exhaustive list of the states with less than one metric ton of CO_2 per capita. There are sixty-one states that fall into this category (World Bank 2015b).

7 Examples include France at 5.2, Germany at 8.9, Italy at 6.7, Spain at 5.8, Sweden at 5.5, and the UK at 7.1.

References

5Gyres. 2015. "Microbeads." *5Gyres.org*. http://www.5gyres.org/microbeads.

Ackerly, Brooke, and Jacqui True. 2010. *Doing Feminist Research in Political and Social Science*. New York, NY: Palgrave Macmillan.

Adams, Carol. 1990. *The Sexual Politics of Meat: A Feminist-Vegetarian Critical Theory*. Malden, MA: Polity.

Adger, W. Neil, et al. 2014. "Human Security." http://ipcc-wg2.gov/AR5/images/uploads/WGIIAR5-Chap12_FGDall.pdf.

Adger, W. Neil, Jon Barnett, F. S. Chapin III, and Heidi Ellemor. 2011. "This Must Be the Place: Underrepresentation of Identity and Meaning in Climate Change Decision-Making." *Global Environmental Politics*. 11(2): 1–25.

Agarwal, Bina. 2009. "Gender and Forest Conservation: The Impact of Women's Participation in Community Forest Governance." *Ecological Economics*. 68(11): 2785–99.

Agyeman, Julian. 2013. *Introducing Just Sustainabilities: Policy, Planning, and Practice*. New York, NY: Zed Books.

Agyeman, Julian, Robert D. Bullard, and Bob Evans, eds. 2003. *Just Sustainabilities: Development in an Unequal World*. Cambridge, MA: MIT Press.

Agyeman, Julian, and Bob Evans. 2004. "'Just Sustainability': The Emerging Discourse of Environmental Justice in Britain?" *Geographical Journal*. 170(2): 155–64.

Ali, Saleem H., and Mary A. Ackley. 2011. "Foreign Investment and Environmental Justice in an Island Economy: Mining, Bottled Water, and Corporate Social Responsibility in Fiji." In

Environmental Inequalities Beyond Borders: Local Perspectives on Global Injustices, eds. JoAnn Carmin and Julian Agyeman. Cambridge, MA: MIT Press, pp. 67–84.

Alston, Margaret. 2010. "Gender and Climate Change in Australia." *Journal of Sociology*. 47(1): 53–70.

Alston, Margaret. 2014. "Gender Mainstreaming and Climate Change." *Women's Studies International Forum*. 47: 287–94.

Andonova, Liliana, Michele M. Betsill, and Harriet Bulkeley. 2009. "Transnational Climate Governance." *Global Environmental Politics*. 9(2): 52–73.

Angus, Ian, and Simon Butler. 2011. "Panic Over 7 Billion: Letting the 1% Off the Hook." *Different Takes*. 73: 1–4.

Arora-Jonsson, Seema. 2011. "Virtue and Vulnerability: Discourses on Women, Gender and Climate Change." *Global Environmental Change*. 21: 744–51.

Ascher, William, Toddi Steelman, and Robert Healy. 2010. *Knowledge and Environmental Policy: Re-Imagining the Boundaries of Science and Politics*. Cambridge, MA: MIT Press.

Associated Press. 2015. "France Warns of Security Risks Caused by Global Warming." *Guardian*. http://www.theguardian.com/environment/2015/oct/14/france-warns-of-security-risks-caused-by-global-warming.

Aumônier, Simon, Michael Collins, and Peter Garrett. 2008. "An Updated Lifecycle Assessment Study for Disposable and Reusable Nappies." https://www.gov.uk/government/uploads/system/uploads/attachment_data/file/291130/scho0808boir-e-e.pdf.

Baechler, Günther. 1998. *Violence through Environmental Discrimination*. Boston, MA: Kluwer Academic.

Bandarage, Asoka. 1997. *Women, Population and Global Crisis: A Political-Economic Analysis*. London, UK: Zed Books.

Barke, Richard P., Hank Jenkins-Smith, and Paul Slovic. 1997. "Risk Perception of Men and Women Scientists." *Social Science Quarterly*. 78: 167–76.

Barnett, Jon. 2001. *The Meaning of Environmental Security: Ecological Politics and Policy in the New Security Era*. New York, NY: Zed Books.

Barr, Stewart, Andrew Gilg, and Gareth Shaw. 2011. "Citizens, Consumers and Sustainability: (Re)Framing Environmental Practice in an Age of Climate Change." *Global Environmental Change*. 21: 1224–33.

Baxter, Brian H. 2000. "Ecological Justice and Justice as Impartiality." *Environmental Politics*. 9(3): 43–64.

Beckerman, Wilfred, and Joanna Pasek. 2001. *Justice, Posterity, and the Environment*. Oxford, UK: Oxford University Press.

Benería, Lourdes. 2003. *Gender, Development, and Globalization: Economics as if People Mattered.* London, UK: Routledge.

Bensouda, Fatou. 2014. "Gender Justice and the ICC." *International Feminist Journal of Politics.* 16(4): 538–542.

Best, Henning, and Martin Lanzendorf. 2005. "Division of Labour and Gender Differences in Metropolitan Car Use: An Empirical Study in Cologne, Germany." *Journal of Transport Geography.* 13: 109–21.

Betsill, Michele M. 2014. "Transnational Actors in International Environmental Politics." In *Advances in International Environmental Politics*, eds. Michele M. Betsill, Kathryn Hochstetler, and Dimitris Stevis. New York, NY: Palgrave Macmillan, pp. 185–210.

Betsill, Michele M., Kathryn Hochstetler, and Dimitris Stevis, eds. 2014. *Advances in International Environmental Politics.* 2nd edn. New York, NY: Palgrave Macmillan.

Blaikie, Piers, Terry Cannon, Ian Davis, and Ben Wisner. 1994. *At Risk: Natural Hazards, People's Vulnerability and Disasters.* New York, NY: Routledge.

Boserup, Ester. 1992. *The Conditions of Agricultural Growth: The Economics of Agrarian Change under Population Pressure.* New York, NY: Earthscan.

Bowser, Gillian. 2015. "Ambition, Transparency and Differentiation: Women at the COP21." http://www.huffingtonpost.com/gillian-bowser/ambition-transparency-and_b_8821966.html.

Brack, Duncan. 2002. "Combatting International Environmental Crime." *Global Environmental Change.* 12: 143–7.

Bradshaw, Sarah. 2015. "Engendering Development and Disasters." *Disasters.* 39(1): 54–75.

Brand, Christian, and Brenda Boardman. 2008. "Taming of the Few: The Unequal Distribution of Greenhouse Gas Emissions from Personal Travel in the UK." *Energy Policy.* 36: 224–38.

Braun, Yvonne A., and Assitan Sylla Traore. 2015. "Plastic Bags, Pollution, and Identity: Women and the Gendering of Globalization and Environmental Responsibility in Mali." *Gender and Society.* 29(6): 863–87.

Bretherton, Charlotte. 1998. "Global Environmental Politics: Putting Gender on the Agenda?" *Review of International Studies.* 24(1): 85–100.

Bretherton, Charlotte. 2003. "Movements, Networks, Hierarchies: A Gender Perspective on Global Environmental Governance." *Global Environmental Politics.* 3(2): 103–19.

Briggs, Laura. 2010. "The Pill in Puerto Rico and Mainland United States: Negotiating Discourses of Risk and Decolonization." In

Governing the Female Body: Gender, Health, and Networks of Power, eds. Lori Reed and Paula Saukko. Albany, NY: SUNY Press, pp. 159–85.

Brockington, Dan. 2002. *Fortress Conservation: The Preservation of the Mkomazi Game Reserve, Tanzania.* Indianapolis, IN: Indiana University Press.

Brown, Phil. 2007. *Toxic Exposures: Contested Illnesses and the Environmental Health Movement.* New York, NY: Columbia University Press.

Brown Weiss, Edith. 1989. *In Fairness to Future Generations: International Law, Common Patrimony, and Intergenerational Equity.* Dobbs Ferry, NY: Transnational.

Brown Weiss, Edith. 1992. "In Fairness to Future Generations and Sustainable Development." *American University International Law Review.* 8(1): 19–26.

Buckingham, Susan. 2004. "Ecofeminism in the Twenty-First Century." *Geographical Journal.* 170(2): 146–54.

Buckingham, Susan, and Rakibe Kulcur. 2009. "Gendered Geographies of Environmental Injustice." *Antipode.* 41(4): 659–83.

Buckingham, Susan, Dory Reeves, and Anna Batchelor. 2005. "Wasting Women: The Environmental Justice of Including Women in Municipal Waste Management." *Local Environment: The International Journal of Justice and Sustainability.* 10(4): 427–44.

Bullard, Robert D. 1990. *Dumping in Dixie: Race, Class, and Environmental Quality.* Boulder, CO: Westview Press.

Bullard, Robert D. 2005. "Environmental Justice in the Twenty-First Century." In *The Quest for Environmental Justice: Human Rights and the Politics of Pollution*, ed. Robert D. Bullard. San Francisco, CA: Sierra Club Books, pp. 19–42.

Bullard, Robert D., and Damu Smith. 2005. "Women Warriors of Color on the Front Line." In *The Quest for Environmental Justice*, ed. Robert D. Bullard. San Francisco, CA: Sierra Club Books, pp. 62–84.

Bunch, Charlotte. 1987. *Passionate Politics: Feminist Theory in Action.* New York, NY: St. Martin's Press.

Burke, Jason. 2014. "India's Population Policies, Including Female Sterilisation, Beset by Problems." *Guardian.* http://www.theguardian.com/world/2014/nov/13/india-population-growth-policy-problems-sterilisation-incentives-coercion.

Buzan, Barry, and Lene Hansen. 2009. *The Evolution of International Security Studies.* New York, NY: Cambridge University Press.

Buzan, Barry, Ole Wæver, and Jaap de Wilde. 1998. *Security: A New Framework for Analysis.* Boulder, CO: Lynne Rienner.

Cairns, Rose, and Andy Stirling. 2014. "'Maintaining Planetary Systems' or 'Concentrating Global Power?' High Stakes in Contending Framings of Climate Geoengineering." *Global Environmental Change*. 28: 25–38.

Carson, Rachel. 1962. *Silent Spring*. New York, NY: Houghton Mifflin.

Casey, Emma, and Lydia Martens, eds. 2007. *Gender and Consumption: Domestic Cultures and the Commercialisation of Everyday Life*. New York, NY: Ashgate.

Chamberlain, Gethin. 2012. "UK Aid Helps to Fund Forced Sterilisation of India's Poor." *Guardian*. http://www.theguardian.com/world/2012/apr/15/uk-aid-forced-sterilisation-india.

Chant, Sylvia. 2008. "The 'Feminisation of Poverty' and the 'Feminisation' of Anti-Poverty Programmes: Room for Revision?" *Journal of Development Studies*. 44(2): 165–97.

Chasek, Pamela S., David L. Downie, and Janet Welsh Brown. 2006. *Global Environmental Politics*. 4th edn. Cambridge, MA: Westview Press.

Chawla, Prabhu. 2014. "Blame Family Planning Anathema on Those Who Have Made It a Protocol of Tragedy." *New Indian Express*. http://www.newindianexpress.com/prabhu_chawla/columns/Blame-Family-Planning-Anathema-on-Those-Who-Have-Made-It-a-Protocol-of-Tragedy/2014/11/16/article2524955.ece.

Choucri, Nazli. 1974. *Population Dynamics and International Violence*. Lexington, MA: Lexington Books.

Christian Aid. 2007. "Human Tide: The Real Migration Crisis." http://reliefweb.int/sites/reliefweb.int/files/resources/47F1DFB56 96BEE43C12572DB0035D16A-Full_Report.pdf.

Clapp, Jennifer. 2012. *Food*. Malden, MA: Polity.

Clapp, Jennifer, and Linda Swanston. 2009. "Doing Away with Plastic Shopping Bags: International Patterns of Norm Emergence and Policy Implementation." *Environmental Politics*. 18(3): 315–32.

Clements, Ben. 2012. "The Sociological and Attitudinal Bases of Environmentally-Related Beliefs and Behaviour in Britain." *Environmental Politics*. 21(6): 901–21.

Coleman, Eric A., and Esther Mwangi. 2013. "Women's Participation in Forest Management: A Cross-Country Analysis." *Global Environmental Change*. 23(1): 193–205.

Collinson, Patrick, and Adam Vaughan. 2016. "UK Consumes Far Less Than a Decade Ago – 'Peak Stuff' or Something Else?" *Guardian*. http://www.theguardian.com/uk-news/2016/feb/29/uk-consumes-far-less-ons-crops-energy-metals-average-material-consumption.

Commission of the European Communities. 2008. "Communication from the Commission to the European Parliament, the Council, the European Economic and Social Committee and the Committee of the Regions on the Sustainable Consumption and Production and Sustainable Industrial Policy Action Plan." http://eur-lex.europa.eu/legal-content/EN/TXT/PDF/?uri=CELEX:52008DC0397&from=EN.

Conca, Ken. 2012. "Environmental Human Rights: Greening 'The Dignity and Worth of the Human Person'." In *Handbook of Global Environmental Politics*, ed. Peter Dauvergne. Northampton, MA: Edward Elgar, pp. 403–18.

Connelly, Matthew. 2006. "Population Control in India: Prologue to the Emergency Period." *Population and Development Review*. 32(4): 629–67.

Coole, Diana. 2013. "Too Many Bodies? The Return and Disavowal of the Population Question." *Environmental Politics*. 22(2): 195–215.

Cooper, David, and Joy Palmer, eds. 1995. *Just Environments: Intergenerational, International and Inter-Species Issues.* New York, NY: Routledge.

Corburn, Jason. 2005. *Street Science: Community Knowledge and Environmental Health Justice.* Cambridge, MA: MIT Press.

Corry, Olaf. 2012. "Securitisation and 'Riskification': Second-Order Security and the Politics of Climate Change." *Millennium: Journal of International Studies*. 40(2): 235–58.

Côté, Isabelle M., and Emily S. Darling. 2010. "Rethinking Ecosystem Resilience in the Face of Climate Change." *PLoS Biology* 8(7).

Crenshaw, Kimberlé. 1989. "Demarginalizing the Intersection of Race and Sex: A Black Feminist Critique of Antidiscrimination Doctrine, Feminist Theory and Antiracist Politics." *University of Chicago Legal Forum* 140: 139–67.

Crenshaw, Kimberlé. 1994. "Mapping the Margins: Intersectionality, Identity Politics, and Violence Against Women of Color." In *The Public Nature of Private Violence*, eds. M. A. Fineman and R. Mykitiul. New York, NY: Routledge, pp. 93–120.

Crist, Eileen, and Philip Cafaro. 2012. *Life on the Brink: Environmentalists Confront Overpopulation.* Athens, GA: University of Georgia Press.

Cuff, Madeleine. 2016. "Survey: British Public among the Least Concerned about Climate Change." *Guardian*. http://www.theguardian.com/environment/2016/feb/01/survey-british-public-among-the-least-concerned-about-climate-change.

Cutter, Susan L. 1995. "The Forgotten Casualties: Women, Children, and Environmental Change." *Global Environmental Change*. 5(3): 181–94.

Dalby, Simon. 2009. *Security and Environmental Change*. Malden, MA: Polity.

Dalby, Simon. 2013. "Environmental Dimensions of Human Security." In *Environmental Security: Approaches and Issues*, eds. Rita Floyd and Richard A. Matthew. New York, NY: Routledge, pp. 121–38.

Daley, Shannon. 2013. "Closing the Gap between Law and Reality: Women's Constitutional Rights in Afghanistan." *Connecticut Journal of International Law*. 29: 329.

Dankelman, Irene. 2002. "Climate Change: Learning from Gender Analysis and Women's Experiences of Organising for Sustainable Development." In *Gender, Development, and Climate Change*, ed. Rachel Masika. Oxford, UK: Oxfam GB, pp. 21–9.

Dankelman, Irene. 2010. *Gender and Climate Change: An Introduction*. Sterling, VA: Earthscan.

Dauvergne, Peter. 2005. "Dying of Consumption: Accidents or Sacrifices of Global Morality?" *Global Environmental Politics*. 5(3): 35–47.

Dauvergne, Peter. 2008. *The Shadows of Consumption: Consequences for the Global Environment*. Cambridge, MA: MIT Press.

Dauvergne, Peter. 2010. "The Problem of Consumption." *Global Environmental Politics*. 10(2): 1–10.

Dauvergne, Peter, and Jennifer Clapp. 2016. "Researching Global Environmental Politics in the 21st Century." *Global Environmental Politics*. 16(1): 1–12.

Dauvergne, Peter, and Jane Lister. 2013. *Eco-Business: A Big-Brand Takeover of Sustainability*. Cambridge, MA: MIT Press.

Davidson, Mélanie Josée, and Catherine Krull. 2011. "Adapting to Cuba's Shifting Food Landscapes: Women's Strategies of Resistance." *Cuban Studies*. 42: 59–77.

Deda, Paola, and Renata Rubian. 2004. "Women and Biodiversity: The Long Journey from Users to Policy-Makers." *Natural Resources Forum*. 28(3): 201–4.

Deere, C. D., A. D. Oduro, H. Swaminathan, and C. Doss. 2013. "Property Rights and the Gender Distribution of Wealth in Ecuador, Ghana, and India." *Journal of Economic Inequality*. 11(2): 249–65.

Deligiannis, Tom. 2013. "The Evolution of Qualitative Environment-Conflict Research: Moving Towards Consensus." In *Environmental Security: Approaches and Issues*, eds. Rita Floyd and Richard A. Matthew. New York, NY: Routledge. pp. 36–63.

de Soysa, Indra. 2013. "Environmental Security and the Resource Curse." In *Environmental Security: Approaches and Issues*, eds. Rita Floyd and Richard A. Matthew. New York, NY: Routledge, pp. 64–81.

Detraz, Nicole. 2012. *International Security and Gender*. Malden, MA: Polity.

Detraz, Nicole. 2014. *Environmental Security and Gender*. New York, NY: Routledge.

Detraz, Nicole, and Michele M. Betsill. 2009. "Climate Change and Environmental Security: For Whom the Discourse Shifts." *International Studies Perspectives*. 10(3): 304–21.

Detraz, Nicole, and Dursun Peksen. 2016. "The Effect of IMF Programs on Women's Economic and Political Rights." *International Interactions*, 42(1): 81–105.

Detraz, Nicole, and Leah Windsor. 2014. "Evaluating Climate Migration: Population Movement, Insecurity and Gender." *International Feminist Journal of Politics*. 16(1): 127–46.

Deudney, Daniel. 1990. "The Case Against Linking Environmental Degradation and National Security." *Millennium: Journal of International Studies*. 19(3): 461–76.

Di Chiro, Giovanna. 2015. "A New Spelling of Sustainability: Engaging Feminist-Environmental Justice Theory and Practice." In *Practising Feminist Political Ecologies: Moving Beyond the "Green Economy,"* eds. Wendy Harcourt and Ingrid L. Nelson. London, UK: Zed Books, pp. 211–37.

Donner, William, and Havidán Rodríguez. 2008. "Population Composition, Migration and Inequality: The Influence of Demographic Changes on Disaster Risk and Vulnerability." *Social Forces*. 87(2): 1089–114.

Döös, Bo R. 2002. "Population Growth and Loss of Arable Land." *Global Environmental Change*. 12: 303–11.

Dove, Michael R. 2006. "Indigenous People and Environmental Politics." *Annual Review of Anthropology*. 35: 191–208.

Doyle, Timothy. 2005. *Environmental Movements in Minority and Majority Worlds: A Global Perspective*. New Brunswick, NJ: Rutgers University Press.

Dresner, Simon. 2008. *The Principles of Sustainability*. Sterling, VA: Earthscan.

Dryzek, John S. 2003. *Green States and Social Movements: Environmentalism in the United States, United Kingdom, Germany, & Norway*. New York, NY: Oxford University Press.

Dryzek, John S. 2005. *The Politics of the Earth: Environmental Discourses*. 2nd edn. New York, NY: Oxford University Press.

Eakin, Hallie, and Maggie L. Walser. 2007. "Human Vulnerability to Global Environmental Change." In *Encyclopedia of Earth*, ed.

C. J. Cleveland. Washington, DC: Environmental Information Coalition, National Council for Science and the Environment. https://eoearthlive.wordpress.com/article/Human_vulnerability_to_global_environmental_change.

Eaton, Heather, and Lois Ann Lorentzen, eds. 2003. *Ecofeminism and Globalization: Exploring Culture, Context, and Religion.* New York, NY: Rowman & Littlefield.

Eckersley, Robyn. 2004. *The Green State: Rethinking Democracy and Sovereignty.* Cambridge, MA: MIT Press.

Eckersley, Robyn. 2007. "Ecological Intervention: Prospects and Limits." *Ethics and International Affairs.* 21(3): 293–316.

Ehrlich, Paul. 1968. *The Population Bomb.* Cutchogue, NY: Buccaneer Books.

Ekins, Paul. 2000. *Economic Growth and Environmental Sustainability: The Prospects for Green Growth.* New York, NY: Routledge.

Elborgh-Woytek, Katrin, et al. 2013. "Women, Work, and the Economy: Macroeconomic Gains from Gender Equity." http://www.imf.org/external/pubs/ft/sdn/2013/sdn1310.pdf.

Elliott, Lorraine. 2006. "Cosmopolitan Environmental Harm Conventions." *Global Society.* 20(3): 345–63.

Elmhirst, Rebecca. 2011. "Introducing New Feminist Political Ecologies." *Geoforum.* 42(2): 129–32.

Elson, Diane. 2014. "Economic Crises from the 1980s to the 2010s: A Gender Analysis." In *New Frontiers in Feminist Political Economy*, eds. Shirin Rai and Georgina Waylen. New York, NY: Routledge, pp. 189–212.

Elson, Diane, and Tonia Warnecke. 2011. "IMF Policies and Gender Orders: The Case of the Poverty Reduction and Growth Facility." In *Questioning Financial Governance from a Feminist Perspective*, eds. Brigitte Young, Isabella Bakker, and Diane Elson. New York, NY: Routledge, pp. 110–31.

Emmott, Stephen. 2015. "Though Climate Change Is a Crisis, the Population Threat Is Even Worse." *Guardian.* http://www.the-guardian.com/commentisfree/2015/dec/04/climate-change-population-crisis-paris-summit.

Enarson, Elaine. 2012. *Women Confronting Natural Disaster: From Vulnerability to Resilience.* Boulder, CO: Lynne Rienner.

Enarson, Elaine, and Lourdes Meyreles. 2004. "International Perspectives on Gender and Disaster: Differences and Possibilities." *International Journal of Sociology and Social Policy.* 24(10/11): 49–93.

Enloe, Cynthia. 2004. *The Curious Feminist: Searching for Women in a New Age of Empire.* Berkeley, CA: University of California Press.

Enloe, Cynthia. 2007. *Globalization and Militarism: Feminists Make the Link*. New York, NY: Rowman & Littlefield.

EPA. 2014. "Polychlorinated Biphenyls (PCBs)." http://www.epa.gov/wastes/hazard/tsd/pcbs/about.htm.

EU. 2009. "Strategy for Sustainable Development." http://eur-lex.europa.eu/legal-content/EN/TXT/?uri=URISERV%3Al28117.

European Commission. 2016. "Sustainable Development." http://ec.europa.eu/environment/eussd.

European Environment Agency. 2012. "Unsustainable Consumption: The Mother of All Environmental Issues?" http://www.eea.europa.eu/highlights/unsustainable-consumption-2013-the-mother .

Evershed, Nick. 2015. "Australia's Population Growth Rate Reaches Lowest Point in Almost 10 Years." *Guardian*. http://www.theguardian.com/news/datablog/2015/sep/25/australias-population-growth-rate-reaches-lowest-point-in-almost-10-years.

Fan, Mei-Fang. 2006. "Environmental Justice and Nuclear Waste Conflicts in Taiwan." *Environmental Politics*. 15(3): 417–34.

FAO. 2006a. "Livestock's Long Shadow: Environmental." ftp://ftp.fao.org/docrep/fao/010/a0701e/a0701e.pdf.

FAO. 2006b. "The Right to Food in Practice: Implementation at the National Level." http://www.fao.org/docrep/016/ah189e/ah189e.pdf.

FAO. 2011. "Climate Change, Water and Food Security." http://www.fao.org/docrep/014/i2096e/i2096e.pdf.

FAO. 2012. "FAO Statistical Yearbook 2012." http://www.fao.org/economic/ess/ess-publications/ess-yearbook/yearbook2012/en.

Federici, Silvia. 2009. "The Devaluation of Women's Labour." In *Eco-Sufficiency and Global Justice: Women Write Political Ecology*, ed. Ariel Salleh. New York, NY: Pluto Press, pp. 43–65.

Fisher, Monica, and Edward R. Carr. 2015. "The Influence of Gendered Roles and Responsibilities on the Adoption of Technologies that Mitigate Drought Risk: The Case of Drought-Tolerant Maize Seed in Eastern Uganda." *Global Environmental Change*. 35: 82–92.

Floyd, Rita, and Richard A. Matthew, eds. 2013. *Environmental Security: Approaches and Issues*. New York, NY: Routledge.

Ford, Robert E., and Kim T. Adamson. 1995. "The Population–Environment Nexus and Vulnerability Assessment in Africa." *GeoJournal*. 35(2): 207–16.

Foreman, Dave, and Laura Carroll. 2015. *Man Swarm: How Overpopulation is Killing the Wild World*. New York, NY: LiveTrue Books.

Fothergill, Alice. 2004. *Heads Above Water: Gender, Class, and Family in the Grand Forks Flood*. New York, NY: SUNY Press.

Fuchs, Doris A., and Sylvia Lorek. 2005. "Sustainable Consumption Governance: A History of Promises and Failures." *Journal of Consumer Policy.* 28(3): 261–88.

Fukuda-Parr, Sakiko. 2015. "Re-Framing Food Security as if Gender Equality and Sustainability Mattered." In *Gender Equality and Sustainable Development,* ed. Melissa Leach. New York, NY: Earthscan, pp. 82–104.

Fulfer, Katy. 2013. "The Capabilities Approach to Justice and the Flourishing of Nonsentient Life." *Ethics and the Environment.* 18(1): 19–38.

Gaard, Greta. 1998. *Ecological Politics: Ecofeminists and the Greens.* Philadelphia, PA: Temple University Press.

Gaard, Greta. 2011. "Ecofeminism Revisited: Rejecting Essentialism and Re-Placing Species in a Material Feminist Environmentalism." *Feminist Formations.* 23(2): 26–53.

Gaard, Greta. 2015. "Ecofeminism and Climate Change." *Women's Studies International Forum.* 49: 20–33.

Gaarder, Emily. 2011. "Where the Boys Aren't: The Predominance of Women in Animal Rights Activism." *Feminist Formations.* 23(2): 54–76.

Gender and Water Alliance. 2006. "Bangladesh: Gender Mainstreaming Processes in Community-Based Flood Risk Management." http://www.genderandwater.org/page/5839.

GenderCC. 2011. "A Closer Look at the Numbers: GenderCC Discussion Paper on Population Growth, Climate Change and Gender." http://www.gendercc.net/fileadmin/inhalte/Dokumente/ UNFCCC_conferences/COP17/GenderCC_discussion_paper_ on_population_-_FINAL.pdf.

GenderCC. 2012. "Gender and Climate Change Activities at COP 18- Doha 2012." *Gender CC.* http://gendercc.net/genderunfccc/ unfccc-conferences/doha-2012.html.

GenderCC. 2015. "A Reality Check on the Paris Agreement from the Women and Gender Constituency." http://gendercc.net/genderunfccc/unfccc-conferences/paris-2015.html.

Ghodsee, Kristen. 2007. "Potions, Lotions and Lipstick: The Gendered Consumption of Cosmetics and Perfumery in Socialist and Post-Socialist Urban Bulgaria." *Women's Studies International Forum.* 30: 26–39.

Gleditsch, Nils Petter. 2012. "Whither the Weather? Climate Change and Conflict." *Journal of Peace Research.* 49(1): 3–9.

Glenn, Evelyn Nakano. 2008. "Yearning for Lightness: Transnational Circuits in the Marketing and Consumption of Skin Lighteners." *Gender and Society.* 22(3): 281–302.

Goldstone, Jack A. 1991. *Revolution and Rebellion in the Early Modern World.* Berkeley, CA: University of California Press.

Goldsworthy, Heather. 2010. "Women, Global Environmental Change, and Human Security." In *Global Environmental Change and Human Security*, eds. Richard A. Matthew, et al. Cambridge, MA: MIT Press, pp. 215–36.

Gosine, Andil. 2005. "Dying Planet, Deadly People: 'Race'-Sex Anxieties and Alternative Globalizations." *Social Justice*. 32(4): 69–86.

Gottlieb, Robert. 2005. *Forcing the Spring: The Transformation of the American Environmental Movement*. Washington, DC: Island Press.

Graeger, Nina. 1996. "Environmental Security?" *Journal of Peace Research* 33(1): 109–16.

Guha, Ramachandra, and Joan Martinez-Alier. 1997. *Varieties of Environmentalism: Essays North and South*. London, UK: Earthscan.

Guha-Sapir, Debarati, Philippe Hoyois, and Regina Below. 2015. "Annual Disaster Statistical Review 2014: The Numbers and Trends." http://cred.be/sites/default/files/ADSR_2014.pdf.

Guzmán, José Miguel, George Martine, Gordon McGranahan, Daniel Schensul, et al., eds. 2009. *Population Dynamics and Climate Change*. New York: NY: UNFPA.

Hajer, Maarten. 1995. *The Politics of Environmental Discourse: Ecological Modernization and the Policy Process*. London, UK: Oxford University Press.

Happaerts, Sander, and Hans Bruyninckx. 2014. "Sustainable Development: Institutionalization of a Contested Policy Concept." In *Advances in International Environmental Politics*, eds. Michele M. Betsill, Kathryn Hochstetler, and Dimitris Stevis. New York, NY: Palgrave Macmillan, pp. 300–327.

Harcourt, Wendy, ed. 1994. *Feminist Perspectives on Sustainable Development*. Atlantic Highlands, NJ: Zed Books.

Harcourt, Wendy, and Ingrid L. Nelson, eds. 2015. *Practising Feminist Political Ecologies: Moving Beyond the "Green Economy."* London, UK: Zed Books.

Hardin, Garrett. 1968. "The Tragedy of the Commons." *Science*. December 13: 1243–8.

Harding, Sandra. 1991. *Whose Science? Whose Knowledge? Thinking from Women's Lives*. Ithaca, NY: Cornell University Press.

Harding, Sandra. 1993. *The Science Question in Feminism*. Ithaca, NY: Cornell University Press.

Harris, Paul G., and Jonathan Symons. 2013. "Norm Conflict in Climate Governance: Greenhouse Gas Accounting and the Problem of Consumption." *Global Environmental Politics*. 13(1): 9–29.

Hartmann, Betsy. 1995. *Reproductive Rights and Wrongs: The Global Politics of Population Control*. Boston, MA: South End Press.

Hartmann, Betsy. 1999. "Population, Environment, and Security: A New Trinity." In *Dangerous Intersections: Feminist Perspectives on Population, Environment, and Development*, eds. Jael Silliman and Ynestra King. Cambridge, MA: South End Press, pp. 1–23.

Hartmann, Betsy. 2010. "Rethinking Climate Refugees and Climate Conflict: Rhetoric, Reality and the Politics of Policy Discourse." *Journal of International Development*. 22(2): 233–46.

Hartmann, Betsy, Anne Hendrixson, and Jade Sasser. 2015. "Population, Sustainable Development and Gender Equality." In *Gender Equality and Sustainable Development*, ed. Melissa Leach. New York: Routledge, pp. 56–81.

Hartmann, Betsy, and Hilary Standing. 1985. *Food, Saris and Sterilization: Population Control in Bangladesh*. London, UK: Bangladesh International Action Group.

Hartmann, Betsy, Banu Subramaniam, and Charles Zerner, eds. 2005. *Making Threats: Biofears and Environmental Anxieties*. New York: Rowman & Littlefield.

Harvard Humanitarian Initiative. 2015. "Resources and Resourcefulness: Gender, Conflict, and Artisanal Mining Communities in Eastern Democratic Republic of the Congo." http://www-wds. worldbank.org/external/default/WDSContentServer/WDSP/IB/2 015/04/24/090224b082e03858/1_0/Rendered/PDF/Resources0and00epublic0of0the0Congo.pdf.

Harvey, Fiona. 2015. "COP21 is Too Male Dominated and Has Male Priorities, Says UN Special Envoy." *Guardian*. http://www. theguardian.com/environment/2015/dec/08/cop21-is-too-male-dominated-and-has-male-priorities-says-un-special-envoy.

Hawkins, Roberta, and Diana Ojeda. 2011. "Gender and Environment: Critical Tradition and New Challenges." *Environment and Planning D: Society and Space*. 29: 237–53.

Headey, Derek, and Shenggen Fan. 2010. "Reflections on the Global Food Crisis." http://ebrary.ifpri.org/utils/getfile/collection/p15738coll2/id/5724/filename/5725.pdf.

Hemmati, Minu, and Ulrike Röhr. 2009. "Engendering the Climate-Change Negotiations: Experiences, Challenges, and Steps Forward." *Gender and Development*. 17(1): 19–32.

Holdren, John P., and Paul R. Ehrlich. 1974. "Human Population and the Global Environment: Population Growth, Rising Per Capita Material Consumption, and Disruptive Technologies Have Made Civilization a Global Ecological Force." *American Scientist*. 62: 282–92.

Homer-Dixon, Thomas. 1991. "On the Threshold: Environmental Changes as Causes of Acute Conflict." *International Security* 16(2): 76–116.

Homer-Dixon, Thomas. 1999. *Environment, Scarcity, and Violence.* Princeton, NJ: Princeton University Press.

Hopwood, Bill, Mary Mellor, and Geoff O'Brien. 2005. "Sustainable Development: Mapping Different Approaches." *Sustainable Development.* 13: 38–52.

Hultgren, John. 2015. *Border Walls Gone Green: Nature and Anti-Immigrant Politics in America.* Minneapolis, MN: University of Minnesota Press.

Human Rights Watch. 2012. "India: Target-Driven Sterilization Harming Women." *Human Rights Watch.* https://www.hrw.org/news/2012/07/12/india-target-driven-sterilization-harming-women.

Hunter, Lori M. 2005. "Migration and Environmental Hazards." *Population and Environment.* 26(4): 273–302.

Huppert, Herbert E., and R. Stephen J. Sparks. 2006. "Extreme Natural Hazards: Population Growth, Globalization and Environmental Change." *Philosophical Transactions of the Royal Society A.* 364: 1875–88.

ICISS. 2001. *The Responsibility to Protect: Report of the International Commission on Intervention and State Sovereignty.* Ottawa, Canada: International Development Research Centre. http://www.iciss.ca/pdf/Commission-Report.pdf.

IFPRI. 2015. "Global Hunger Index: Armed Conflict and the Challenge of Hunger." http://ebrary.ifpri.org/utils/getfile/collection/p15738coll2/id/129681/filename/129892.pdf.

Ikeme, Jekwu. 2003. "Equity, Environmental Justice and Sustainability: Incomplete Approaches in Climate Change Politics." *Global Environmental Change.* 13: 195–206.

IPCC. 2012. "Managing the Risks of Extreme Events and Disasters to Advance Climate Change Adaptation." http://www.ipcc-wg2.gov/SREX/images/uploads/SREX-All_FINAL.pdf.

IPCC. 2014. "Climate Change 2014 Synthesis Report: Summary for Policymakers." http://ipcc.ch/pdf/assessment-report/ar5/syr/AR5_SYR_FINAL_SPM.pdf.

IUCN. 1980. "World Conservation Strategy: Living Resource Conservation for Sustainable Development." https://portals.iucn.org/library/efiles/html/WCS-004/cover.html.

Ivanova, Maria. 2015. "COP21: Why More Women Need Seats at the Table." http://www.cnn.com/2015/11/23/opinions/cop21-women-need-participate.

Jackson, Tim. 2009. "Prosperity Without Growth? The Transition to a Sustainable Economy." http://www.sd-commission.org.uk/data/files/publications/prosperity_without_growth_report.pdf.

Jaggar, Alison M. 2014. "Gender and Global Justice: Rethinking Some Basic Assumptions of Western Political Philosophy." In *Gender and Global Justice*, ed. Alison M. Jaggar. Malden, MA: Polity, pp. 1–17.

Johnson, Jane M. F., Alan J. Franzluebbers, Sharon Lachnicht Weyers, and Donald C. Reicosky. 2007. "Agricultural Opportunities to Mitigate Greenhouse Gas Emissions." *Environmental Pollution*. 150(1): 107–24.

Johnson, McKenzie F., et al. 2014. "Network Environmentalism: Citizen Scientists as Agents for Environmental Advocacy." *Global Environmental Change*. 29: 235–45.

Johnsson-Latham, Gerd. 2006. "Initial Study of Lifestyles, Consumption Patterns, Sustainable Development and Gender: Do Women Leave a Smaller Ecological Footprint than Men?" http://www.government.se/content/1/c6/06/72/73/1bd9aa9c.pdf.

Johnsson-Latham, Gerd. 2007. "A Study on Gender Equality as a Prerequisite for Sustainable Development." http://www.atria.nl/epublications/2007/study_on_gender_equality_as_a_prerequisite_for_sustainable_development.pdf.

Johnstone, Barbara. 2002. *Discourse Analysis*. New York: Blackwell.

Jorgenson, Andrew K., Brett Clark, and Jeffrey Kentor. 2010. "Militarization and the Environment: A Panel Study of Carbon Dioxide Emissions and the Ecological Footprints of Nations, 1970–2000." *Global Environmental Politics*. 10(1): 7–29.

Juran, Luke. 2012. "The Gendered Nature of Disasters: Women Survivors in Post-Tsunami Tamil Nadu." *Indian Journal of Gender Studies*. 19(1): 1–29.

Kaplan, Robert D. 1994. "The Coming Anarchy." *Atlantic Monthly*. February. http://www.theatlantic.com/magazine/archive/1994/02/the-coming-anarchy/4670.

Karlsson, Sylvia, Tanja Srebotnjak, and Patricia Gonzales. 2007. "Understanding the North–South Knowledge Divide and Its Implications for Policy: A Quantitative Analysis of the Generation of Scientific Knowledge in the Environmental Sciences." *Environmental Science and Policy*. 10(7–8): 668–84.

Keller, Ann Campbell. 2009. *Science in Environmental Policy: The Politics of Objective Advice*. Cambridge, MA: MIT Press.

Kerr, Rachel Bezner. 2005. "Food Security in Northern Malawi: Gender, Kinship Relations and Entitlements in Historical Context." *Journal of Southern African Studies*. 31(1): 53–74.

King, Ynestra. 1995. "Engendering a Peaceful Planet: Ecology, Economy, and Ecofeminism in Contemporary Context." *Women's Studies Quarterly*. 23: 15–21.

Klein, Julia A., et al. 2014. "Unexpected Climate Impacts on the Tibetab Plateau: Local and Scientific Knowledge in Findings of Delayed Summer." *Global Environmental Change*. 28: 141–52.

Knapp, Eli J., Dennis Rentsch, Jennifer Schmitt, Claire Lewis, et al. 2010. "A Tale of Three Villages: Choosing an Effective Method for Assessing Poaching Levels in Western Serengeti, Tanzania." *Oryx: The International Journal of Conservation*. 44(2): 178–84.

Koizumi, Tatsuji. 2014. "Biofuels and Food Security." In *Biofuels and Food Security: Biofuel Impact on Food Security in Brazil, Asia and Major Producing Countries*, ed. Tatsuji Koizumi. Cham: Springer, pp. 103–21. http://dx.doi.org/10.1007/978-3-319-05645-6_7.

Krause, Keith, and Michael C. Williams. 1996. "Broadening the Agenda of Security Studies: Politics and Methods." *Mershon International Studies Review*. 40(2): 229–54.

Kronsell, Annica. 2013. "Gender and Transition in Climate Governance." *Environmental Innovation and Societal Transitions*. 7: 1–15.

Kuran, Timur, and Edward J. McCaffery. 2008. "Sex Differences in the Acceptability of Discrimination." *Political Research Quarterly*. 61(2): 228–38.

Laestadius, Linnea I., Roni A. Neff, Colleen Barry, and Shannon Frattaroli. 2014. "'We Don't Tell People What to Do': An Examination of the Factors Influencing NGO Decisions to Campaign for Reduced Meat Consumption in Light of Climate Change." *Global Environmental Change*. 29: 32–40.

Lather, Patti. 1991. *Getting Smart: Feminist Research and Pedagogy with/in the Postmodern*. New York, NY: Routledge.

Lavelle, Marianne, and Marcia Coyle. 1992. "Unequal Protection: The Racial Divide in Environmental Law (a Special Investigation)." *National Law Journal*. 15(3): 52–4.

Leach, Melissa, Lyla Mehta, and Preetha Prabhakaran. 2015. "Sustainable Development: A Gendered Pathways Approach." In *Gender Equality and Sustainable Development*, ed. Melissa Leach. New York, NY: Routledge, pp. 1–33.

Lekhi, Rohit, and Peter Newell. 2006. "Environmental Injustice, Law and Accountability." In *Rights, Resources and the Politics of Accountability*, eds. Peter Newell and Joanna Wheeler. New York, NY: Zed Books, pp. 186–204.

Lewis, Tania, and Emily Potter, eds. 2011. *Ethical Consumption: A Critical Introduction*. New York, NY: Routledge.

Lipschutz, Ronnie D. 2009. "The Sustainability Debate: Déjà Vu All Over Again?" *Global Environmental Politics*. 9(4): 136–41.

Litfin, Karen T. 1999. "Constructing Environmental Security and Ecological Interdependence." *Global Governance.* 5(3): 359–78.

Litfin, Karen T. 2012. "Thinking Like a Planet: Gaian Politics and the Transformation of the World Food System." In *Handbook of Global Environmental Politics*, ed. Peter Dauvergne. Northampton, MA: Edward Elgar, pp. 419–30.

Littler, Jo. 2011. "What's Wrong with Ethical Consumption?" In *Ethical Consumption: A Critical Introduction*, eds. Tania Lewis and Emily Potter. New York, NY: Routledge, pp. 27–39.

Liverman, Diana M. 2001. "Vulnerability to Global Environmental Change." In *Global Environmental Risk*, eds. J. X. Kasperson and R. E. Kasperson. Tokyo, Japan: UN University, pp. 201–16.

Low, Nicholas, and Brendan Gleeson. 1998. *Justice, Society and Nature: An Exploration of Political Ecology.* New YorkY: Routledge.

Lykke, Nina. 2009. "Non-Innocent Intersections of Feminism and Environmentalism." *Women, Gender and Research.* 18: 36–44.

MacDonald, Rhona. 2005. "How Women Were Affected by the Tsunami: A Perspective from Oxfam." *Public Library of Science Medicine.* 2(6): 474–5.

MacGregor, Sherilyn. 2004. "From Care to Citizenship: Calling Ecofeminism Back to Politics." *Ethics and the Environment.* 9(1): 56–84.

MacGregor, Sherilyn. 2006. *Beyond Mothering Earth: Ecological Citizenship and the Politics of Care.* Toronto, Canada: UBC Press.

MacGregor, Sherilyn. 2009. "A Stranger Silence Still: The Need for Feminist Social Research on Climate Change." *Sociological Review.* 57(2): 124–40.

MacQuarrie, Patrick, and Aaron T. Wolf. 2013. "Understanding Water Security." In *Environmental Security: Approaches and Issues*, eds. Rita Floyd and Richard A. Matthew. New York, NY: Routledge, pp. 169–86.

Madrid, Ashifa Kassam, et al. 2015. "Europe Needs Many More Babies to Avert a Population Disaster." *Guardian.* http://www.theguardian.com/world/2015/aug/23/baby-crisis-europe-brink-depopulation-disaster.

Malthus, Thomas Robert. 2007. *An Essay on the Principle of Population.* Mineola, NY: Dover Publishers.

Maniates, Michael. 2001. "Individualization: Plant a Tree, Buy a Bike, Save the World?" *Global Environmental Politics.* 1(3): 31–52.

Maniates, Michael, and John M. Meyer, eds. 2010. *The Environmental Politics of Sacrifice.* Cambridge, MA: MIT Press.

Mann, Susan A. 2011. "Pioneers of U.S. Ecofeminism and Environmental Justice." *Feminist Formations*. 23(2): 1–25.

Mantilla, Franklina. 2012. "Review of Gender Mainstreaming in UNEP." http://unep.org/eou/Portals/52/Reports/Review%20of%20Gender%20Mainstreaming%20in%20UNEP_final%20report%20with%20annexes.pdf.

Martinez-Alier, Joan. 2002. *The Environmentalism of the Poor: A Study of Ecological Conflicts and Valuation*. Cheltenham, UK: Edward Elgar.

Martinez-Alier, Joan. 2014. "The Environmentalism of the Poor." *Geoforum*. 54: 239–41.

Martinez-Alier, Joan, et al. 2014. "Between Activism and Science: Grassroots Concepts for Sustainability Coined by Environmental Justice Organizations." *Journal of Political Ecology*. 21: 19–60.

Mason, Michael. 2008. "The Governance of Transnational Environmental Harm: Addressing New Modes of Accountability/Responsibility." *Global Environmental Politics*. 8(3): 8–24.

Matthew, Richard, Jon Barnett, Bryan McDonald, and Karen L. O'Brien, eds. 2010. *Global Environmental Change and Human Security*. Cambridge, MA: MIT Press.

Matthew, Richard A., and Ted Gaulin. 2002. "The Ecology of Peace." *Peace Review*. 14(1): 33–9.

McCright, Aaron M. 2010. "The Effects of Gender on Climate Change Knowledge and Concern in the American Public." *Population and Environment*. 32(1): 66–87.

McCright, Aaron M., and Riley E. Dunlap. 2011. "Cool Dudes: The Denial of Climate Change Among Conservative White Males in the United States." *Global Environmental Change*. 21: 1163–72.

McCurry, Justin. 2007. "Japanese Minister Wants 'Birth-Giving Machines', aka Women, to Have More Babies." *Guardian*. http://www.theguardian.com/world/2007/jan/29/japan.justinmccurry.

McCurry, Justin. 2015. "Japanese Politician in Sexism Row after Call for Women to Have More Babies." *Guardian*. http://www.theguardian.com/world/2015/sep/30/japanese-politician-yoshihide-suga-in-sexism-row-after-call-for-women-to-have-more-babies.

McDonald, Bryan L. 2010. *Food Security*. Malden, MA: Polity.

McLaughlin, Paul, and Thomas Dietz. 2008. "Structure, Agency and Environment: Toward an Integrated Perspective on Vulnerability." *Global Environmental Change*. 18: 99–111.

McMichael, A. J. 2003. "Global Climate Change: Will It Affect Vector-Borne Infectious Diseases?" *Internal Medicine Journal*. 33: 544–55.

MEA. 2005. "Ecosystems and Human Well-Being." http://www.unep.org/maweb/documents/document.356.aspx.pdf.

Mégret, Frédéric. 2009. "Beyond the 'Salvation' Paradigm: Responsibility to Protect (Others) vs the Power of Protecting Oneself." *Security Dialogue*. 40(6): 575–95.

Mellor, Mary. 2003. "Gender and the Environment." In *Ecofeminism and Globalization: Exploring Culture, Context, and Religion*, eds. Heather Eaton and Lois Ann Lorentzen. New York, NY: Rowman & Littlefield, pp. 11–22.

Merchant, Carolyn. 1996. *Earthcare: Women and the Environment*. New York. NY: Routledge.

Mies, Maria, and Vandana Shiva. 1993. *Ecofeminism*. London, UK: Zed Books.

Mitchell, Gordon, and Danny Dorling. 2003. "An Environmental Justice Analysis of British Air Quality." *Environment and Planning A*. 35: 909–29.

Mohai, Paul, David Pellow, and J. Timmons Roberts. 2009. "Environmental Justice." *Annual Review of Environment and Resources*. 34: 405–30.

Mol, Arthur P. J. 2003. *Globalization and Environmental Reform: The Ecological Modernization of the Global Economy*. Cambridge, MA: MIT Press.

Mosberg, Marianne, and Siri H. Eriksen. 2015. "Responding to Climate Variability and Change in Dryland Kenya: The Role of Illicit Coping Strategies in the Politics of Adaptation." *Global Environmental Change*. 35: 545–57.

Najam, Adil. 2005. "Why Environmental Politics Looks Different from the South." In *Handbook of Global Environmental Politics*, ed. Peter Dauvergne. Northampton, MA: Edward Elgar, pp. 111–26.

Nalbone, Jennifer. 2015. "Unseen Threat: How Microbeads Harm New York Waters, Wildlife, Health and Environment." http://ag.ny.gov/pdfs/Microbeads_Report_5_14_14.pdf.

Nash, Roderick. 2001. *Wilderness and the American Mind*. New Haven, CT: Yale University Press.

Neefjes, Koos. 1999. "Ecological Degradation: A Cause for Conflict, a Concern for Survival." In *Fairness and Futurity: Essays on Environmental Sustainability and Social Justice*, ed. Andrew Dobson. New York, NY: Oxford University Press, pp. 249–78.

Nelson, Jennifer. 2003. *Women of Color and the Reproductive Rights Movement*. New York, NY: New York University Press.

Nelson, Julie A. 2015. "Is Dismissing Environmental Caution the Manly Thing to Do? Gender and the Economics of Environmental Protection." *Ethics and the Environment*. 20(1): 99–122.

Neumayer, Eric, and Thomas Plümper. 2007. "The Gendered Nature of Natural Disasters: The Impact of Catastrophic Events on the Gender Gap in Life Expectance, 1981–2002." *Annals of the Association of American Geographers*. 97(3): 551–66.

Newell, Peter. 2005. "Race, Class and the Global Politics of Environmental Inequality." *Global Environmental Politics*. 5(3): 70–94.

Newell, Peter. 2012. *Globalization and the Environment: Capitalism, Ecology and Power*. Malden, MA: Polity.

Newell, Peter, and Matthew Paterson. 2010. *Climate Capitalism: Global Warming and the Transformation of the Global Economy*. Cambridge, UK: Cambridge University Press.

Nightingale, Andrea. 2006. "The Nature of Gender: Work, Gender, and Environment." *Environment and Planning D: Society and Space*. 24: 165–85.

Nightingale, Andrea. 2011. "Bounding Difference: Intersectionality and the Material Production of Gender, Caste, Class and Environment in Nepal." *Geoforum*. 42(2): 153–62.

Norgaard, Kari, and Richard York. 2005. "Gender Equality and State Environmentalism." *Gender and Society*. 19(4): 506–22.

Nye, Joseph S., and Sean M. Lynn-Jones. 1988. "International Security Studies: A Report of a Conference on the State of the Field." *International Security*. 12(4): 5–27.

O'Brien, Karen L. 2006. "Are We Missing the Point? Global Environmental Change as an Issue of Human Security." *Global Environmental Change*. 16: 1–3.

O'Brien, Karen L., and Robin M. Leichenko. 2000. "Double Exposure: Assessing the Impacts of Climate Change within the Context of Economic Globalization." *Global Environmental Change*. 10(3): 221–32.

Okereke, Chukwumerije, and Mark Charlesworth. 2014. "Environmental and Ecological Justice." In *Advances in International Environmental Politics*, eds. Michele M. Betsill, Kathryn Hochstetler, and Dimitris Stevis. New York, NY: Palgrave Macmillan, pp. 328–55.

Oswald Spring, Úrsula. 2008. *Human, Gender and Environmental Security: A HUGE Challenge*. Bonn, Germany: UNU Institute for Environment and Human Security.

Oum, Young Rae. 2003. "Beyond a Strong State and Docile Women: Reproductive Choices, State Policy and Skewed Sex Ratio in South Korea." *International Feminist Journal of Politics*. 5(4): 420–46.

Oxfam. 2010. "Gender, Disaster Risk Reduction, and Climate Change Adaptation: A Learning Companion." https://www.gdnonline.org/resources/OxfamGender&ARR.pdf.

Oxford Research Group. 2014. "Sustainable Security." *Oxford Research Group: Building Bridges for Global Security*. http://www.oxfordresearchgroup.org.uk/ssp.

Paasi, Anssi. 2005. "Globalisation, Academic Capitalism, and the Uneven Geographies of International Journal Publishing Spaces." *Environment and Planning A*. 37(5): 769–89.

Paavola, Jouni. 2006. "Justice in Adaptation to Climate Change in Tanzania." In *Fairness in Adaptation to Climate Change*, eds. W. Neil Adger, et al. Cambridge, MA: MIT Press, pp. 201–22.

Park, Jacob, Matthias Finger, and Ken Conca. 2008. "The Death of Rio Environmentalism." In *The Crisis of Global Environmental Governance: Towards a New Political Economy of Sustainability*, eds. Jacob Park, Ken Conca, and Matthias Finger. New York, NY: Routledge, pp. 1–12.

Parr, Adrian. 2009. *Hijacking Sustainability*. Cambridge, MA: MIT Press.

Parr, Adrian. 2012. *The Wrath of Capital: Neoliberalism and Climate Change Politics*. New York, NY: Columbia University Press.

Pasgaard, Maya, Bo Dalsgaard, Pietro K. Maruyama, Brody Sandel, et al. 2015. "Geographical Imbalances and Divides in the Scientific Production of Climate Change Knowledge." *Global Environmental Change*. 35: 279–88.

Pasgaard, Maya, and Niels Strange. 2013. "A Quantitative Analysis of the Causes of the Global Climate Change Research Distribution." *Global Environmental Change*. 23(6): 1684–93.

Paterson, Matthew. 2001. *Understanding Global Environmental Politics: Domination, Accumulation, Resistance*. New York, NY: Palgrave.

Peluso, Nancy, and Michael Watts. 2001. "Violent Environments." In *Violent Environments*, eds. Nancy Peluso and Michael Watts. Ithaca, NY: Cornell University Press, pp. 3–38.

Perez, C., et al. 2015. "How Resilient Are Farming Households and Communities to a Changing Climate in Africa? A Gender-Based Perspective." *Global Environmental Change*. 34: 95–107.

Phillips, Tom. 2015. "China Ends One-Child Policy after 35 Years." *Guardian*. http://www.theguardian.com/world/2015/oct/29/china-abandons-one-child-policy.

Pimentel, D., et al. 2007. "Ecology of Increasing Diseases: Population Growth and Environmental Degradation." *Human Ecology*. 35(6): 653–68.

Piotrowski, Jan. 2015. "Women's Views Missing at COP 21." *SciDev.Net*. http://www.scidev.net/global/gender/scidev-net-at-large/women-views-missing-at-cop-21.html.

Pirages, Dennis Clark, and Theresa Manley DeGeest. 2004. *Ecological Security: An Evolutionary Perspective on Globalization*. Boulder, CO: Rowman & Littlefield.

Plumwood, Val. 1993. *Feminism and the Mastery of Nature.* New York, NY: Routledge.

Plumwood, Val. 2002. *Environmental Culture: The Ecological Crisis of Reason.* New York, NY: Routledge.

Plumwood, Val. 2006. "Feminism." In *Political Theory and the Ecological Challenge*, eds. Andrew Dobson and Robyn Eckersley. New York, NY: Cambridge University Press, pp. 51–74.

Portugese, Jacqueline. 1998. *Fertility Policy in Israel: The Politics of Religion, Gender, and Nation.* Westport, CT: Praeger.

Pricope, Narcisa, Gregory Husak, David Lopez-Carr, Christopher Funk, et al. 2013. "The Climate–Population Nexus in the East African Horn: Emerging Degradation Trends in Rangeland and Pastoral Livelihood Zones." *Global Environmental Change.* 23: 1525–41.

Princen, Thomas. 2002. "Consumption and Its Externalities: Where Economy Meets Ecology." In *Confronting Consumption*, eds. Thomas Princen, Michael Maniates, and Ken Conca. Cambridge, MA: MIT Press, pp. 23–42.

Princen, Thomas. 2003. "Principles for Sustainability: From Cooperation and Efficiency to Sufficiency." *Global Environmental Politics.* 3(1): 33–50.

Princen, Thomas. 2005. *The Logic of Sufficiency.* Cambridge, MA: MIT Press.

Princen, Thomas. 2012. "A Sustainability Ethic." In *Handbook of Global Environmental Politics*, ed. Peter Dauvergne. Northampton, MA: Edward Elgar, pp. 466–79.

Princen, Thomas, Michael Maniates, and Ken Conca. 2002. *Confronting Consumption.* Cambridge, MA: MIT Press.

Puechguirbal, Nadine. 2010. "Discourses on Gender, Patriarchy and Resolution 1325: A Textual Analysis of UN Documents." *International Peacekeeping.* 17(2): 172–87.

Puri, Lakshmi. 2015. "Women and Girls Are Essential Climate Actors." *UN Women.* http://www.unwomen.org/en/news/stories/2015/12/lakshmi-puri-at-globe-internationals-annual-legislators-summit#sthash.cPitfdcU.dpuf.

Ravishankar, Sandhya. 2016. "Manatees to the Rescue? Cities Offer Ideas to Solve Chennai's Flooding Problem." *Guardian.* http://www.theguardian.com/cities/2016/mar/02/100-resilient-cities-ideas-to-solve-chennai-flooding-problem-manatees.

Rawls, John. 1971. *A Theory of Justice.* New York, NY: Belknap.

Reddy, Bhavya. 2015. "If Sustainable Living Is Seen as 'Feminine', That's Bad for the Planet – and Women." *Guardian.* http://www.theguardian.com/commentisfree/2015/oct/20/if-sustainable-living-feminine-bad-for-planet-and-women.

Reid, Megan. 2013. "Disasters and Social Inequalities." *Sociology Compass*. 7(11): 984–97.

Riebeek, Holli. 2005. "The Rising Cost of Natural Hazards." *Earth Observatory*. March 28.

Roberts, J. Timmons, and Bradley C. Parks. 2009. "Ecologically Unequal Exchange, Ecological Debt, and Climate Justice: The History and Implications of Three Related Ideas for a New Social Movement." *International Journal of Comparative Sociology*. 50(3–4): 385–409.

Robertson, Thomas. 2012. *The Malthusian Moment: Global Population Growth and the Birth of American Environmentalism*. New Brunswick, NJ: Rutgers University Press.

Rocheleau, Dianne. 2015. "A Situated View of Feminist Political Ecology from My Networks, Roots and Territories." In *Practising Feminist Political Ecologies: Moving Beyond the "Green Economy,"* eds. Wendy Harcourt and Ingrid L. Nelson. London, UK: Zed Books, pp. 29–66.

Rocheleau, Dianne, Barbara Thomas-Slayter, and Esther Wangari, eds. 1996. *Feminist Political Ecology: Global Issues and Local Experiences*. New York, NY: Routledge.

Ross, Michael. 2004. "What Do We Know about Natural Resources and Civil War?" *Journal of Peace Research*. 41(3): 337–56.

Runyan, Anne Sisson, and V. Spike Peterson. 2013. *Global Gender Issues in the New Millennium*. 4th edn. Boulder, CO: Westview Press.

Sachs, Carolyn, and Margaret Alston. 2010. "Global Shifts, Sedimentations, and Imaginaries: An Introduction to the Special Issue on Women and Agriculture." *Signs: Journal of Women in Culture and Society*. 35(2): 277–87.

Salleh, Ariel, ed. 2009. *Eco-Sufficiency and Global Justice: Women Write Political Ecology*. New York, NY: Pluto Press.

Sandilands, Catriona. 1999. *The Good-Natured Feminist: Ecofeminism and the Quest for Democracy*. Minneapolis, MN: University of Minnesota Press.

Sapra, Sonalini. 2009. "Participatory Democracy and Social Justice: The Politics of Women's Environmental Action in India." Dissertation. Vanderbilt University.

Schlosberg, David, and David Carruthers. 2010. "Indigenous Struggles, Environmental Justice, and Community Capabilities." *Global Environmental Politics*. 10(4): 12–35.

Seager, Joni. 1993. *Earth Follies: Coming to Feminist Terms with the Global Environmental Crisis*. New York, NY: Routledge.

Seager, Joni. 1999. "Patriarchal Vandalism: Militaries and the Environment." In *Dangerous Intersections: Feminist Perspectives on Population, Environment, and Development*, eds. Jael Silliman and Ynestra King. Cambridge, MA: South End Press, pp. 163–88.

Seager, Joni. 2003. "Rachel Carson Died of Breast Cancer: The Coming of Age of Feminist Environmentalism." *Signs: Journal of Women in Culture and Society.* 28(3): 945–72.

Seager, Joni. 2006. "Noticing Gender (or Not) in Disasters." *Geoforum.* 37(1): 2–3.

Sen, Gita. 2004. "Women, Poverty, and Population: Issues for the Concerned Environmentalist." In *Green Planet Blues: Environmental Politics from Stockholm to Johannesburg*, eds. Ken Conca and Geoffrey Dabelko. Boulder, CO: Westview Press, pp. 358–367.

Shaw, D. John. 2007. *World Food Security: A History since 1945.* New York, NY: Palgrave Macmillan.

Shiva, Vandana. 1989. *Staying Alive: Women, Ecology, and Development.* Atlantic Heights, NJ: Zed Books.

Shiva, Vandana. 1993. "The Impoverishment of the Environment." In *Ecofeminism*, Maria Mies and Vandana Shiva. London, UK: Zed Books, pp. 70–90.

Shiva, Vandana. 2008. *Soil Not Oil: Environmental Justice in an Age of Climate Crisis.* Berkeley, CA: North Atlantic Books.

Sikor, Thomas, and Peter Newell. 2014. "Globalizing Environmental Justice?" *Geoforum.* 54: 151–7.

Simon, Julian L. 1990. *Population Matters: People, Resources, Environment, and Immigration.* New Brunswick, NJ: Transaction.

Slovic, Paul, Torbjörn Malmfors, C. K. Mertz, Nancy Neil, et al. 1997. "Evaluating Chemical Risks: Results of a Study of the British Toxicology Society." *Human and Experimental Toxicology.* 16: 661–75.

Smith, N., and A. Leiserowitz. 2013. "American Evangelicals and Global Warming." *Global Environmental Change.* 23: 1009–17.

Smithers, Rebecca. 2013. "One-Third of Fish Caught in Channel Have Plastic Contamination, Study Shows." *Guardian.* http://www.theguardian.com/environment/2013/jan/24/fish-channel-plastic-contamination.

Spitzner, Meike. 2009. "How Global Warming is Gendered." In *Eco-Sufficiency and Global Justice: Women Write Political Ecology*, ed. Ariel Salleh. New York, NY: Pluto Press, pp. 218–229.

Stein, Rachel, ed. 2004. *New Perspectives on Environmental Justice: Gender, Sexuality, and Activism.* New Brunswick, NJ: Rutgers University Press.

Stevis, Dimitris. 2014. "The Trajectory of International Environmental Politics." In *Advances in International Environmental*

Politics, eds. Michele M. Betsill, Kathryn Hochstetler, and Dimitris Stevis. New York, NY: Palgrave Macmillan, pp. 13–44.

Sturgeon, Noël. 1997. *Ecofeminist Natures: Race, Gender, Feminist Theory and Political Action*. New York, NY: Routledge.

Sturgeon, Noël. 2009. *Environmentalism in Popular Culture: Gender, Race, Sexuality, and the Politics of the Natural*. Tucson, AZ: University of Arizona Press.

Sultana, Farhana. 2009. "Fluid Lives: Subjectivities, Gender and Water in Rural Bangladesh." *Gender, Place and Culture*. 16(4): 427–44.

Sultana, Farhana. 2011. "Suffering For Water, Suffering From Water: Emotional Geographies of Resource Access, Control and Conflict." *Geoforum*. 42(2): 163–72.

Sundström, Aksel, and Aaron M. McCright. 2014. "Gender Differences in Environmental Concern among Swedish Citizens and Politicians." *Environmental Politics*. 23(6): 1082–95.

Swatuk, Larry A. 2005. "From Project to Context: Community Based Natural Resource Management in Botswana." *Global Environmental Politics*. 5(3): 95–124.

Swatuk, Larry A. 2006. "Environmental Security." In *Advances in International Environmental Politics.*, eds. Michele M. Betsill, Kathryn Hochstetler, and Dimitris Stevis. New York, NY: Palgrave Macmillan, pp. 203–36.

Terry, Geraldine. 2009. "No Climate Justice Without Gender Justice: An Overview of the Issues." *Gender and Development*. 17(1): 5–18.

Terry, Geraldine, and Caroline Sweetman, eds. 2009. *Climate Change and Gender Justice*. London: Practical Action in association with Oxfam GB.

Thiele, Leslie Paul. 2013. *Sustainability*. Malden, MA: Polity.

Thomas, Vinod, Jose Ramon G. Albert, and Rosa T. Perez. 2013. "Climate-Related Disasters in Asia and the Pacific." http://www.adb.org/publications/climate-related-disasters-asia-and-pacific.

Thompson, Paul M., and Parvin Sultana. 1996. "Distributional and Social Impacts of Flood Control in Bangladesh." *Geographical Journal*. 162(1): 1–13.

Tickner, J. Ann. 2001. *Gendering World Politics: Issues and Approaches in the Post-Cold War Era*. New York, NY: Columbia University Press.

Torras, Mariano, and James K. Boyce. 1998. "Income, Inequality, and Pollution: A Reassessment of the Environmental Kuznets Curve." *Ecological Economics*. 25: 147–60.

Trombetta, Maria Julia. 2008. "Environmental Security and Climate Change: Analysing the Discourse." *Cambridge Review of International Affairs*. 21(4): 585–602.

True, Jacqui. 2003. *Gender Globalization and Postsocialism: The Czech Republic after Communism.* New York, NY: Columbia University Press.

True, Jacqui. 2012. *The Political Economy of Violence Against Women.* New York, NY: Oxford University Press.

UK Office for National Statistics. 2016. "UK Environmental Accounts: How Much Material is the UK Consuming?" http://www.ons.gov.uk/economy/environmentalaccounts/articles/ukenvironmentalaccountshowmuchmaterialistheukconsuming/ukenvironmentalaccountshowmuchmaterialistheukconsuming.

UN. 1995. "Beijing Declaration and Platform for Action." http://www.un.org/womenwatch/daw/beijing/pdf/BDPfA%20E.pdf.

UN. 2002. "Gender Mainstreaming: An Overview," ed. Office of the Special Adviser on Gender Issues and Advancement of Women. http://www.un.org/womenwatch/osagi/pdf/e65237.pdf.

UN. 2011. "The Global Social Crisis: Report on the World Social Situation 2011." http://www.un.org/esa/socdev/rwss/docs/2011/rwss2011.pdf.

UN. 2014. "Preliminary Draft: International Water Quality Guidelines for Ecosystems." http://www.unep.org/esm/Portals/50159/Preliminary%20draft%20international%20water%20quality%20guidelines%20for%20ecosystems_Sept14.pdf.

UN. 2015. "Transforming Our World: The 2030 Agenda for Sustainable Development." https://sustainabledevelopment.un.org/sdgs.

UN DESA. 2013. "Demographic Components of Future Population Growth." http://www.un.org/en/development/desa/population/publications/pdf/technical/TP2013-3.pdf.

UN DESA. 2015. "World Population Prospects: Key Findings and Advance Tables." http://esa.un.org/unpd/wpp/Publications/Files/Key_Findings_WPP_2015.pdf.

UNDP. 2015. "Human Development Report 2015: Work for Human Development." http://hdr.undp.org/sites/default/files/2015_human_development_report.pdf.

UNDSD. 1992. "Agenda 21." http://sustainabledevelopment.un.org/content/documents/Agenda21.pdf.

UNEP. 1992. "Rio Declaration on Environment and Development." http://www.unep.org/Documents.Multilingual/Default.asp?documentid=78&articleid=1163.

UNEP. 2005. "Feature Focus: Gender, Poverty and Environment." *GEO Yearbook 2004/5:* 55–70.

UNEP. 2014. "Valuing Plastics: The Business Case for Measuring, Managing and Disclosing Plastic Use in the Consumer Goods Industry." http://www.slideshare.net/sustainablebrands/valuing-

plastic-the-business-case-for-measuring-managing-and-disclos
ing-plastic-use-in-the-consumer-goods-industry-36391779.

UNEP. 2015. "About UNEP: The Organization." http://www.unep.
org/Documents.Multilingual/Default.asp?DocumentID=43&Arti
cleID=1554&l=en.

UNESCO. 2010. "Gender Dimensions of Biodiversity." http://
unesdoc.unesco.org/images/0018/001897/189762e.pdf.

UNFCCC. 2013. "Report of the Conference of the Parties on its
Eighteenth Session." http://unfccc.int/resource/docs/2012/cop18/
eng/08a03.pdf.

UNFCCC. 2015. "Adoption of the Paris Agreement: Proposal
by the President." http://unfccc.int/documentation/documents/
advanced_search/items/6911.php?priref=600008831.

UNGA. 2015. "Transforming Our World: The 2030 Agenda for
Sustainable Development." http://www.un.org/ga/search/view_
doc.asp?symbol=A/70/L.1&Lang=E.

Uraguchi, Zenebe Bashaw. 2010. "Food Price Hikes, Food Security,
and Gender Equality: Assessing the Roles and Vulnerability of
Women in Households of Bangladesh and Ethiopia." *Gender and
Development*. 18(3): 491–501.

Urban, Jessica Leann. 2007. "Interrogating Privilege/Challenging
the 'Greening of Hate'." *International Feminist Journal of Politics*. 9(2): 251–64.

Varga, Csaba, István Kiss, and István Ember. 2002. "The Lack of
Environmental Justice in Central and Eastern Europe" *Environmental Health Perspectives*. 110: 662–3.

Wæver, Ole. 1995. "Securitization and Desecuritization." In *On
Security*, ed. Ronnie D. Lipschutz. New York, NY: Columbia
University Press, pp. 46–86.

Wangari, Esther, Barbara Thomas-Slayter, and Dianne Rocheleau.
1996. "Gendered Visions for Survival: Semi-Arid Regions in
Kenya." In *Feminist Political Ecology: Global Issues and Local
Experiences*, eds. Dianne Rocheleau, Barbara Thomas-Slayter,
and Esther Wangari. New York, NY: Routledge, pp. 127–54.

Wapner, Paul. 2010a. *Living Through the End of Nature: The
Future of American Environmentalism*. Cambridge, MA: MIT
Press.

Wapner, Paul. 2010b. "Sacrifice in an Age of Comfort." In *The
Environmental Politics of Sacrifice*, eds. Michael Maniates and
John M. Meyer. Cambridge, MA: MIT Press, pp. 33–60.

Wapner, Paul. 2012. "After Nature: Environmental Politics in a
Postmodern Age." In *Handbook of Global Environmental Politics*, ed. Peter Dauvergne. Northampton, MA: Edward Elgar,
pp. 431–42.

Warlenius, Rikard, Gregory Pierce, and Vasna Ramasar. 2015. "Reversing the Arrow of Arrears: The Concept of 'Ecological Debt' and its Value for Environmental Justice." *Global Environmental Change*. 30: 21–30.

Warren, Karen J. 1997. *Ecofeminism: Women, Culture, Nature*. Bloomington, IN: Indiana University Press.

Warren, Karen J. 2000. *Ecofeminist Philosophy: A Western Perspective on What It Is and Why It Matters*. Boulder, CO: Rowman & Littlefield.

WaterAid. 2016. "WaterAid: What We Do." http://www.wateraid. org/us/what-we-do/the-crisis/women.

WEDO. 2008. "Gender, Climate Change and Human Security: Lessons from Bangladesh, Ghana, and Senegal." http://www. gdnonline.org/resources/WEDO_Gender_CC_Human_Security. pdf.

Westhoek, Henk, et al. 2014. "Food Choices, Health and Environment: Effects of Cutting Europe's Meat and Dairy Intake." *Global Environmental Change*. 26: 196–205.

Weston, Burns H. 2012. "The Theoretical Foundations of Intergenerational Ecological Justice: An Overview." *Human Rights Quarterly*. 34(1): 251–66.

White, Gregory. 2011. *Climate Change and Migration: Security and Borders in a Warming World*. New York, NY: Oxford University Press.

White, Rob. 2008. *Crimes Against Nature: Environmental Criminology and Ecological Justice*. New York, NY: Routledge.

WHO. 2008. "Climate Change Will Erode Foundations of Health." *WHO*. http://www.who.int/mediacentre/news/releases/2008/ pr11/en.

Wilcox, Chris, Erik Van Sebille, and Britta Denise Hardesty. 2015. "Threat of Plastic Pollution to Seabirds Is Global, Pervasive, and Increasing." *Proceedings of the National Academy of Sciences*. 112(38): 11899–904.

Willsher, Kim. 2014. "French Stores Accused of Imposing 'Woman Tax.'" *Guardian*. http://www.theguardian.com/world/2014/nov/ 04/french-stores-woman-tax-pricing-investigation.

Wilson, Kalpana. 2012. "Population Control, the Cold War and Racialising Reproduction." In *Race, Racism and Development: Interrogating History, Discourse and Practice*, Kalpana Wilson. New York, NY: Zed Books, pp. 69–96.

Wilson, Kalpana. 2014. "Britain Must End Its Support for Sterilisation in India." *Guardian*. http://www.theguardian.com/commen tisfree/2014/nov/14/britain-end-support-forced-sterilisation-india-chhattisgarh.

Winston, Andrew. 2015. "Can the Planet Handle China's New Two-Child Policy?" *Guardian.* http://www.theguardian.com/ sustainable-business/2015/nov/24/china-two-child-policy-sustainable-population.

World Bank. 2012. "Gender Equality and Development." http:// siteresources.worldbank.org/INTWDR2012/Resources/7778105-1299699968583/7786210-1315936222006/Complete-Report. pdf.

World Bank. 2015a. "GDP (Current US$)." http://data.worldbank. org/indicator/NY.GDP.MKTP.CD/countries/1W?display=graph.

World Bank. 2015b. "CO_2 Emissions (Metric Tons per Capita)." http://data.worldbank.org/indicator/EN.ATM.CO2E.PC.

World Commission on Environment and Development. 1987. "From One Earth to One World." In *Our Common Future*, World Commission on Environment and Development. Oxford, UK: Oxford University Press, pp. 1–23.

Xiao, Chenyang, and Dayong Hong. 2010. "Gender Differences in Environmental Behaviors in China." *Population and Environment.* 32: 88–104.

Xiao, Chenyang, and Aaron M. McCright. 2014. "A Test of the Biographical Availability Argument for Gender Differences in Environmental Behaviors." *Environment and Behavior.* 46: 241–63.

Index